Management of Regeneration

This text provides readers of all levels with an understanding of the choices, challenges and dilemmas that face regeneration managers. By synthesising theory with practice and examining management, policy and social issues, the authors encourage readers to evolve their criticality within a clear theoretical framework. Strategic processes are explained and new forms of local, sub-regional and regional management examined. *Management of Regeneration* explores current initiatives in order to present good practice in a one-stop resource that will be essential reading for all those studying or working within regeneration and public management.

Features include current case vignettes, learning objectives, key themes boxes and a review and reflection section at the end of each chapter.

John Diamond is Senior Lecturer in Urban Policy Studies at Edge Hill College of Higher Education, UK.

Joyce Liddle is Lecturer in Strategic Management at Durham Business School, University of Durham, UK.

Management of Regeneration

Choices, challenges and dilemmas

John Diamond and Joyce Liddle

Routledge
Taylor & Francis Group

LONDON AND NEW YORK

First published 2005
by Routledge
2 Park Square, Milton Park, Abingdon, Oxon OX14 4RN

Simultaneously published in the USA and Canada
by Routledge
270 Madison Ave., New York, NY 10016

Routledge is an imprint of the Taylor & Francis Group

© 2005 John Diamond and Joyce Liddle

Typeset in Perpetua and Bell Gothic by
Taylor & Francis Books
Printed and bound in Great Britain by
Antony Rowe Ltd, Chippenham, Wiltshire

British Library Cataloguing in Publication Data
A catalogue record for this book is available from the British Library

Library of Congress Cataloging-in-Publication Data
Diamond, John, 1954–
    Management of Regeneration: Choices, challenges and
    dilemmas/John Diamond and Joyce Liddle
    p. cm.
    Includes bibliographical references and index.
    ISBN 0-415-33420-9 (hard cover) – ISBN 0-415-33421-7 (soft cover)
    1. Urban renewal – Great Britain. 2. Urban policy – Great Britain.
    3. Sociology, Urban – Great Britain. 4. Globalization. I Liddle, Joyce
    1952– II. Title.
    HT178.G7D53 2005
    307.3'416'0941–dc22

ISBN 0–415–33420–9 (hbk)
ISBN 0–415–33421–7 (pbk)

Contents

Illustrations

FIGURES

TABLES

Preface

UK approaches to contemporary regeneration have undergone a 'renaissance' since 1997 and the election of New Labour. A mixture of innovative and, at times, contradictory sets of initiatives has been launched, in which the new site of intervention is the 'neighbourhood' or the 'community'. For those directly involved in the design, delivery and management of these schemes a substantially new skill set and knowledge base is required. These new developments necessitate not just the acquisition of a new language of regeneration but also a shift in thinking. We try to show in what follows that the current wave of regeneration initiatives involves much more than the physical redevelopment of a defined area; it also has profound social, organisational and political implications for those living and working in the area which last after the regeneration caravan has moved on.

Perhaps the most significant change that has occurred is that current regeneration initiatives are taking place through 'partnerships' with local communities. Rather than engaging in physical and social renewal *of* local communities, the current aspiration is to develop an approach *with* local communities. This shift in focus represents not only a change in emphasis but also a qualitative shift in thinking and practice.

As we try to show in this book, this thinking should be informed by a grasp of the particular circumstances in the neighbourhood where the initiative is taking place. Each neighbourhood has a distinctive local history and while there are general social and economic factors which have shaped the degeneration of communities in the UK, how they get played out in each locality will differ. The challenge, as it always has been, is to seek to match the specific needs of one community with the resources available, and, at the same time, to reconcile the limited priorities of UK regeneration initiatives with the expectations and aspirations of those living and working in a particular place at a particular time.

We believe that the value of this book lies in its attempt to draw upon the experience of practitioners to inform (and, hopefully, to shape) current debates and practice. We will illustrate the theoretical debates which follow by reference to real lived experiences. In so doing we are inviting you to share in the reflections of practice which are discussed below.

We argue that it is by developing our skills of analysis and reflection that we can view our own practice in a different way. These skills have the potential to redefine our own practice and to create the opportunities to renegotiate the priorities of our work with those to whom we are accountable. It is by explicit reference to the challenges, choices and dilemmas of existing practitioners that we hope to influence practice. We have organized the book so that at the end of Chapters 2, 4, 5, 6 and 7 you are invited to share the reflections of current practitioners. In a very real sense this is not, yet, another 'how to' book. The critical reflections of these chapters are about enabling you to consider a particular issue through the experience of those engaged in the complexities and lived experience of practitioners and managers.

We have organized the book as follows.

Chapter 1 attempts to place current initiatives in context. By taking the Neighbourhood Renewal Strategy as a starting point we explore the changing (and competing) discourse of regeneration. We examine the ways in which apparently different approaches to regeneration over the past 30 years have come together in a centrally driven set of initiatives. In particular, we reflect upon not only how current approaches attempted to address an agenda defined by need and exclusion, but also how the structures established to deliver such initiatives are, also, shaping the institutions of the local state. The current approach of regeneration appears to encompass pre-figurative institutions which challenge existing organisations and arrangements. Is this deliberate? Or is it an unintended consequence?

Chapter 2 addresses the context within which learning and skill development for regeneration managers is taking place. We review the different approaches to learning currently under consideration and anticipate future developments. A particular emphasis in this chapter is the role of accreditation and the discussion concerning how different levels of understanding and skill development can be accommodated within a training and staff development programme.

Chapter 3 provides both a literature review and a theoretical framework within which concepts of strategic decision making can be considered. Regeneration managers may occupy different roles in the formation of strategic policy making. On one level they have responsibility for the implementation of already defined strategic objectives. On another level they are expected to develop a strategic framework for a regeneration initiative as part of a succession (or exit) strategy.

Chapter 4 looks at the differing roles and responsibilities participating agencies and organisations play in regeneration initiatives. These 'stakeholders' in the process and practice can occupy different and competing roles. They may be present only to provide additional points of reference or guidance. But they may have a direct and significant interest in the outcome of the initiatives. They may be part of the commissioning and monitoring process. In short, they may have a vested interest in the initiative. How are these roles, relationships and interests managed and sustained?

In addition the chapter explores the differing models of leadership which are emerging through the regeneration experience. The primary focus of this book (and its intended audience) is those directly involved in the management and delivery of area-based interventions. But alongside these regeneration managers can be found key community-based 'leaders' as well as front line staff or single agency staff who occupy important roles in facilitating and enabling change at a local level. These individuals occupy, potentially, key leadership roles. How are they identified, supported and developed?

Chapter 5 explores different models of partnership from strategic partnership to local delivery partnerships. In particular, we argue that while the notion of partnership has become the new conventional wisdom in the delivery of services, it is often the site of both stated and unstated conflict and boundary disputes between competing agencies. We suggest that a more critical reflection on the nature of developing and sustaining partnerships is necessary. Specifically, we illustrate the relationship between skill development and partnership development by identifying the particular skills and approaches which may contribute to partnership 'success' or 'failure'.

Chapter 6 explores the literature and models present in the discussion over 'capacity building'. Like the notion of partnership, this is a contested concept. For example, it is not always clear whose capacity is being built. Arguably, the capacity of agencies and professionals to engage successfully with local communities is left unexplored. Drawing upon the experience of local community activists and community-based projects we seek to show that it is in this arena that the present (and next) generation of regeneration managers will be tested to demonstrate whether they have the capacity to work with and alongside local communities.

Chapter 7 draws upon a number of implicit themes from the earlier chapters by focusing upon the issues of governance and accountability. Arguably we are in a transformative phase of an emerging (and contested) form of new public governance. It is important to distinguish between explicit and implicit forms of accountability present in the experience of regeneration managers, and, at the same time, to try and imagine the nature of governance present and implied by the forms of decision-making and partnership formation.

Chapter 8 places some of these debates in an international context. We can explore the relationships between UK regeneration strategies and practice and those in Europe and across the world by identifying similar approaches and models. But we can also think of these relationships in the context of 'globalisation' and the ways in which industrial societies have sought to adjust to the decline of their manufacturing bases and the growth of the service/high-tech economies.

At the end of each chapter we include a review and reflection section. We have drawn upon the real experiences of regeneration professionals across the UK. It is here that we hope you will reflect upon your own experience, identify your needs and begin to develop your own strategies. To help you to do this we have identified a set of questions to assist in this process of reflection. We have, in the spirit of the book's aim, developed these through our conversations with local managers and practitioners.

Acknowledgements

We are very well aware that this book could not have been written without the support and guidance of a number of friends and colleagues. In particular we would like to say thank you to Carole Brocken (CLPS office) at Edge Hill College of HE. We would also like to record our thanks to those who have been willing to discuss our ideas, including Colette Crossdale, Mindy Docker, Anne Kearney, Andrew Nelson and Stuart Speeden.

Thanks are also due to the many full- and part-time MBA, MA and MSc students over the years who may have unwittingly contributed new thoughts and approaches to regeneration, based on their practical experience. Other current practitioners in whose debt we remain are Mark Lloyd, Brian Brown, Jeff Riddell, John Smith and Chief Inspector Dave Pryer.

We would also like to thank Emma Joyes and Francesca Heslop at Routledge for their help and advice.

Introduction

The central arguments of this book are that those currently engaged in regeneration management are working in a period of change and transformation, and that as a consequence successful practitioners need to apply more than generic managerial skills in order to work effectively.

This period of change and transformation can be understood, we suggest, by reference to the following:

- Changing structures of governance and accountability.
- Existing and emerging local networks of practitioners and residents.
- Changing roles of existing agencies and their interaction.
- Emerging networks of interest groups.
- Generational change in those engaged in regeneration management.

In this introduction we set out to identify why we believe these factors are significant and to indicate how we want to explore them in the book. Our starting point for this discussion is that while the acquisition of generic management skills is necessary, it is not sufficient if practitioners are not only to grasp the significance of the changes which are taking place but also to shape these changes in their own locality.

CHANGING STRUCTURES OF ORGANIZATION AND ACCOUNTABILITY

It is self-evident that the organizational boundaries within which much regeneration activity takes place have changed significantly over the past 10 years and that they are likely to continue to expand and change over the next decade.

The argument for change maintains that very little can be accomplished by a single organization acting alone. In an era when organizational boundaries are loosening and becoming more complex and problematic, most agencies need partners, not only horizontally in alliances, but vertically around relationships with users. As a consequence, increasingly new standards of delivery are now matched by exhortations to 'join up' practice and involve service users. The current New Labour government's aim for a radical modernization of public services depends on its ability to make a reality of 'holistic' government and 'joined-up thinking'.

These new arrangements do lead to a blurring of the boundaries between the state, the market and civil society. Multi-agency partnerships are now regarded as the most effective means of achieving common goals. Indeed, it is not just the present Labour government which is promoting this approach. The European Commission is a key factor in promoting and requiring change. At a regional or local level those engaged in regeneration management have to take account of the European perspective if only to secure funding.

Given this new context it seems to us that the regeneration managers who have to 'sense-make' and manage within these new forms of governance are having difficulty in adjusting to the new forms of public service delivery. Indeed those hierarchical and organizationally specific forms of accountability embedded in the traditional governmental system of delivery are no longer appropriate for a new experimental world of regeneration. While change is uneven we can see at a local level attempts to restructure local authorities away from service departments to a 'thematic' model which is an attempt to facilitate a more strategic and 'joined-up' approach. At the same time as a result of central government initiatives all local authorities are engaged with some form of restructuring in order to participate in local partnerships, deliver the new agenda in children's services and prepare community plans. We suggest that 'new action spaces' have been created, and that managers at different levels of the hierarchy are being expected to work horizontally and vertically. This means that very senior strategists are working alongside operational people and front line staff, within and outside the public sector. The role of professionals is becoming blurred, as state and non-state actors pool resources and expertise to achieve commonly agreed objectives.

Therefore, many of the new arrangements for regeneration are emergent and experimental. These developments create new models of governance and accountability with innovative and entrepreneurial actors in public, private and other sectors seeking to identify particular initiatives/projects for regeneration.

Despite these changes professionals within regeneration are expected to work across boundaries, on specific area-based programmes, and yet still operate within other forms of regional and sub-regional and local governance. It is this 'uncertainty' which neatly illustrates our suggestion that this phase is one of transformation and long-term change.

EXISTING AND EMERGING NETWORKS OF PRACTITIONERS AND RESIDENTS

We argue that the current (and next) generation of regeneration managers need to be able to inform their decisions and choices by reference to the network of agencies and initiatives already present in a locality. Partnership mapping or establishing a database of initiatives is not only about ensuring you have an up-to-date awareness of what is happening in your area, but also about understanding the complex social/personal/political dimensions of those networks. In a very real sense these networks are transforming our received understanding of local and civic culture within the UK. One important consequence, we argue, of the move to embed 'the partnership' approach at a local, sub-regional or regional level is that it challenges the existing legitimacy of our political institutions at the local level. This is more than the issue of accountability and governance for regeneration initiatives. It is about the way in which partnerships have been given particular roles and responsibilities which marginalise or even remove existing structures and organizations from participation themselves in the decision-making processes.

As we discuss in the following chapters these emerging forms of local governance are not yet fixed. Indeed, regeneration initiatives are often the site of struggle and contest over how power in decision making is being exercised. In this location of dispute sit regeneration managers seeking to navigate their way through warring factions.

Regeneration initiatives have often been used as places of experimentation. As we suggest in the UK there is a long (and contested) history of the ways in which successive governments have used (usually) urban policy initiatives to react to specific events or to pilot new forms of delivery. The differences, since 1997, we maintain, are that the reforms introduced have both a long life expectancy and a direct impact on existing institutions at the local level.

To add to the complexity of this picture we explore the ways in which the 'partnership' model(s) create new relationships between both practitioners and residents. Often these networks cover a defined geographical area, but they may also exist at local, sub-regional/regional or national levels too. An element of this complexity is the way in which New Labour have promoted 'networks' as part of their Neighbourhood Renewal Strategy (NRS). Thus, alongside Local Strategic Partnerships (LSPs), Community Empowerment Networks (CENs) have been formed to promote the interests of the voluntary and community sector. Regeneration managers are, therefore, likely to find themselves liaising with and/or participating in a variety of professional/practitioner networks. While these developments may help to increase the local knowledge of practitioners, they do, also, have the potential to add to the pressure managers find themselves under.

CHANGING ROLES OF EXISTING AGENCIES AND THEIR INTERACTION

Regeneration activity has resulted in more partnership working spanning different sectors; however, most is concerned with the sharing of information and plans, or consultation with other partners or communities. Actual decisions about activities tend to be made intra-organizationally rather than inter-organizationally. Progress on joint planning or commissioning has been uneven; there is no discernible shift in resources or responsibilities.

But we can see the evolution of and development of 'new' agencies to address the so-called 'wicked issues'. It is, often, in the regeneration areas that we can observe the development of these new organizational structures. Since 1997 the plethora of initiatives in health, education, social exclusion, young people, anti-social behaviour and crime reduction has resulted in changed relationships between existing agencies and the creation of new agencies.

For those engaged in the management of regeneration activity these developments pose new dilemmas and choices. The need to make 'sense' of what is happening and to negotiate working relationships with these new and evolving agencies are of major importance. As these new agencies create their own sense of identity and purpose, existing practitioners need to establish clarity on their changing roles and responsibilities and to identify potential areas of collaboration, information exchange and joint working.

EMERGING NETWORKS OF INTEREST GROUPS

Regeneration projects are, inevitably, a complex web of quite different interest groups. Some of these will be professionalized welfare agencies seeking to limit the extent to which the initiative intervenes across their known and defined boundaries. Other interest groups will be from the voluntary and community sector which themselves may be administered by professionalized interested groups. And a third set of interest groups may reside in city hall and may combine the professionalized interest groups of elected councillors and senior officers.

All of these different groups share a set of common assumptions (although usually unacknowledged) that they will seek to shape the regeneration project in their definition of what is needed and how it is to be delivered. In addition most contemporary regeneration managers have an additional set of external reference points. These are a combination of their peers and are, nominally, represented by the Government Office for the Regions (GOR).

These interest groups not only function at different levels and exercise different levels of power and influence, but are, sometimes, in conflict with each other. Regeneration managers will, therefore, be seeking to find the agreed space within which they can work and, at the same time, attempting to create additional space within which consensus can be achieved.

GENERATIONAL CHANGE

We also want to argue that there may be important developments taking place which are likely to result in a 'capacity gap' in those able to undertake these complex roles. This potential gap is partly a result of the increasing number of initiatives being introduced. It is, also, a generational issue. We have observed how many existing senior regeneration managers come with a background in community development or community work practice. As such approaches became unfashionable in the 1980s these individuals switched careers. As a consequence the skill pool which might match existing needs with potential practitioners has been significantly reduced. If we are right then this enhances the case for training and staff development, but it also raises an important issue of whether such training can be a substitute for the kind of experience to be found working in neglected and marginalized neighbourhoods. It may, however, strengthen the case for facilitating the development of local residents who have the capacity to benefit from such opportunities.

At a national level the current Neighbourhood Renewal Strategy has recruited a significant number of 'advisers' to liaise with local initiatives. This, too, has reduced the pool of experience and expertise at a local or sub-regional level. The particular sets of skills we are suggesting that this generation of regeneration managers brings (awareness of local dynamics, managing conflict, having a sense of local politics and who the key players are) may, of course, in some circumstances act as an inhibiting factor. There is a positive strength in being an 'outsider' and having to negotiate new alliances rather than being an 'insider' and anticipating what the local dynamics are instead of examining them critically, and helping to develop and to sustain new networks.

In a real sense, therefore, this book is attempting to address this issue of the 'capacity gap'. We start from the assumption that generic managerial 'skills', while relevant, are not a substitute for the challenges facing this new generation of regeneration managers. On the contrary, the challenges, choices and dilemmas they face are more significant than those who gained their experience in the 1970s and 1980s. The organizational (and political) culture is different. The demands are greater and the expectations are higher.

In the following chapters we seek to set out what those challenges are and we start with an attempt to review how we got here.

Chapter 1

Context setting

KEY THEMES

- Reflecting on regeneration initiatives: a story of continuity or discontinuity?
- Changing and challenging approaches to regeneration activity.
- Understanding failure.
- Neighbourhood renewal: a new initiative?

LEARNING POINTS

By the end of this chapter we hope that you will be able to:

- Identify the ways in which regeneration initiatives have been defined over the past 30 years.
- Reflect upon the ways in which explanations of success or failure are contested interpretations.
- Locate your own experience or knowledge in the context of what you read and thought.
- Begin to identify the challenges, choices and dilemmas faced by regeneration professionals.

INTRODUCTION

A difficulty for those engaged in regeneration management is to balance the demands of the present with the expectations (and doubts) of those who live in the neighbourhoods where activity is taking place. A very real challenge for both managers and residents is to develop a shared picture of what the neighbourhood could be like over a 10-year time frame. To have credibility these attempts at imagining the future or developing a shared vision have to be rooted in a sense of what is real. One coping strategy is to see current initiatives as the focus of dialogue and debate and an opportunity to break with the past. As we try to show in this chapter, there is a real sense of the way in which 'regeneration activity' has been redefined and reassessed over the past 30 years. The story of regeneration initiatives has been one where each new strategy has been claimed as making a break with the past. There are some good reasons why this may be both useful and appropriate (as we suggest below). However, for those involved in the day-to-day coordination and delivery of activity and projects it may be more appropriate to adopt a slightly different approach.

By adopting a different 'lens' – one which seeks to see the neighbourhood as those who live there see it – an alternative interpretation may emerge. This 'alternative' would suggest that for residents the wave of successive initiatives represents a 'norm' of both instability and predictability. The 'instability' derives, often, from the short-term nature of such interventions and the nature of the relationships between those who manage and/or decide the type of intervention and those who live in an area and are the 'object' of the intervention. The 'predictability' comes from the assumption that at some point a new initiative will be announced without reference to the perceived or spoken needs of those who live there. In that sense, while regeneration managers may see current initiatives as a break from the past (and there are good reason why this might be the case), local residents may adopt a scepticism which sees them as part of a process with a long history.

As we try to suggest in this chapter it is important to locate contemporary initiatives in the context of what has gone before. This is necessary for four good reasons:

1   The current neighbourhood renewal strategy claims to be radically different from previous regeneration initiatives.
2   The formation and funding, at a local level, of 'networks' of community representatives represents a shift in thinking and practice.
3   There has been an emphasis on the training and with it the 'professionalization' of regeneration managers.
4   There is an emerging political consensus on the importance of 'localism'.

We are not suggesting that these reasons alone are shaping the policy and practice of local regeneration teams. We do recognize that within each regeneration initiative there will be a different set of histories which will inform the way in which the initiative is managed, delivered and experienced. We are suggesting that it is important to take account of these histories (which may not be shared or even acknowledged by all participants) and to place current practice in the context of change. It is for these reasons that we argue (in the introduction) that contemporary regeneration managers need to have a variety of skills and a broad understanding of the dynamics in play at a local level.

We want now to trace the development of the current neighbourhood renewal strategy and to reflect upon how and in what ways it can be said to be a 'break with the past'.

REFLECTING UPON REGENERATION INITIATIVES – A STORY OF CONTINUITY OR DISCONTINUITY?

The 'story' of UK-based regeneration initiatives is, at first sight, one of discontinuity. It also appears to be one which is defined by the political priorities of whichever party is in government. This complex history of 'discontinuity' can be traced back to the 1960s. As we show below, the origins and development of the Urban Programme in the late 1960s provide a useful point of reference when exploring the significance of the Neighbourhood Renewal Strategy (NRS). But there is another, potentially more significant reason for referencing the current NRS with the Urban Programme. A number of current neighbourhood renewal/ regeneration managers (and neighbourhood renewal advisers) come from the generation of practitioners who were active in a number of initiatives associated with the Urban Programme. They both provide and are part of the collective regeneration memory and experience. They act as an alternative thread to UK-based regeneration practice stretching back over 30 years. These points of reference are important. Their importance rests partly in their cumulative knowledge or experience. It also provides an alternative lens through which UK regeneration activity may be understood and evaluated. Further, it represents a generation which may soon be 'lost' to existing managers and practitioners. And so we may lose not only a rich vein of experience, but also ways of understanding and reflecting upon the continuity (or discontinuity) between the past and the present.

Since 1997 the Blair government has developed two major regeneration programmes. The New Deal for Communities (NDC) and the NRS are, in some ways, a continuation of earlier initiatives. They share many of the same characteristics of contemporary UK regeneration programmes. They are based upon area-based initiatives (ABIs), adding additional layers of monitoring and delivery to existing systems and claiming to engage in facilitating a partnership between the public, private and voluntary sectors.

The significance of these initiatives derives from their focus on inter-agency working and the need to develop a clear succession (or exit) strategy which is dependent upon the capacity of existing local state agencies and local communities to ensure that change is maintained. In the UK the analysis which underscores these new programmes is partly based upon an evaluation of earlier schemes and partly upon the experience of Labour during the Thatcher years. Both indicate that it is necessary to create the conditions for effective collaboration between welfare agencies and to develop a local or neighbourhood response (Burgess *et al.* 2001; Filkin *et al.* 2001; Newman 2001). In addition there is an assumption that changes in service delivery and more effective managerial systems will effect the reforms necessary.

The present government would appear to have embraced the 'partnership' approach as the means to achieve social and urban regeneration. Its assumed capacity to achieve these goals is most clearly illustrated with reference to the report from the Social Exclusion Unit (1998) which noted that:

> Administrative fragmentation is a pervasive problem at local level too. Local authorities are just as likely as Whitehall to fall victim to 'departmentalism'; many other key local agencies are not within the local authority sphere at all. Routine joint planning, where key local services come together to tackle and prevent similar problems is rare. In many places partnership working still tends only to happen when there is a special programme to apply for or where there is a particularly acute local problem. The quality of partnerships varies hugely.
>
> (1998: 38)

From the outset we can make a number of generalized observations. First, that in making use of the term 'partnership' the present government is laying claim to some concept of 'equality'. The implication in a number of studies from the Audit Commission and the Social Exclusion Unit (and the associated policy statements) is that this represents not only a more effective way of delivering services but also a means by which different 'voices' can be heard and acknowledged. We think that this assumption needs to be challenged. While there may be evidence that the delivery of services can be affected positively by bringing different agencies together it is by no means proven as is illustrated below. As Mayo (1997) and Schaecter and Loftman (1997) demonstrate, it is debatable whether 'partnerships' enable local community organizations to feel that their views and experiences are 'valid' and can shape policy decisions. Indeed, it is often the case that the forums in which local community groups are asked to participate are inimical to such a process.

During the 1990s there had been a significant shift in the form and content of urban regeneration policy. The introduction of both City Challenge and the Single Regeneration Budget (SRB) by the Conservatives signalled the arrival of an apparently different mechanism by which regeneration initiatives were to be managed. Central to this process was the requirement to establish quasi 'stand-alone' agencies from the local authority to manage and to deliver initiatives. The responsibility for monitoring and 'supervising' these area-based approaches was devolved to regional government offices.

The role of the local authority was, and to some extent remains, ambiguous. It occupied the role of the 'sponsor' to the strategy. The process whereby bids were made and negotiations between potential partnerships conducted were carried out on behalf of the local authority. It was, in one sense, *the* local agency. However, the 'day-to-day' responsibility for managing the process was devolved to a small team of officers appointed (or seconded) by the authority (often on fixed term contracts) who were 'supervized' by locally established boards (usually including local councillors and representatives from other key agencies (or stakeholders) in the area.

The successful delivery of both City Challenge and SRB was predicated upon the establishment of good inter-agency working. In part this was built into the structure and organization of the process. By identifying a thematic approach to regeneration it was evident that individual agencies working alone would not be able either to secure additional funds through the initiative or to meet their stated outcomes. In one sense it is possible to argue that what was being proposed was a positive attempt to reduce the departmental barriers for effective working.

This approach was reflecting an emerging consensus across the political and academic spectrum (Stewart and Taylor 1995) which argued that, at minimum, area-based regeneration needed inter-agency co-operation and co-ordination. This approach had, clearly, informed the decentralization experiments in the 1980s in a number of Labour-run local authorities (Burns *et al*. 1994) and had been one of the criticisms of the earlier regeneration approaches of the Conservatives' urban development corporations (Leach *et al*. 1996).

This need to identify ways in which development time can be built into the process of establishing partnerships is a theme which is repeated in a number of studies (Booth 1997; Leach and Wilson 1998; Mayo 1997; Schaectar and Loftman 1997).

In seeking to identify a model for discussion which draws together the need to address the 'failings' of elected members and professionals to engage fully with the experiences of local people (Mayo 1997) and the practicalities of local organizations navigating their way around the complexities of the SRB bidding processes (Nevin *et al*. 1997) we need to think creatively about how to support those who feel excluded or marginalized. Many studies (Brownhill and Darke 1998; Skelcher *et al*. 1996; Taylor 1995) focused on the needs of local organizations.

Both the NDC and the NRS place a high priority on empowering middle and senior managers to exercise control over 'their' resources. In the UK (and especially in England) these changes have been accompanied by reforms within local government. As a result locally elected councillors have even *less* power than before. The reforms of public agencies began in the 1980s and have continued under New Labour. Health, housing and education, all of which used to be *locally* managed and delivered, have all (to a greater or lesser degree) been restructured so that 'stand-alone' agencies at a regional or sub-regional basis have responsibility for them.

Perhaps this can be best illustrated by changes to social housing in the UK. In order to secure resources for improvements in housing New Labour have 'encouraged' the transfer of the housing stock from local government to housing associations or other equivalent agencies. To ensure this change tenants have to vote in its favour. In many cases this has happened and the campaigns to support or to reject such proposals are a useful indicator of the degree of resistance to such moves (Younge 2002). The significance of these reforms is, partly, in the way they change the relationship between the tenant and the landlord (the local authority), which may be welcomed, and, more interestingly, the removal of public housing from local control and the impact this has for locally developed services and the wider public interest.

Changes within local government have resulted in an even greater centralization of decision making at the local level. Councillors who are not part of the 'cabinet' at city hall are, in effect, excluded from the decision-making process. The models of reform introduced by New Labour reflect the US influence. But these changes, though important in the short to medium term, are not perhaps as significant as the impact of the NRS.

Under the NRS, local strategic partnerships are being set up to improve the co-ordination of public and welfare agencies (including the police) in local areas (Russell 2001). These partnership boards (which are prescribed by central government) are not subject to local democratic accountability.

It is here that we can see the relative power and authority of the new cadre of regeneration managers (Diamond 2001; 2002a) who are able to exercise managerial direction within their initiatives. The capacity of the community-based sector effectively to influence the priorities and practice of the NDC is very limited. And it is subject to competing interpretations over what is possible.

The NDC approach reflects the priorities and assumptions of what is possible (and desirable) in neighbourhood regeneration. It involves the identification by external agencies of a specific physical area within which a number of initiatives will be located. The classification of a neighbourhood by external welfare and professional agencies is a process in which 'local' actors (tenants and/or residents) are included only after the event.

This, in effect, establishes the notion of a dependent and passive neighbourhood, a notion which is at the core of contemporary regeneration (Byrne 2001; Powell 1999). Thus, there is a dichotomy between the language used by regeneration professionals in which they seek the involvement of local people, and their exclusion from the initial phase of the process. The neighbourhood is assumed to be incapable of engaging with the regeneration agenda and, in fact, is disempowered from the start. The agencies created to manage and to implement the regeneration initiative are, themselves, often drawn from the outside. In the UK, a growing army of 'wandering' regeneration specialists has been created. They usually work on temporary contracts for the lifetime of the project. They may be seconded from local welfare agencies, so many have some knowledge of the area, but they rarely live within the area which is subject to the regeneration process.

Local involvement is usually restricted to those who are active in local residents' groups who find themselves co-opted into the initiative. Thus, for some individuals (and possibly their families), the 'benefits' of involvement may be associated with an enhanced status, an opportunity to influence particular (but discrete) aspects of the initiative, an opportunity (perhaps) to secure a job (albeit temporarily) and a 'place at the table' to meet with the senior managers and professionals. This process of incorporation is not new and has been a feature of UK regeneration strategies since the mid 1960s. In effect, what is happening is that the capacity of the local community to intervene is restricted to those who 'sign up' to the initiative.

As a strategy of containing potential discontent and alternative perspectives it can be very effective. The balance of power within any regeneration initiative is, therefore, significantly weighted in favour of the status quo. Yet, the long-term success of any initiative is partly dependent upon the capacity of local people to sustain their neighbourhood networks and street-based (or community) organizations after the professionals have left. It is, also, dependent upon a sustained investment in jobs and training (Atkinson 1998; Banks *et al.* 2003; Jowitt and Chapman 2001; Mayo and Taylor 2001; Purdue *et al.* 2000).

The initial focus has often been on securing 'flagship' developments to draw in economic investment. But such prestige initiatives may not meet the needs of local people.

There is, therefore, a basic mismatch between the needs of local groups and the policies which are assumed appropriate and relevant by the regeneration initiatives. This basic flaw in contemporary regeneration initiatives should not surprise us. It stems from an assumption which implies that 'communities' lack the skills and knowledge to engage sufficiently with the local state and that alternative community-based perspectives cannot be guaranteed to 'fit' with the needs of the external agencies. In this sense the implicit model of the community is a deficit model and, of course, this has implications. Given this, the task for the local state is to 'repair' the local neighbourhood sufficiently to make it safe for inward investment and development. The local state restructures localities so as to ensure its own competitive advantage over other cities and places (Cockburn 1977; Peck and Tickell 1995; Peck and Ward 2002). At the same time, however, these initiatives raise community expectations and pressure local initiatives to address specific and neighbourhood concerns. The space is, therefore, open to local lobbying and a struggle ensues in the identification of short-term priorities and the allocation of resources (Mayo 1997; Taylor 1995).

For these reasons we can see the ways in which increasing the capacity of local people to engage with the regeneration initiative can lead to conflict and challenge. The need to manage such potential conflict has become a real issue for many regeneration initiatives (Diamond 2002b); it is not the case that one can simply 'read off' who is involved, though, at a local neighbourhood or ward level.

The key regeneration managers will experience a tension in their relationships with local agencies, local residents and those who manage and/or fund the initiative. Local political elites will seek to exercise direct or indirect influence on regeneration initiatives. The key political leadership in a number of areas have delegated responsibility for initiatives to senior regeneration managers. As a consequence local politicians have even less voice than before.

At an initiative level there will be inter- and intra-organizational tension. The needs of the economic development teams, for instance, are likely to have priority over the needs and aspirations of the community or resident groups. In part this tension is sustained by the setting of performance indicators against which staff are judged and there may be a competing sense of time and place. For those who are involved in tenant and resident liaison, the immediate needs of local groups will influence their given priorities. As they seek to renegotiate these they will have to look for 'space' within which to operate. Yet they remain managerially accountable to senior staff who often have neither the time nor the space to engage in such reflection.

The community groups present will, themselves, reflect some of these tensions. There are, of course, important questions about the accountability and representativeness of local community leaders. Some groups will have regeneration 'sponsors' who do receive support and resources. Where this is so it inevitably increases their dependence on the regeneration agency but it can also increase their distance from other community groups or activists.

The varied networks and partnerships which are associated with such initiatives increase the potential to separate local activists from their neighbourhoods, and they also lead to ambiguity in decision making and accountability. Local community or regeneration boards may be places of formal decision making but it is important to recognize the significance of informal decision making, and to locate its sources.

The focus, in the UK, on neighbourhood (or area-based) initiatives is, itself, rooted in a past which goes back to the late 1960s (Higgins et al. 1983). Successive governments (both Labour and Conservative) have accepted the notion that urban poverty and civic disengagement can be addressed by area- or locally-based renewal schemes. While there have been differences of emphasis during this period (from policies aimed at improving the physical infrastructure to explicit strategies for addressing social exclusion) the underlying assumption has remained the same.

This consensus, evident in the policy and practice, suggests that a common conceptual framework is in place, a framework which promotes the concept of the 'active' citizen within very clear constraints and boundaries. There is little ideological party difference, in the UK, in terms of supporting the role of the voluntary- and community-based sectors. 'Active' voluntary associations are encouraged as long as they do not challenge the status quo. The promotion of an independent (and critical) voluntary- and community-based sector is, at best, tolerated and, at worse, finds itself marginalized from the decision-making processes.

Current regeneration initiatives on partnership and inter-agency working originated in the experiences and reflections of practitioners, policy makers and academics in the 1980s (Diamond 2004). It is here that differences of emphasis and focus are at their most explicit. While it might appear that, during the early 1980s, real theoretical, ideological and conceptual debate took place, the period resulted in a new political consensus which informed public policy in the present.

The debates in the early 1980s in the UK focused very specifically on the role and purpose of local government and the extent to which it could be innovative and independent of the centre (in London). Opposition to the Thatcher government was mainly located in the large urban authorities of the major cities in the UK and the decentralization of local services was part of this opposition.

The development of policies aimed at decentralising local services and enhancing local democratic structures was often described as 'going local' (Burns et al. 1994; Hambleton and Hoggett 1984). The advocates of this were predominantly Labour Party councillors, political activists and academics in the London area and a number of urban authorities. They advocated change for a number of reasons. As some commentators suggested at the time (Boddy and Fudge 1984), these 'going local' approaches, if successful, would demonstrate that Labour could deliver services effectively (following defeats in the 1979 and 1983 General Elections); would provide an alternative power base to challenge the 'New Right' policies of the Thatcher government; would enhance the status and authority of local democratic institutions; and would 'empower' local people to participate in the decision-making processes at a local level.

To achieve these broad goals a number of strategies were adopted. Services were physically decentralized from city hall. Neighbourhood offices (or one-stop shops) were opened up across local authorities where local people could gain access to information and advice on a number of services, including housing, welfare rights, planning and social services. Large, bureaucratic, local state welfare agencies (housing and social services) were broken down into flatter, less hierarchical forms of management. Issues of gender, race and sexual equality were emphasized, with local authorities developing their own policies on anti-racism and equal opportunities in employment and service provision. Coalitions of interest between the local authority and the community and voluntary sectors were developed. Policies on resident and tenant participation were developed and implemented. Special units were created within city halls to develop these approaches and to co-ordinate their implementation.

While these approaches did represent a radical shift in thinking, they failed on balance to achieve the aims they had set themselves.

REASONS FOR FAILURE

There are three possible reasons for this failure:

1 Resistance from welfare and social professionals.
2 Lack of an analysis of power.
3 Lack of community participation.

The primary focus for change emphasized the failure of public social and welfare services to respond adequately to the needs of their users. The critique of the bureaucratic and professionalized welfare services identified their size and the closed world of professional agencies as being resistant to resident or user criticisms and demands for greater access. Seeing these agencies as obstacles to local democracy, the focus was on the need to reform the way services were organized and to improve the ways in which they were delivered.

This critique can be summarized thus:

> program specialization; centralization of executive authority; institutional constraints; hierarchic distance, the civil service merit system – promotion derived from a closed bureaucratic culture; municipal unions; inter-governmental dependence.
>
> (Mudd 1984: 1322)

Those categories could apply to the critique offered by pluralists and the 'new left' of the inadequacies of public welfare services. The recommendations, though, focus more narrowly on the development of decentralized strategies which encompass changes in the organization of service delivery, the devolvement of decision-making power to lower level officers and, occasionally, the inclusion of extended roles for elected members. The issue of empowerment of local communities was not addressed in a coherent or systematic way. The issues of organizational structures within the service delivery departments dominated the internal discussions held between service professionals and elected members. It was assumed that these changes would empower users but this was rarely directly addressed – except in a conventional and formalistic manner (as evidenced by proposals to establish neighbourhood forums to 'empower' local communities).

As a contrast Yin and Yates (1975) make the point that the identification of outcomes associated with decentralization strategies in terms of their territorial focus and the degree of client involvement in the administration of services (p. 29) is essential. They suggest five potential outcomes for decentralization policies, each of which is associated with increased client control over the services delivered.

15

The outcomes they identify are:

1   An increase in the flow of information between the servers and the served.
2   An improvement in service officials' attitudes.
3   An improvement in clients' attitudes.
4   An improvement in services delivered.
5   An increase in client control.

(1975: 30–31)

They suggest that in terms of evaluating the success of decentralization policies it is important to note that:

> One of the most significant implications of decentralization is that it brings the analysis of service problems down to the street level … decentralized service delivery makes the particularity of neighbourhood services its central concern.
>
> (1975: 187–189)

To facilitate the specific concerns of neighbourhoods in determining the allocation, distribution and evaluation of resources, Yin and Yates set out seven 'distinct decentralization strategies that have been used, sometimes in isolation and sometimes in combination with each other, in nearly every decentralization innovation' (1975: 26).

The seven strategies suggested by Yin and Yates include:

- community relations policies – to build informal relationships between service officials and clients;
- physical redeployment – to relocate facilities and staff to serve the needs of a specific neighbourhood;
- administrative decentralization – to grant officials greater discretionary authority and autonomy;
- grievance mechanism – to establish procedures for receiving complaints from clients;
- employment of neighbourhood residents – who represent or who are clients in a particular service area;
- neighbourhood institutions – to develop separate institutions outside the established bureaucracy to fulfil neighbourhood needs;
- political decentralization – the attempt to give clients control over a service being delivered to a specific neighbourhood.

(1975: 26–27)

Nearly 30 years later we can see in the NRS an attempt to bring about change which reflects this model. As we show in Chapter 4, such approaches are not easy to achieve and we can expect resistance from a number of interest groups.

The introduction of reform within local government aimed at introducing a 'localized' dimension to service delivery combined with organizational changes to transfer day-to-day responsibility to front line staff was not (*per se*) either a 'radical' or an 'empowering' strategy. Furthermore the aim of securing greater 'client control' over services, as suggested by Yin and Yates, does not necessarily follow from decentralization of functional services onto a neighbourhood basis.

What we are suggesting is that the absence of an analysis which combines an understanding of the functional role of local services within local government and their political and power relationship with the central and local state leads to the emphasis on the issues of content rather than process.

During the late 1970s and 1980s the UK was going through a period of profound economic crisis. Unemployment in the industrial urban centres of the UK was rising. The Thatcher government adopted social and economic policies which accentuated the process of economic and industrial restructuring. At the same time the government sought to reduce the financial and political autonomy of local government. This seriously restricted the power of local authorities to act independently. The 'municipal socialist' or 'new left' agenda included the development of local economic strategies to minimize the global and national impact of unemployment. As their relative power diminished, their ability to introduce local and innovative social and economic programmes was reduced too – the economic crisis was also a political crisis (Gyford 1985). In the mid 1980s the Thatcher government defeated a national miners' strike, local authorities accepted the demands of central government and the new Labour leader Neil Kinnock distanced himself and the national party from the 'going local' agenda.

UNDERSTANDING FAILURE

Financial and political weakness at the local level reveals the limited conceptual understanding, at the time, of the power of capital and the state to meet its needs. The work of Fainstein and colleagues (Fainstein and Fainstein 1982; Fainstein *et al.* 1986) is particularly useful here, in clarifying these relationships. Their analysis does, in the view of these writers, provide a model which continues to inform current debates. It has been augmented by the wider literature on globalization. As Clarke (2004) has argued, while some see the neo-globalization effect as widespread, specifically:

- the marketization of public services;
- the preoccupation with 'zone' initiatives;

- the 'consumer' being dominant;
- the emphasis on competition;
- the depoliticization of management and public services.

the critical point he makes is that the globalization effect is uneven and (sometimes) contradictory. The value to us of the 1980s' approach by Fainstein and Fainstein is that it 'captures' different trends and moments in the uneven development of the urban crisis. They point to specific trends which we discuss below, and while they are describing the US experience, the broad trends can be (and are) replicable across Europe and other Western economies.

Fainstein and Fainstein's framework is informed by their contention that 'capitalists require state intervention in the urban system' (1982: 11). They locate the relationship between local policies and the central state within the needs and demands of the economic system, claiming that 'if the state only does capital's bidding, it still carries out functions that capital cannot do by itself and can effect transformations that change the nature of social relations' (p. 279).

This model requires us to see the development of policy in its relationship with social and economic policies. They use the descriptive and interpretative device of locating change and conflict within a continuum of policy initiatives, identifying three phases of urban policy making and attempting to understand the actual process of policy making in each stage. Though the model is based upon their analysis of US urban policy making, it provides a conceptual base which can be applied to the experience in UK policy.

The three types of city 'regimes' they identify are the 'directive'; the 'concessionary'; and the 'conserving' (Fainstein and Fainstein 1982: 258–260). The directive regime covers the period from 1950 to 1964. It is during this time that the state supported large-scale urban redevelopment programmes throughout the USA. Their claim is that capital needs state institutions and agencies to meet the social policy needs which capital cannot provide. Large-scale provision of the necessary infrastructure, housing programmes, education facilities and administration are illustrative of the social policy needs of capital. These policies may also reflect a coincidence of interest between the needs of capital and the needs of local communities. In particular, Fainstein and Fainstein claim, they may be considered to advance the needs and interests of working-class communities and sections of society dispossessed through gender and race. During this period Fainstein and Fainstein suggest there is little opposition to these policies from these groups.

It is during the second phase of urban policy making, the development of the concessionary regime (1965–1981), that opposition to the state is exercised. The Fainstein and Fainstein model identifies the period during which there was significant social unrest in the USA as a period in which the state was required to be responsive to working-class/black women's demands in order to preserve its legitimacy. In this period the state introduced policies to meet educational, political and social inequalities through the War on Poverty programmes, and through the allocation of resources to local community and neighbourhood groups. The state is required to introduce such policies in order to preserve social and political control of the institutions and distribution of power with society.

The third phase — that of the conserving regime — corresponds to the increasing financial and economic crisis of the central state. Fainstein and Fainstein suggest that the period from 1981 onwards reflects the inability of capital to reconcile its needs for structural changes within the labour market and the industrial and economic base with the social policy demands of the working class. They describe the process of fiscal retrenchment as follows:

> The needs of the city are redefined in physical terms.... Civil service unions dare not fight the cutbacks ... as taxpayer hostility limits their power to retain jobs.... The aims of the government are directed at achieving improved fiscal management, dismissing redundant staff and generally improving the investment climate.
>
> (1982: 182–184)

This model locates the implementation of urban policy at the central and local levels within constraints determined by the needs of capital. Those making policy in the city and the interests of capital are not determined by the institutions of the state (such as the political and administrative mechanisms for enabling parliamentary democracy to be administered, or the bureaucracy of the state to supervize and evaluate social policy), but the specific and particular needs of capital will be shaped by capital's interaction with the institutions of the state.

What Fainstein and Fainstein provide is a way of exploring the paradigm shifts which have taken place in the UK over the past 30 years. Thus, while the model for decentralization developed in the 1980s explicitly sought to equate improved service delivery with local democracy, the context within which initiatives took place focused on the former. Fainstein and Fainstein, therefore, offer a model which enables us to elucidate the internal dynamics of change and to bring it to the foreground of any analysis.

In the mid 1980s it was argued that the needs of the central state took precedence over the reforms being introduced at the local level. More significantly, the advocates of decentralization lacked an analysis of the 'state' to explain their relationship to the centre. This failure to analyse the interlocking relationship between economic development, public policy making and service delivery is critical. In the UK the absence of such an interpretation resulted in the development of local initiatives which had little chance of success. This was particularly evident when examining policies introduced to enhance local democracy and citizen engagement.

The third possible explanation for failure can be found in the understanding of community participation. While some advocates of change (Hoggett 1997) were aware that rearranging the administrative and managerial structures was necessary but not sufficient to ensure change, the issue of community engagement became peripheral. There were attempts in a number of authorities to establish local community forums. But while the issues for discussion were broad, the potential to effect change was very limited. The actual advantage, for some community activists, of attending such meetings was perceived as minimal.

The relative failures of these initiatives, in places where decentralization was seen as a priority, are revealing. They suggest that advocates of 'going local' had failed to grasp the significance of what they were seeking to do. Resistance to change from professional agencies was evident. But it also suggests that there is a real dilemma for those proposing radical change. The task is made difficult because of the lack of participation at the local level. For enthusiasts of neighbourhood management and community participation the difficulty focuses on whether improved service delivery needs to come first before the public are engaged.

The broader issue which undermined the potential of such processes to effect change was the emergence of the 'new managerialism' in UK local government (Speeden and Diamond 1993). The reforms introduced both at a local level and by the centre emphasized the need for enhanced managerial and professional powers.

As a number of commentators (Gaster 1995; Hoggett 1991) have indicated, the significance of managerial skills, in decision making, resource allocation and delivery of services, was transformed during the late 1980s and 1990s in the UK.

Thus, the failure of the going local experiments in the early 1980s exposed significant weaknesses in theoretical and conceptual understanding of the power and dynamics of the local state by their advocates. But, they also resulted in a shift in power (at a local level) back to key senior managers. In addition, community engagement became translated into 'consumer' or 'customer' involvement. This redefinition of the citizen as consumer was profound and significant.

Independent policy organizations such as the Institute for Public Policy Research (IPPR), the Commission for Local Democracy (CLD) and the New Local Government Network (NLGN) all played an important role in setting the public policy agenda for New Labour after 1997 (Stoker 1996; 1998).

The work of the IPPR in promoting citizens' panels and citizens' juries (Coote and Lenaghan 1997) cannot be underestimated. Citizens' panels were sponsored by a number of local authorities. They provided a representative sample of the local electorate which could be polled to gather their views on a number of issues identified by the local authority. They were seen as a way of aiding the policy-making process and, thus, the decision-making process at the local level (Diamond et al. 1997; Speeden and Diamond 1993). They have been taken up by local authorities as a valuable addition to existing systems. But, while they have provided a rich resource of data to inform the local authority, they are an essentially passive exercise.

Citizens juries, too, have been less successful in the UK than their advocates hoped. There is little evidence of their effecting policy changes at a local level. They are clearly seen by local agencies as advisory. They provide a 'space' for views to be heard but they have no direct impact on decision making.

Since 1997 there has been some evidence of a change in policy. The Blair government through its neighbourhood renewal approach does make an explicit reference to improving the capacity of local groups and people to participate. In part this is because the initiatives are short term and there is a need to ensure a presence after the resources are spent.

But the dominance of managerial and professional interests remains. We are moving beyond the third phase (identified by Fainstein and Fainstein) to one in which co-option is the key. The partnership boards and multiplicity of networks established do confer a status and legitimacy on those few community representatives present. But they are (or are at risk of becoming) 'professionalized' too.

The case for independent voices and support to local networks remains strong. There is evidence in the UK (Diamond 2004) that initiatives can develop which have a critical voice present to give advice and guidance to local groups.

CONCLUSION

Regeneration initiatives in both the UK and the USA grew out of the social and economic restructuring of urban centres. In the UK the issues of poverty, race and class were identified as the key catalysts for growing discontent in the industrial cities. The need to 'reclaim' the city (and especially the inner core) was seen as necessary if the decline of key cities was to be halted.

The strategies adopted in the UK involved a number of elements including the redevelopment of the inner core to make it attractive for investment and innovation; the depoliticization of welfare and service delivery by the enhancement of voluntary sector agencies and the separation of their activities from local government; the promotion of the 'partnership' model to welfare and social agencies; and the assertion of 'managerialism' at the expense of local politics.

To develop and to implement these strategies it is possible to identify a number of approaches. In a context where the city and the urban environment were undergoing profound change to meet the needs of capital and the market, the emergence of new managerialism was critical. UK city and local authorities experimented with changes to the way services were organized. The concept of 'neighbourhood' city halls or one-stop shops with multi-agency teams and devolved decision-making powers was developed and refined. To some extent the 'stand-alone' regeneration agency in the UK has been an inevitable part of this process.

An important part of this process has been the further detachment of the regeneration professionals from the localities and neighbourhoods in which they work. These restructuring processes were taking place during the social and economic crises of the past 25 years. At a city level local political and business elites

21

have attempted to establish their 'place' within a supranational league of world or European cities.

In this context the place and role of local-community-based groups appears marginal. To redress these inequalities in power and decision-making local groups need to form their own networks and alliances to act as a political counterpoint to the regeneration managerialists. At a local level, there is a tradition (and potential) to question the decision makers and policy makers. And, as Clarke (2004) argues, to make the case for reclaiming the public realm. It is an approach which can be found by looking at the Rogers Report (see Table 1.1) and those who are arguing for an increased emphasis on the significance of civic society.

Table 1.1 *Can we make a patchwork quilt? Urban regeneration from 1969 to the present*

Initiative or organisation	Operational period	Description
Urban Programme	1969–1992	The first major government programme to be targeted on inner cities, its aim was to rebuild confidence and encourage investment, latterly in 57 priority areas
Urban Development Corporations (UDCs)	1981–1998	Twelve English quangos set up to regenerate designated areas of our major towns and cities
Enterprise Zones (EZs)	1981–1996	Fast-track planning and financial incentives for developers and occupiers willing to take the risk on unpopular commercial locations
Urban Development Grant	1982–1988	Provided financial support for a wide range of urban development projects involving the private sector which would otherwise not have taken place
Estate Action	1985–1994	Aimed to help local authorities transform unpopular housing estates into places where people wanted to live
City Grant	1988–1994	Offered direct gap funding to the private sector for development schemes in priority urban areas which otherwise would not have been commercially viable
Housing Action Trusts	1992–	Comprehensive quango-led transfer and redevelopment of social housing stock for a number of large social housing estates
City Challenge	1992–1998	The first real attempt at a competitive bidding programme for regeneration funding. Resulted in 31 five-year programmes, managed by partnerships who all received the same amount of money

Continued on next page

Table 1.1 (cont.)

Initiative or organisation	Operational period	Description
English Partnerships	1993–	National quango which subsumed City Grant, Derelict Land Grant and English Estates; grew quickly to a budget of over £400 million but then lost its regional offices and budgets to the Regional Development Agencies (RDAs). Now regrouping as a national body following a merger with the Commission for New Towns, but with an uncertain set of functions
Single Regeneration Budget (SRB) Challenge Fund	1994–	A rolling programme of bidding rounds for local partnerships to secure resources for up to seven years for a mix of economic, social and physical regeneration schemes. Now in Round 5, it has become targeted on the most deprived local authority areas
Estates Renewal Challenge Fund	1996–	Local authorities compete for government resources to regenerate deprived estates based on the transfer of the stock to a housing association or housing company to allow a mix of public and private sector funding for renewal

Source: Adapted from the Rogers Report (1999)

DISCUSSION POINTS

- What are the strengths/weaknesses for you of thinking about the overview of the regeneration experience provided here?
- What have been the central drivers for change in regeneration management?
- How far have public policy initiatives been shaped by review and reflection?
- How have issues of equality and diversity informed regeneration practices?

FURTHER READING

Clarke, J. (2004) 'Dissolving the Public Realm? The Logic and Limits of Neo-liberalism', *Journal of Social Policy* 33(1): 27–48

Higgins, J., Deakin, N., Edwards, J. and Wicks, M. (1983) *Government and Urban Poverty*, London: Blackwell

Social Exclusion Unit (1998) *Bringing Britain Together: A National Strategy for Neighbourhood Renewal*, HMSO Cm 4045, London: Stationery Office

USEFUL WEB SITES

Community Cohesion Unit – www.communitycohesion.gov.uk

Commission for Racial Equality – www.cre.gov.uk

Home Office – www.homeoffice.gov.uk

Local Government Association – www.lga.gov.uk

Neighbourhood Renewal Unit – www.neighbourhood.gov.uk www.renewal.net

Neighbourhood Statistics – www.neighbourhoodstatistics.gov.uk

Chapter 2

Learning new skills and competences

KEY THEMES

- The impact of the changing context and social and economic factors on learning and skills development within regeneration.
- The need for innovative initiatives, and the creation of learning and skills development in design, delivery and management of schemes.
- A review of different approaches to learning, by drawing on some US and UK public leadership, policy learning and transfer literature.
- The role of accreditation and how different levels of understanding and skills development can be accommodated within training and staff development programmes.
- The demand for innovation, risk management and entrepreneurial action and reflection on new roles, responsibilities and ways of working.

LEARNING POINTS

By the end of this chapter we hope that you will be able to:

- Identify the changing context and demand for new skills and competences.
- Reflect upon new 'action spaces' for decision making.
- Consider types of skills demanded and barriers to overcome.
- Identify deficiencies in your own skills base, examine management development needs and redefine your own practice.
- Consider types of learning and how policy transfer occurs.

INTRODUCTION

Regeneration management is governed by mandates and funding regimes quite different to those you may have been familiar with when you entered your professional careers. The hierarchical and top-down bureaucracies many of you will have entered when professionally trained have been replaced by more flexible and networked organizational forms, many requiring a wholly new set of skills, competences and expertise to deliver the modernising agenda. Multi-agency professionals are increasingly required to work beyond their own organizational and professional boundaries in partnership and to pool resources in an effort to achieve commonly agreed regeneration objectives. Moreover, the need to draw in communities and other stakeholder groups to formulate and implement regeneration initiatives has illustrated the significance of stakeholder management as a key area of activity. More in-depth evaluation of this particular skill need follows in Chapter 4. New action spaces have been created in which policy experimentation and learning are essential to future success, but the paucity of guidance from central government leaves many managers at a loss as to how to proceed. Learning from best practice and benchmarking activities with other external sources have become the preferred means of adaptation and continuous learning in very messy, ambiguous and contested territories.

Specifically in this chapter we emphasize that the intensification of a mixed economy of public services and the consequent changing relations of politicians, administrators, providers and publics have brought a new emphasis on innovation, creativity, entrepreneurship and risk in the public sector. Arguably regeneration managers are now urged to come up with innovative managerial practices to deal with the sometimes contradictory dimensions of quality and targets and the different aspects of risk associated with them. Moreover, they are expected to instigate mechanisms to monitor and evaluate programmes and auditing and reporting of activities. It is important to recognize that new forms of organizations and changes to funding regimes are challenging traditional bureaucratic practices with consequent requirements for competences/skills that can be used to manage more fluid and entrepreneurial situations.

At the same time improved quality and performance to satisfy all stakeholder demands, as well as partnerships, networks or other collaborative arrangements, and new methods of financing of public services (e.g. through private finance) are demanding innovation and risk management in public service provision. We argue that despite the concepts of innovation, entrepreneurialism and risk taking in public service delivery being relatively new ideas, many external forces are keenly impacting on the work of regeneration managers. In an era of change, you will increasingly be required to be innovative, entrepreneurial and risk taking. Moreover, managers need a wholly new set of attributes, skills and competences that allow them, and their organizations, to be more innovative, entrepreneurial and risk taking.

In this chapter we draw out the main points of the modernising agenda, in particular the centrality of experimentation, continuous learning from best practice elsewhere, and policy transfer not only to show the new challenges you are being presented with in a rapidly changing world, but also to identify the types of skills and competences that are essential to manage professional, organizational and individual performance.

In the context of greater outcome and impact measures and other forms of target setting, scrutiny and auditing, regeneration managers who are able to act more entrepreneurially, innovatively and creatively, take risks and be experimental must carry out their roles by identifying the barriers to achieving objectives. It is also imperative that you develop the social and political skills to deal with conflicting values, and accommodate other views of how best to bring about change.

By reflecting on the changed national modernising context, and the dynamic local decision-making action spaces you are required to work in, within your day-to-day strategic and operational roles, this chapter should enlighten you and provide a better understanding of the need for new skills and competences. It should enable you to identify your own strengths, weaknesses and management development needs. Policy transfer, lessons drawing from best practice and benchmarking are not uncontentious concepts, but they have been identified as a central thrust of the modernising agenda, and will remain vitally important aspects of your future managerial roles and responsibilities.

POLICY LEARNING AND TRANSFER

As we seek to explain, searching for lessons from past or current experience to improve practice is not recent. Aristotle developed general propositions on good governance by observing differences in how different states addressed common problems (*The Politics*, Book 4, Section 3). Furthermore, generalising across space and time by trial and error, or identifying similarities and differences, can counteract perceptions that specific situations are unique, as well as reducing parochialism and isolationism (Rose 1993: 13). Arguably, combining and synthesising elements to produce a wholly new programme provides the inspiration and stimulus for novel programmes of action (Rose 1993). However, the multiplicity of factors, specific conditions, power and resource distribution or prevalent political values can combine to undermine the technical feasibility of lesson drawing, but these limitations can be overcome by systematic comparisons to diagnose emergent problems.

It is clear that there have been many diverse approaches and methods of investigating policy learning and transfer, and recent attempts have been subjected to scrutiny and criticism. Nationally the Cabinet Office, Social Inclusion Unit and Neighbourhood Renewal Unit have issued discussion reports on policy learning and transfer of innovative ideas, whereas OECD has sponsored comparative bench-marking studies, study visits, temporary assignments, use of foreign experts on policy design, monitoring and evaluation (Luxembourg Conference 2002), in the belief that transnational learning can improve the quality of policy making (Stampfer 2002). This was evident in the case of Estonia where policy instruments and capac-ities were developed by using foreign expertise (Parna 2002). Policy effectiveness improved in both Holland and Sweden when, over time, policy makers visited other countries for personal involvement in policy making (Bockholt 2002).

Comparative research on policy networks has been criticized for its failure to recognize the significance of dialectic processes of learning within networks shaped by policy environments, or how networks are formed, evolve, transform and ter-minate in response to broader social, political and economic change processes (Hay and Richards 2000). Often, the politics and conflicts in all processes of network development have been ignored in previous work.

For those working in regeneration, social learning theory can explore how policy makers learn, or fail to learn, from both past experience and policy lessons by showing how learning depends on past legacies. As such, promoters of effective policy learning are usually experts on policy, and states need to operate without societal or pluralistic considerations for effective policy learning to be achieved (Greener 2001). The technical expertise needed for policy learning tends to be the preserve of expert officials (Hall 1993), but this is not always the case. Indeed regeneration managers are not experts in the field as they seek tried and tested ways of formulating and implementing strategies for change within an experimental milieu.

We agree with the view that good practice in one context may not necessarily be so in another (Tomlinson 2002), and all changes are bound to a particular time. However, comparisons can aid policy development by isolating the sources of vari-ance in governance (Peters 1988: 3–5).

NEW PROFESSIONAL ROLES WITH A CHANGING CONTEXT

In addition to this variance, little attention has been paid in the literature to the new roles, responsibilities and capabilities needed by regeneration managers to perform effectively in completely different environments. Not only are they taking on roles as community champions or leading change processes, but the increased need to work in partnership with communities and partners beyond their own organizational boundaries, and stimulate cultural change, have implications in terms of the way they perceive their roles. The cross-cutting nature of activities and the vertical rather than horizontal and bureaucratic nature of managing has altered the patterns, practices and performance of managers in the maelstrom of regener-ation. Delivering services to a disparate groups of clients in an ever more complex, ambiguous environment and the move from a supplier-driven to a customer-focused basis have had dramatic effects on managerial functions and approaches.

We suggest that professionalism has always been a driving force in service delivery, but the multi-professional input into decision making and the need to deliver in collaboration with other agencies have created major problems in who does what, how, and more importantly, as will be explored more fully in Chapter 6, who is accountable for actions. Thus, as budgets, programmes and projects are aligned, confusion over whether or not managers are equipped with the correct skills mix has become an important consideration.

For those engaged in regeneration, managing the tensions of performing well as community champions and motivating or leading multi-agency partnerships is critical to understanding the processes. We argue that the complex and adaptable systems of regeneration, composed of a diversity of agents interacting with each other, generate novel and innovative benefits for a whole system. There is a positive strength in developing leadership in multi-agency working partnerships, by encouraging a process of change, shared among others in a system (Gordon 2002). As the lines between public, private and non-profit have become blurred and sectors are converging (Kellerman and Webster 2001; Mumford *et al.* 2003), the environments inhabited by regeneration managers are fuzzy, and there is insufficient critical mass of scholarly work on public sector leadership to develop effective guidance (Kellerman and Webster 2001).

A difficulty for those managing regeneration is in understanding the changing context, which includes:

- A growing recognition that major external and internal forces such as non-interventionist policies of nation states have altered the balance between government and other agencies.
- Diversification of decision making throughout a wide range of organizations.
- A restructuring of inter-governmental relationships as the more prevalent form of governance.
- Rapid global and technological changes and interdependence and competition between nation states have increased competitive pressures.
- A shrinking of budgets to support social programmes.

It is generally agreed that no single organization acting alone can solve the multi-faceted social and economic problems. The need to mainstream finance and solve an increasing number of linked problems means that alliances must be formed horizontally and vertically around relationships with stakeholder groups of service users, consumers and other partner organizations. Standards of service delivery and measurable outcomes and targets have forced managers to work in 'joined-up' ways, but unfortunately little thought has been given to exactly how they can do this without requisite training, and what some of the problems might be in a complete alteration of existing ways of working.

We argue that these new systems of 'governance' have blurred the boundaries between the state, the market and civil society, and engage a plurality of multi-agency partnerships to achieve common goals. In the 'outcome-focused' new world of public policy it is argued that systems must be organized around 'what works' in the interface between organizations, rather than within the boundaries of single organizations (DETR 1999) and there is a clear need to address some of the 'wicked' or' cross-cutting' issues. It is important to identify not only 'what works', but crucially 'what works, for whom and in what circumstances' (Gray and Jenkins 2001: 220). Some commentators had regarded service delivery mechanisms based on bureaucratic, producer-led organizational structures as the key problem in aggravating problems in the 1980s, which *exacerbated* the existing limitations on centrally directed resources and restricted local discretion.

A FRAGMENTED POLITY

Nowadays it is generally accepted that the public policy system is characterized by issues or problems lying outside any one area of professional expertise and this creates barriers in the boundaries between different administrative jurisdictions. Earlier writers had drawn boundaries around 'action spaces' where decisions were made, and the imagery of networks allowed a picture of the linkages between actors and agencies in complex and varied sectors (Friend *et al*. 1974). The subtleties of formal and informal relationships could then be discerned and, by locating the action spaces within a broader policy arena, showed the problems inherent in top-down planned strategies. The turbulence of the environment, multiple account-abilities, technicalities of implementation and execution added to the problems.

Writers had differences of opinion on just how fragmented the polity had become during the efficiency drives of the 1980s and 1990s. Some argued that a fragmented locality system had replaced a previously integrated one (J. Stewart 1982, quoted in Rhodes 1998: 18), whereas others have long considered the UK system of government as a 'fragmented and differentiated polity' (Rhodes 1998: 3). Rejecting the unitary and integrated basis of the polity, Rhodes considered the state as a system of central/local interdependence in which territories have equal importance to the centre. This alternative view of policy making had located local authorities within networks of public and private 'non-local sources of policy change'; or a milieu of governmental, professional and corporate institutions where no single organization dominated (Rhodes 1998: 3). Policy was therefore messy, complex, functionally differentiated and shaped by numerous factors and diverse political and non-political actors. This labyrinthine system that replaced the machine bureaucracy created problems of poor co-ordination and control, as well as unintended consequences.

Many of the new service domains, in which you will be expected to work in partnership, have few mandatory guidelines, and this limits the scope for innovation, creativity and entrepreneurialism. The lack of mandatory guidance within regeneration presents major problems in who is responsible for which activities and managers may be reluctant to act entrepreneurially or take risks while they are accountable for spending on programmes. There are considerable ambiguities in untried and essentially experimental forms of governance, a situation made worse by confusion on contradictory, overlapping and duplicated sets of central government programmes and initiatives. Arguably, central control is as intense as ever, with a rhetoric of devolved implementation; however, this has not been matched by a willingness to trust front line deliverers with discretionary powers (Gray and Jenkins 2001: 216).

A very real challenge to Weberian formalization, centralization and bureaucratic procedures and displaced, generalized, top-down, command and control public sector management approaches with more flexible arrangements has led to:

- fragmentation;
- organizational segregation;
- decentralized decision making across formal organizational boundaries.

  (Bogason 2000: 10)

We agree with the view that as public sector professionals are juxtaposed alongside other non-state actors, new communication processes between different groups and agencies have become more important than top-down formal hierarchies. This has created situations in which cultural and professional differences, varied institutional histories and contradictory working practices have emerged. Adaptable and flat networks require managers with wholly new sets of skills and competences, with the capacity to communicate across boundaries. 'Situation-oriented' rather than 'bureaucratically rule-bound' managers are more crucially needed in the regeneration milieu.

As we attempt to explain, differences do exist between the sectors despite some private sector approaches proving to be successful in the public sector, but there remain problems in applying private sector ideas in public sector environments. It is important not to fall into the trap of believing there is no difference in leadership in public, private and voluntary sectors. The key difference is the political context in which leaders clash openly on major issues, interactions between politicians, public managers and stakeholders, and the pressure for short-termist solutions (Bovaird and Loeffler 2003: 69).

LEADERSHIP IN REGENERATION

In seeking to develop some models of learning and skills development we drew on the existing literature on leadership, and Chapter 4 gives a much deeper evaluation of the significance of leadership in engaging stakeholders. However, it became evident that existing work is heavily grounded in the belief that it is the interpersonal influence of visionary individuals who 'do' things, rather than leadership being a 'process', shared among others in a system (Gordon 2002). As the lines between public, private and non-profit have become blurred and sectors are converging (Kellerman and Webster 2001; Mumford *et al*. 2003), the environments inhabited by public managers have become fuzzy. However, social scientists have failed to create a critical mass of scholarly work on public sector leadership (Kellerman and Webster 2001).

Research indicates that leaders in public sector organizations are now expected to work alongside a variety of stakeholders in new organizational forms, such as partnerships, networks and collaborative arrangements to achieve overall aims. The messy and ambiguous settings lead managers to attempt to make sense and develop some order and clarity. While nor denying the importance of the role of visionary public managers who lead communities, we would suggest that this has to be done alongside many other actors in a holistic way.

Arguably, much of the literature on skills and competences has been developed on the basis of understanding what individual managers need within specific (usually private) companies but there are few studies of those operating in politically charged or politically led organizations, and fewer still looking at the types of skills needed in multi-agency partnerships where boundaries are blurred.

The modernising public sector environment now requires:

- Consumerism/citizen involvement.
- Greater democratization.
- The need to build capacities and improve quality and performance.
- A requirement for skills mixes located in different people at different times.
- An understanding that no one organization or person possesses all the skills and competences to undertake activities.
- Effective performance by regeneration managers, who synthesize past experience, skills, knowledge, behaviours and competences within organizational, but increasingly in cross-boundary, settings.

Most existing frameworks are bounded within an organizational setting and do not take account of the outward focus of public organizations. Managers now work in new contexts with other partner organizations, communities and businesses/voluntary and charitable sectors or other traditional auxiliary bodies (such as trade unions, churches, universities, sporting clubs, etc.) and this leads to important questions, such as:

- Do the public managers in regeneration have a set of individual skills or organizational skills they can use to contribute to overall local needs?
- What new skills are required to work in completely different ways with partners and communities?
- If there are deficiencies, how can these be remedied and by which organization?

RECENT INITIATIVES

Some recent initiatives have been introduced to answer these questions, as follows:

- The Regeneration Exchange (to exchange good practice).
- BURA (British Urban Regeneration Association) which has developed an accreditation process for regeneration practitioners.
- Learning Curve.
- Universities, in-house and external consultants.

Furthermore, in the north-east of England, the five regional universities have recently instigated a Joint Universities Regeneration Prospectus with the aim of providing web access to a one-stop shop on information. It contains courses relevant to professionals, policy makers, practitioners and local residents seeking to develop skills and knowledge that can be applied to regeneration and neighbourhood renewal in the region (one of the authors is the Durham link person on this). This is supported by the Universities for the NE, One North East, the RDA, Government Office NE, other agencies and the NE Centre of Excellence for Regeneration. The web site went live in 2004. Additionally, One North East, the RDA, is currently mapping regeneration expertise, with a view to aligning identified training and development needs.

As public agencies (such as local authorities) instigate structural changes to the way they conduct business, we suggest that this will benefit skills development. By devolving or decentralising services through area committees, LSPs or other mechanisms, opportunities are created for learning from best practice, or learning from other professional groups, as well as from communities.

Important cultural changes are being encouraged as a result of using consultants or academics, brought into forums as change agents (both authors have been involved in such activities). In this way public managers/communities are able to share experiences of how services can be delivered. This facilitates greater understanding of the context within which service provision takes place, allows an identification of key stakeholders and strategic issues, and reveals the barriers to achieving commonly agreed objectives. Away days (and many partnerships have engaged in such activities) serve to alter gradually the cultures and working practices of each participant.

As an example, in a city council in the north-east the following activities were used as learning opportunities during the development of a leisure strategy (developed by one of the authors):

- internal and external stakeholder workshops;
- consultation meetings with communities, trade unions and council members;
- focus groups of hard-to-reach groups;
- creativity days and exhibitions;

- benchmarking;
- challenge days;
- surveys;
- expert panels.

All were designed to help the authority learn more about its context, processes and linkages, as well as helping to improve its best value and regeneration processes.

Internally many local authorities are experimenting with new skills and competence development, by developing formal programmes on management development. This is organized by consultants who provide short courses, or by sending staff off to specified programmes of education/training, such as the BURA accreditation mentioned previously. New innovative ways of involving the communities and other groups in decision making have been encouraged, and through village appraisals and evolving community networks there are attempts to achieve cross-pollination of ideas on better decision making.

The Neighbourhood Renewal Unit (NRU) has identified the need to build up the capacities of professionals, practitioners, policy makers and communities in deprived areas, and set up Learning Curve. This was launched on 21 October 2003 by Barbara Roche, Minister for Social Exclusion, in Manchester and takes forward the £21.6 million Skills and Knowledge Programme launched in December 2002, to ensure that there are comprehensive learning and development strategies for neighbourhood renewal. It is a 23-point action plan to target people working in regeneration, to fill the gaps in skills and knowledge at national, regional and neighbourhood levels. It is designed to provide a framework of skills, development and behaviours for delivering effective neighbourhood renewal (NRU, Skills and Knowledge: see http://www.neighbourhood.gov.uk/sandk.asp?pageid=36).

The Improvement and Development Agency has developed a model to support self-sustaining improvement in local government, and Leadbeater (2003: 135–177) argues that there are no magic recipes, only the need for a skilful combination of the good-quality basic ingredients of strong leadership, demanding performance management, sound financial systems and constant customer focus.

To create public learning requires a whole-system approach to:

- Involve the whole system, develop shared understanding of current realities and collective vision for the future.
- Develop key questions on gaps between current and desired state, to agree publicly with stakeholders on the way ahead.
- Develop a climate in the parts of their own organizations to gain commitment and combat coercion.
- Challenge rhetoric of collaboration and partnership as opposed to competition.

34

- Place a high value on learning in human resource processes and performance and appraisal.
- Develop and value a learning ethos, discourage action fixated behaviours.
- Reinforce learning, discourage competition and short-term target setting, and incorporate into pay and reward systems.

(Adapted from Attwood *et al.* 2003: 94)

In attempting to regenerate locales managers are breaking away from old-style urban managerialism and resource allocation processes, and the new managerialism involving many stakeholder agencies and communities means that specific initiatives are collaboratively developed to regenerate local areas. Whether or not this new managerialism is capable of bringing the necessary changes has a lot to do with the skills and capacities of the actors involved, but may also be due to the fact that

> all mechanisms for governing are prone to failure, because there are limitations to effective interventions in the market. Secondly partnerships operate on a scale and over time periods where objectives may be difficult to achieve and the difficulties in developing effective inter-personal, inter-organizational and inter-systemic co-ordination are considerable. Failure is normal rather than abnormal and requires constant review of co-ordinating mechanisms, and greater legitimacy by participatory politics to involve a wider group of stakeholders (p. 14). State managers have short term horizons and are open to lobbying, they have bounded rationality, limited information, uncertainty, time pressures, multiple, contradictory and sometimes infeasible goals, costs and benefits that differ from public goals and external resistance, outputs are difficult to measure.
>
> (B. Jessop, in Stoker 2000: 30)

THE NEW SKILLS AND COMPETENCIES FOR REGENERATION

Regeneration managers inhabit an environment in which they are expected to:

- create entrepreneurial change in government;
- turn crises and adversity into opportunity;
- champion causes, act as leaders and develop collaboration;
- develop a civic infrastructure based on informal networks;
- establish and maintain visions, goals and trust;
- obtain resources (financial and non financial) from external bodies.

(Osborne and Gaebler 1992)

35

or who are:

- embedded in a social milieu where complex interactions take place;
- operating in dynamic, uncertain environments;
- making systematically organized choices;
- creating change and seizing opportunities;
- transforming political and social arenas;
- setting agendas and developing innovative ideas;
- taking risks (but not for monetary gain).

(Schneider *et al*.1995)

The literature on entrepreneurialism is growing but the skills needed to manage networks are rarely considered, or given scant attention. However, we argue that inter-agency partnerships and networks, which should be the basis for shared values, often fail due to rivalry and lack of a shared vision. There is little in the network literature to say how networks emerge or are formed, or the political struggles underlying their formation or operation. Squabbles of distribution of power mean that it is imperative for the political, managerial and administrative processes to be properly managed.

Managing networks is problematic for regeneration managers, not least because of the complexity and evolutionary nature, but also because they may change over time and involve many relationships. As kaleidoscopic entities partnerships require negotiation over 'shifting sands', as well as diplomacy, the need to foresee political conflicts, patterns between seemingly chaotic sets of relationships, and an ability to think in a linear way. In dealing with ambiguity and fuzziness, regeneration managers are urged to be tolerant of ambiguity and mess.

While accepting that risk taking has never been a significant element of the portfolio of public servants, we suggest that increasingly it is dominating the regeneration landscape. To date risk taking and entrepreneurial zeal have not been the more consummate skills of senior civil servants (Gray and Jenkins 2001: 214). Neither, until quite recently, has there been a need to activate networks and take on the brokerage mantle of bringing together diverse groups from dissimilar cultures and conflicting values. Managing stakeholder relationships with all the associated mediation, arbitration and facilitation required is perhaps the most challenging aspect of regeneration (Jackson and Stainsby 2000).

As a consequence of the changing policy context state and non-state actors need new skills and competences to enhance traditional ones. Leadership of regeneration partnerships seems to be more of a traditional kind, with local authorities dominating and drawing in other agency representation and community involvement. It is questionable how skilled these officers are in relationship management, which involves identifying the key stakeholders and 'enabling the community to face issues, deal with problems, and realize aspirations in the most effective manner' (Stewart and Taylor 1995: 14). Conflict resolution becomes an essential skill and interview data suggests that informal mechanisms are still the favoured means of achieving consensus on contentious issues.

A key skill for management is the need to recognize intimate links between various and possibly conflicting levels of governance, in particular the ability to know which funding streams can be accessed, and by whom. The potentially divergent needs of accountability on public expenditure, central control of policy making, and sensitivity to local conditions remain problematic for managers, although there have not been many studies into what managers working in the public service actually do, unlike their counterparts in the commercial and private sectors where a long-established body of work exists. Recent research, however, has begun to address the fundamental question 'what do public managers do?', and a collection of findings from an international study reveals some interesting facts. Noordegraf (2000), researching into the Dutch public sector, recognized that senior public servants manage issue streams in the midst of political struggles and 80 per cent of the day is punctuated by interactions caused by meetings and paper-driven activities.

He categorized this process of interactions as follows:

- labelling, interpretation and institutionalization of issue;
- absorption of issues into textual information such as papers, reports and directives;
- identification of the relevant officials, after examination of existing portfolios;
- meetings held, within and beyond organizations and departments;
- plans, policies, budgets drawn up to guide procedures.

This whole process takes place within a political milieu of ministerial and parliamentary meetings, manifesto pledges, and political signals and crises in the external environment. Consequently public servants are always working in ambiguous and complex environments. The instability between issues; difficulties in assessing impacts on actions; level of opposition, and media exposure all force them into accounting for their actions.

New partnership arrangements at sub-regional and local levels could, we argue, be regarded as sitting between the 'public to private continuum' identified by Alford (2001). In this examination both 'ideal types' were regarded as analogous because each produces value for actors in different environments, utilising resources and capabilities, but each differs in the nature of that value, the resources, capabilities and environments in which they carry out strategic decisions. In a purely private sector model a manager's task is to produce the most effective goods and services desired by customers, produce as many as are required at the minimal cost and competitive price (competition in the market place ensures maximization of resource and performance). In the public sector an ideal-type manager is also concerned with transforming resources into tangible or intangible value, but at all stages of the process there is a wider array of possible elements in the values produced, productive capabilities, resources to be called upon, nature of the environments and interactions between environments and organizations. Production of values is public and consumed collectively, underpinned by a legal framework, a potential to correct market failure and a promotion of equity. All of this adds to complexity in applying private sector models of strategy to the activities of public and political activities (Alford 2001: 9).

As Joyce (1999: 172) further suggests, a grounded theory of strategy in a public sector context must be directed towards managing within public and political pressures (e.g. public opinion, elections, pressure groups, changes of government) and it can lead to innovation in services and activities because the consensus needed to satisfy the myriad of competing forces requires leadership, empowerment and co-operation between organizations. The political environment creates a level of entrepreneurialism that is a healthy improvement on strategic management in this field.

Joyce (2000) sees the importance of identifying, monitoring and managing issues and articulates the way senior managers respond to changes in the organizational environment by confronting resource issues, democratic community issues and organizational issues (pp. 51–55). Furthermore he sees that making use of both private and public partnerships can increase economy, efficiency and effectiveness (p. 184) and achieve greater results. To do this, however, involves having an understanding of overlapping mandates and boundaries, co-operating, setting up, internal marketing, project design, conflict and risk management, creating an agenda, selecting the organizational form, having a plan, achieving the objectives and ensuring that the members have the appropriate skills (p. 198) He thinks that public sector managers need to open up and be more communicative with the public, recognising that the bureaucratic model of old administrative structures reinforced paternalistic political and professional attitudes (p. 199). Opening up is seen as critical to accountability, responsiveness and organizational effectiveness, and to achieve this Joyce (2000: 207) urges public sector mangers to:

- be trained in listening and other skills;
- break down professional thinking and paternalistic attitudes;
- shift from an 'administrative' to 'managerial' mindset ;
- build confidence to deal with multiple interests and competition;
- use more entrepreneurial activity.

If these are put into place he argues that there will be a greater supply of ideas, alliances will be constructed to pull resources together in the public interest, and improved economy, efficiency and effectiveness will ensue. The rise of managerialism in state agencies has helped to redefine politics and citizenship on behalf of local communities and the enterprize state; welfare managerialism and public/private partnerships all need to balance economic growth with social needs.

Regeneration managers at all levels of governance are continually managing issue streams and dealing with constant interruptions within a political milieu, as well as having to deal with elected members. There is also a need to label and

38

categorize issues, prioritize and plan budgets, and work with elected members who are accountable through the media and council chambers to the electorate for fundamental aspects of their work. Indeed, arguably these levels of governance are characteristically more complex and have fuzzy boundaries. Jackson and Stainsby (2000) argue that the fuzzy boundaries created by the new networked policy domains require public servants capable of dealing with complexity, negotiating the political struggle over who should be involved, leading and managing stakeholder groups, achieving consensus on aims and objectives, and planning accordingly; building trusting relationships as well as understanding the patterns and flows of information. In short they believe that public servants in future must prepare themselves to abandon linear ways of doing things and tolerate ambiguity and complexity.

Traditionally in economic development and regeneration there has always been a lack of specific statutory guidance, and main actors such as local authority economic development officers undertook a range of tasks and activities based on job role and professionalism rather than by specific rules and regulations. Crocker (2001) defined economic development as 'the improvement of competitive advantage of an area by addressing the consequences of uneven development' and at its core it was regarded as distinguishable from other local government service areas by the focus on 'creating prosperity'. In accepting Crocker's definition it is clear that economic development professionals (as distinguishable from housing managers, land development officers, education officers, or other officials) had to be proactive and entrepreneurial actors who looked for opportunities to intervene and instigate change at different spatial levels. The traditional economic development professional would be expected to carry out a multitude of activities, not least those of supporting business creation and development; advising on sources of finance, availability of sites and infrastructure; and giving assistance on education and training provision. In order to carry out such a broad range of activities, Crocker (2001) separated out the generic and specific skills, as shown in Table 2.1.

Having recognized that not every economic development professional could possibly possess all these skills and competences, a requirement to be creative and

Table 2.1 Generic and specific skills for economic development

Generic	Specific
Literacy	Strategic understanding and objective setting
Numeracy	Planning
Interpersonal	Interventions
Communication	Management
IT skills	Evaluation

Source: Crocker (2001)

innovative underpins them all. Leaving aside the generic skills, if we examine more closely the specific skills in Table 2.1 we can see that Crocker breaks them down as follows:

1   Strategy is delineated into *hard* aspects such as strategic planning, economic and financial analysis, market research, and *soft* aspects such as strategic thinking, creativity, political judgement, managing stakeholders.
2   Planning is delineated into understanding business processes, gathering market intelligence, land use and property evaluation and appraisal.
3   Interventions are delineated into business, labour force, community and infrastructure.
4   Management is delineated into managing teams and individuals, managing finance, projects, programmes, relations across fragmented and diverse political and administrative systems.

Many of the identifiable specific and generic skills are not just relevant to local government officers in the field, but the blurring of boundaries between the public/private and voluntary sectors makes them more applicable to a wider group of professionals in regeneration. All professionals now operating in the multi-agency world of regeneration had previously drawn their expertise from their professional training and experience, and activities were commonly agreed among the communities of professionals. The broader involvement of other multi-professionals has expanded the scope and types of activities needed in regeneration.

Liddle (2001) identified a number of identifiable deficiencies in skills/competences of individuals working in regeneration at local, sub-regional and regional levels of governance in the north-east of England, and they are summarized in Table 2.2.

More recently Southern (2003) showed that as the range of regeneration initiatives had escalated, delivery became the key factor in ensuring successful regeneration. In his opinion the contradictory nature of regeneration, exemplified by many and varied careers and professions, as well as complex funding arrangements, presents particular difficulties. Social, economic and physical renewal is therefore regarded as interesting, energetic, complex and chaotic (p. 1). For Southern, regeneration managers have a primary role in enabling communities to understand the causes of deprivation, and help them to develop capacities. As a cyclical rather than linear process, regeneration managers are urged to develop the skills of analysis, implementation and measuring and evaluating performance, and a continuous circle of identification of new opportunities and problem solving. In the era of outcome measures and target setting it is essential to have regeneration managers who can understand the regime and ensure that communities are centrally involved in shaping the evaluation and monitoring mechanisms. By involving stakeholders in the entire process from project identification through to developing measures of success, it is argued that continuous learning and iteration is needed. In addition

Table 2.2 Skills and competencies

Generic
Working with ambiguity and complexity
Working in different ways, more in keeping with other organisations' styles
Awareness and understanding of other sectors and other sub-regions or regions in the UK
Policy learning between the public and non-public agencies
Female skills: assertiveness, frankness, straight talking (as opposed to male skills such of posturing and macho management)
Presentation skills, particularly for use beyond the region
Research, analytical and critical skills
Generating trust
Communication
Adaptability
Risk taking
Proactivity

Strategic
Synthesis, integration and co-ordination (joined-up strategising)
Exploration and experimentation
Monitoring, reviewing and evaluating strategies and objectives
Networking and managing stakeholder relationships
Environmental analysis (PEST)
Mission and objective setting
Prioritisation of problems
Scenario planning
Leadership
Lobbying

Operational skills
Identifying and drawing in disadvantaged groups
Data and information collection and analysis
Managing stakeholder relationships
Data and information sharing
Accessing funding regimes
PR and promotion of an area
Workload planning
Networking

Team working
Knowledge of how other sectors work (especially values/norms, operating styles, report writing styles, chairing of meetings)
Facilitation skills to deal with large groups from diverse sectors, backgrounds and operating styles
Pooling resources/joint working, integration and achieving a common agenda
Political skills, negotiation, bargaining, brokering
Conflict resolution and managing tensions
Chairing and managing meetings
Identification of vested interests
Achieving transparency
Stress management

to the skills of analysis, implementation and measurement, Southern also recognizes the very wide experience, expertise and portfolio of skills and competences needed to manage the regeneration process. There are general organizational skills of financial planning to support business cases, but more specific skills in human resource management (HRM), strategic thinking, performance management, marketing, risk management, use of technology, as well as relationship management.

The complex terrain of regeneration means that training in many new skills is essential, but despite the recognized need, there has been little formal response. Many partnerships have employed consultants or external speakers to facilitate learning between agency representatives, but much of this has been ad hoc, rather than a planned and proactive programme of training and education.

Roberts (2003), in a survey carried out on behalf of BURA, and supported by NRU and DTI, identified the following areas where regeneration managers would benefit from training:

- strategy building, development, implementation and review;
- research, intelligence, policy understanding and spatial knowledge;
- finance, funding, basic law and regulation;
- partnership building, community engagement, participation;
- economic development and analysis, policics and intervention methods;
- training and other labour market measures;
- needs analysis, social issues, neighbourhood engagement;
- environmental factors, quality of life, urban design;
- property and physical renewal, land and property management;
- management of programmes and projects, monitoring and evaluation;
- performance management, best value;
- succession strategies, mainstreaming initiatives.

As well as cross-cutting issues such as:

- community and public safety, security and welfare;
- equality, ethnicity, gender and other matters;
- disability and other forms of disadvantage;
- other health and welfare matters.

There have been other attempts to create policy learning and transfer of expertise, but none of these initiatives have been fully evaluated.

The Skills and Knowledge Programme was developed during 2002–2003 by the NRU/SEU, and resulted in the recruitment of Neighbourhood Renewal Coordinators for each LSP with the objective of facilitating learning in communities and between LSP partner organizations. As an example of the outcome of such processes East Durham LSP held a number of away days, facilitated by consultants, and supported by Government Office NR Coordinators, The Regeneration Exchange and other agencies. Community Networks were created and Community Appraisals carried out to identify skills gaps. Core skills where training was deemed necessary were found to be:

- Partnership working.
- Listening and learning from others' experience, understanding and objectives.
- Team building, leadership and management.
- Conflict management.
- Problem solving.
- Risk taking.
- Programme and project design and management.
- Understanding of different funding regimes.
- Learning lessons for what has worked across the district and elsewhere.
- Working with communities and building skills with them.

(Neighbourhood Renewal Unit, Government Office, October 2003)

Local Learning Plans are being developed for each LSP, and each region is developing an overall Regional Learning Plan. Neighbourhood Renewal Advisers are the preferred option in helping communities and other multi-agency representatives to develop the requisite skills and development. Community Chest and Community Empowerment Funds are being used to develop local capacities and each region is adhering to a Skills and Innovation Strategy, with plans to establish Regeneration Centres of Excellence. Moreover, government offices have dedicated NR/LSP officers whose sole role is to facilitate understanding, learning and benchmarking between all LSPs. Learning Curve has been established centrally to foster and transfer good practice.

We support the view that politically competent managers are people who expect to experience resistance to their attempts to get things done, but nevertheless keep on taking initiatives, in ways that tend to produce the results they desire (Baddeley and James 1987: 3). Political skills are an essential ingredient for working in pluralistic contexts and partnerships/networks. This requires individuals who are able to read organizational and decision-making processes at all levels. In particular they need to recognize how they can use their own 'power' to influence their organizational culture (p. 9).

To be innovative requires high-quality risk management and safe spaces in which to test out and develop promising ideas (Cabinet Office and DLTR, November 2002). Over the past two decades 'pilots' have been used to test out new policy proposals, some more successful than others. Sure Start is hailed as a successful initiative, with Children's Centres as a follow-on, whereas the Education Maintenance Allowance

(EMA) Pilot was considered a failure because young people in neighbouring areas had differential access to the scheme. Some successful pilots have prompted the use of pathfinders, such as New Deal, Sure Start or zones such as EAZ and HAZ. These latter programmes were criticized for failure to deliver a change agenda because of the relegation of the change process to middle managers (Maddock 2002). Incubators, such as those developing e-government initiatives and innovation in the Office of the e-Envoy, are considered to be a core activity in public services, as they improve performance and public value, and help to respond to citizens' expectations and the needs of users, and to increase service efficiency and cuts costs. If the public sector does not develop new ideas it is likely they will expire (Cabinet Office, October 2003: 2). All innovations can be valuable, the successful and the not so successful, if lessons are learned and knowledge fed back into the continual loop of policy and service development (Cabinet Office, October 2003: 30). Innovative staff are penalized for their efforts to share, negotiate and take risks (Maddock 2002).

Radical modernization of public services requires managers to make a reality of 'holistic' government, 'joined-up thinking' and thus achieve better outcomes across a wide range of policy areas (Wilkinson and Appelbee 1999: 1). To do this they are encouraged to involve stakeholders. Pratchett (2000) argued that the entire role and purpose of local government and the nature of local democracy were under threat. Local authorities were urged to pursue policies in collaboration and partnerships with other agencies as a way of extending local autonomy and local leadership. This could reverse voter apathy and the arcane decision-making structures (Pratchett 2000).

To foster modernization requires social justice and a value base of openness and transparency through more inclusive management practices. However, reversing top-down and more traditional forms of delivery to bottom-up initiatives that include communities of interest will require a nurturing of new stakeholder relationships. These cannot be nurtured overnight, nor do many public servants have the skills to identify and work alongside stakeholders from the various communities. There is a clear gulf between the rhetoric of inclusion and the practices of consulting, listening and involving communities as equal partners.

For Wilkinson and Appelbee (1999: 137–145) issues that need to be addressed to bring about greater regeneration are the need for evidence-based approaches to change by using appropriate research; recovery from the addiction to failing ways of working; taking community involvement seriously; getting beyond zero-sum games and establishing trust; continually searching for improvements in quality, efficiency and effectiveness of services; and an acceptance that real change takes time.

If experimentation, continuous learning from best practice elsewhere, and policy transfer are the central challenges for regeneration managers, the new challenges require new skills and competences for managing professional, organizational and individual performance.

In the north-east of England two recent examples of skills and development within regeneration have been instigated to remedy some of the deficiencies. First a centrally directed programme, entitled 'Neighbourhood Renewal Delivery Skills', to which one of these authors contributed, included the following sessions:

- The national strategy context.
- Building cohesion and avoiding conflict.
- Partnership working and collaboration.
- Performance management.
- Leadership styles.
- Roles, responsibilities and accountabilities.
- Delivering change.

The programme, which was attended by senior managers/directors from regeneration partnerships across England, also included live case studies and visits to current programmes. The objective was to provide the opportunities for current managers and directors to learn from the experience of others. Moreover, the challenges now being faced across different types of regeneration partnerships could be synthesized and used as examples for future scenario building and identification of the 'what if' questions that might occur in the future.

Another, separate, but nevertheless innovative, creative and related example of senior managers coming together to learn across boundaries is the Partnership 10 initiative in Teesside (one of the authors is a contributor and facilitator of this programme). The programme, which commenced in September 2004, is designed for strategic leaders in the Teesside area, and will allow participants to:

- Widen their perception of self and others.
- Understand the external environment partnerships operate within.
- Appreciate the demands of effective leadership of partnerships.
- Heighten awareness of operating in local public sector environments.
- Enhance reflective thinking capacities.

The programme is aimed at exposing leaders to theories, concepts and working practices across the partner organizations, but also encourages proactive and innovative generation of ideas to solve real and current regeneration problems. Real-time collaborative investigation of problems is aimed at improving current performance.

This programme, the first of its kind in the UK, is experimental, experiential and was developed by a constellation of agencies, after rigorous market research found no similar programme available for senior managers. It is aimed at senior managers who want to learn from each other across agency boundaries, within regeneration. The programme is validated by a university in the north-east, but draws on experts from academic and consultancy companies to

45

facilitate the learning. Each module (partnership, citizen and community engagement, governance, strategic thinking, change management and problem resolution) is championed by one partner organization, and there is deliberate overlap between modules to reflect the complex and interconnected world of public management. The 10 participating organizations, hence the title Partnership 10, propose a very senior individual to be part of the programme and each joins a 'learning set', which is the primary method of learning. The programme runs for one year, in the first instance, and each learning set, facilitated by an academic or consultant, will work on live issues where a 'whole systems' approach is needed. Continuous learning will form the basis of approaches to future cross-boundary problem solving.

This initiative is aimed at continuous learning from best practice by benchmarking activities in messy, ambiguous and contested territories and shows collaboration will be used to overcome some of the barriers of attempting to work in isolation. In searching for lessons in other agencies, not only will problems be identified and solved in 'holistic' ways, but also the significance here lies in the capacity to diagnose emergent problems. It is a recognition of the dialectic basis of problem solving, and has great potential for illustrating how one partnership can respond to broader social, political and economic changes in innovative and creative ways.

SUMMARY

We have shown that as management in regeneration is governed by mandates and funding regimes quite different to those experienced in the past, and hierarchical and top-down bureaucracies have been replaced by more flexible and networked organizational forms, a whole new set of skills, competences and expertise is required to deliver the modernising agenda.

Multi-agency professionals now work beyond their own organizational and professional boundaries in partnership, and the need to draw in different communities of interest requires new ways of thinking and working. New action spaces for policy experimentation and learning are essential to future success, but guidance from higher levels of governance leaves many managers at a loss as to how to proceed. Learning from best practice and benchmarking activities with other external sources have become essential to good practice within messy, ambiguous and contested territories.

We have argued that as innovation, creativity, entrepreneurship and risk taking have become more prevalent, then the need to have training and new knowledge is imperative. As managers seek to deal with the sometimes contradictory dimensions of quality and targets, they need new sets of skills for monitoring and evaluation of programmes, and to audit and report on activities.

We advocate the need for new programmes of training to equip managers with the new competences/skills for managing in fluid and entrepreneurial situations. The main question, however, is which body or agency will take responsibility for such training, and how will this be organized? Existing training programmes, we argue, are going some way to remedy the deficiencies, but more focused training and development is essential to improve the effectiveness of regeneration programmes and partnerships.

DISCUSSION POINTS

■ How has the changing context of regeneration management created a need for new skills and competences?
■ What are the key skills and competences needed within regeneration?
■ What training needs are there within regeneration, and what are the barriers to be overcome?
■ Has the debate been informed by private sector management practices, and are they appropriate in public sector settings?

FURTHER READING

Filkin, G. et al. (2001) *Starting to Modernise: The change agenda for local government*, London: New Local Government Network

Joyce, P. (1999) *Strategic Management for the Public Services*, Buckingham: Open University Press

NRU (2002) *The Learning Curve*, London: OPDM

Roberts, P. and Sykes, M. (eds) (2000) *Urban Regeneration: A Handbook*, London: Sage

CASE STUDY

Voluntary sector capacity and learning to support regeneration: VONNE and One Voice Network

The role of voluntary and community organizations is increasingly recognized as a key to help define and implement locally focused regeneration programmes where traditional methods have failed. It is in this context that a research programme – Integrated Regeneration for County Durham and Darlington – was developed, based on the view that the capacity of the voluntary sector to support community regeneration is not only about equipping individuals with skills and capacities that they currently do not possess, but about identifying practical, workable mechanisms and processes to enable the voluntary and community organizations to learn from each other by:

■ Engaging effectively and practically with each other.
■ Engaging with those from other sectors.
■ Managing internal conflict.
■ Maximising mutual collaborative advantage.
■ Maximising leverage on the regeneration process.

The ability of the voluntary sector to demonstrate that it can make a significant contribution to community regeneration at quality and at cost had been recognized at a regional level in the north-east by the establishment of One Voice Network and VONNE (Voluntary Organisations Network North East); both were attempts to bring coherence and co-ordination to a fragmented and disparate set of agencies.

The research, commissioned by One North East (the RDA), Government Office and the NE Assembly, and conducted by interviews across voluntary, community and public sectors, a postal questionnaire administered to 350 community organizations, and interactive workshops, identified the following as prerequisites for developing capacity and learning:

■ financial stability;
■ a focus on delivery;
■ collaboration for delivery efficiency;
■ an effective network of enabling support;
■ building trust;
■ clarification on roles, responsibilities and expectations;
■ definition of real outputs;
■ management of local competitiveness;
■ establishment of core services and standards.

The study also recommended a bold programme of training, partnership working and leadership development for voluntary and community organizations, with a focus on engaging and working collaboratively with regional and sub-regional agencies and partnerships. Furthermore, there was a recommendation that community and voluntary sectors should assist the RDA, One North East and the sub-regional partnerships in developing and appraising projects for funding. This became known as 'third-sector proofing' by asking questions such as 'what role is proposed for the voluntary and community sector in this project? How will this project contribute to the capacity and development of the voluntary and community sector?' There is now a clear recognition of the need for a permanent mechanism for conducting dialogue between the major regional and sub-regional agencies, and the voluntary and community sector. More importantly, the research findings recommend the establishment of a networking forum for dissemination of latest policy initiatives, learning, consultation and feedback. VONNE and One Voice North East (OVNE) have been asked to produce an annual 'state of the voluntary sector' report and promote an event to maximize awareness of the role and contribution of the sector to the regional objectives, and to the economic and social well-being of the region in general.

Strategy

- Strategy: the conventional wisdom and traditional models.
- The changing external and internal environments.
- Top-down managerialism or bottom-up strategy? Hierarchy or democracy?
- Regeneration management and new models of strategic decision making.
- Strategic analysis, choice and implementation: the problems of rational and linear approaches, especially in measuring success.
- Identifying, prioritising and managing stakeholder relationships: the key strategic role?

LEARNING POINTS

By the end of this chapter we hope that you will be able to:

- Identify the central differences between traditional models of strategy and new approaches, by examining critical factors in strategic decision making.
- Reflect upon the changes within the strategic environment and consider the new strategic challenges facing regeneration managers.
- Show how a combination of public, private and voluntary sector collaboration to achieve common objectives challenges conventional wisdom.
- Understand that strategic success depends on the measures and evaluation mechanisms adopted.
- Understand the iterative, cyclical and dynamic nature of strategy within regeneration, and appreciate the need to align hierarchy with democratic approaches to ensure strategic success.
- Reflect upon your own strategic approach, prioritise stakeholder demands and manage future relationships.

INTRODUCTION

As we explained in Chapter 1 there are competing discourses of regeneration, and likewise there are changeable and competing interpretations of strategy. Different approaches to strategy and competing definitions on whether it is about context, content or process have largely been drawn from the business strategy literature. In this chapter we explore the literature to discuss the primary elements of the strategic process, but we also show how important it is to develop a critical way of strategic thinking.

Like the notion of partnership or capacity building, strategy is a contested concept. It is not always clear how the term should be defined, and what contexts shape strategic change. Moreover, there is considerable dispute about the relationship between strategic intent and strategic success, and no one best model fits all situations. Drawing upon some of the problems encountered by managers we seek to show difficulties in adapting existing business strategy to regeneration initiatives.

In particular we reflect on the way that tools, techniques and models drawn from business strategy in commercial, business environments are used (sometimes unwisely) to explain a much more complex set of actors and actions within regeneration.

We argue that current approaches to strategy with the emphasis on rational, linear and prescriptive approaches sit uncomfortably within the complex, cyclical and iterative worlds in which regeneration managers work alongside partners to achieve commonly agreed goals. Not only is it important to reflect on your strategic approach, but in doing so you may better understand why some rational approaches can lead, at best, to unintended consequences, and, at worst, to abject failure.

Arguably, we contend that central government civil servants (and those who set national and regional policies and strategies) have largely relied on the strategy literature to inform their practice, and as a consequence regeneration managers are faced with numerous dilemmas and challenges in responding to top-down, prescriptive instructions from higher authorities, with little recognition of some of the problems inherent in such approaches.

While we argue that private sector techniques, tools and models have become the conventional wisdom, it is also true that recent writers have begun to challenge their efficacy and effectiveness in certain circumstances.

We suggest that a more critical reflection on the various elements of the strategic context, content and processes is a more valid way to develop strategic thinking. Adopting a critical stance would, we argue, better prepare regeneration managers in undertaking their roles more effectively because they would be in a better position to appreciate more fully their specific location in the strategic process. This, we would argue, is more valuable than attempting to achieve rational 'one best way' prescriptive approaches to strategic decision making.

51

We further suggest that a more critical reflection on the nature of the strategic process is vital to developing clarity and an understanding of complex systems within which regeneration managers make essential decisions. Specifically we show the importance of drawing from a variety of models, techniques and tools to address strategic needs in specific public sector or hybrid state, non-state and civic contexts. As managers need to respond to variable types of scrutiny and accountability, and report to higher authorities, we suggest that in considering key strategic processes (social, political, managerial and administrative), changeable contexts of strategy, and being vigilant on the contestable nature of the content of strategic planning, managers may be in a better position to achieve success. If not, then at least we contend that managers may develop a greater understanding of the constraints and frustrations that they need to be aware of, and seek to work around.

Specifically we show that it is vital to synthesize the most appropriate strategic models from a number of available models to enhance decision making, and choose appropriate and feasible strategies acceptable to competing and contradictory stakeholders. Arguably managers spend large chunks of time appeasing stakeholders on different levels and are continually harmonising inputs from the broader and narrower strategic environments.

We also feel that in adapting private sector models to the complex world of regeneration, simple, reductionist and sometimes flawed solutions are used to solve problems, when in fact more complex and debatable choices may be needed. This often leaves regeneration managers to choose from a limited set of options and at a loss to understand how strategic objectives can be achieved. Not only that, but measuring the results of their chosen courses of action becomes oversimplified too.

Specifically the problem with linearity is that it fails to take account of the dynamic and continuous interactions between and within organizations over time. Surviving organizations change structures and directions, and in doing so threaten or provide opportunities for other organizations. Paradoxically, as Stacey (1993: 5–8) shows, interactions over time create (at the same time):

- stability and instability;
- predictability and unpredictability;
- creation and destruction;
- contradictions, dichotomy and paradoxes;
- dilemmas and dualism;
- choices to be made and barriers to be dealt with.

Moreover, we argue that unidirectional, linear connections between cause and effect have led to inadequate understandings of strategic behaviour. Therefore for these, and other, reasons we must be cautious in adapting inappropriate models to unique public sector organizations or those settings in which hybrid public/private/voluntary sector partnerships have developed or are evolving.

SPECIFIC CONTEXTS

Differences do exist between the sectors despite some private sector approaches proving to be successful in the public sector, but there remain problems in applying private sector ideas in public sector environments. It is important not to fall into the trap of believing there is no difference between public, private and voluntary sectors. Arguably, the key difference is the political context in which there are clashes on major issues as interactions between:

- politicians;
- public managers;
- other stakeholders.

We agree with Bovaird and Loeffler (2003: 69) that pressure for short-term solutions means that healthy public organizations are those with:

- Adaptable and innovative cultures.
- Leaders who seek out change in services, customers, service production, procurement and partnership arrangements.
- Decision-making and governance structures to address the democratic deficit, new goals and new cultures.

It is important to understand that regeneration managers have to balance the demands and expectations of the communities and higher levels of authority with what is appropriate, feasible and acceptable. The real challenge is to work with others to develop strategies for the future, and to do so requires continuous negotiation and dialogue with a multitude of stakeholders. What is feasible, appropriate, acceptable in one locale may be inadequate for bringing about change in another locale. For those involved in strategy, there are the twin dilemmas of seeking to achieve targets set by higher levels of governance, at the same time as setting out strategies within given funding levels. Those individuals involved in developing strategies have to match what is required with what can be achieved, and what is possible, given the constraints and frustrations. Managers need to recognize that they may not be in a position to solve all the problems in a defined locale, despite their best efforts, and sometimes they have to satisfice, rather than maximize, their resources. Indeed, as regeneration takes place within a mix of mandatory/statutory requirements, offering limited room for discretion, they must use wise judgement in determining what the problems are, how they can be tackled, and what difficulties may result in inaction or failure to respond to changes in the internal and external environments.

53

New strategic environments, characterized over time by stability and instability, predictability and unpredictability, and the creation and destruction of processes and organizational structures, require, in our view, extraordinary managers who are able to deal with many competing demands and priorities, and have the ability to clarify the 'wood from the trees', as they seek strategic priorities, to bring about the necessary changes.

As we try to suggest in this chapter, it is important to locate regeneration activities in a debate on the nature of strategy, more especially to investigate whether it is concerned with context, content or process, or more significantly, for the purposes of this book, whether it is a learning process in which individuals develop their strategic thinking and judgement on how best to align the strategic fit between internal resources and strengths with the challenges from the environment and context.

This is necessary for six good reasons:

1   No 'one' model satisfies all situations.
2   The context is dynamic.
3   Strategic content is contestable.
4   Processes are socially constructed and dependent on many other factors.
5   There is little evidence to show that strategic decisions equal strategic success.
6   Strategy is iterative, and small incremental steps may be better than recipe book approaches.

We are not suggesting that these reasons alone would add to strategic success, but recognize the need for regeneration managers to develop a set of strategic skills (as was shown in Chapter 2) and that an awareness of these important factors may prepare them better for the strategic environments they inhabit. We are suggesting that existing business strategy models may have some tangential relationship to the realities of regeneration, but can never fully explain the increasingly complex and contestable terrain.

Contemporary regeneration managers need to develop a broad strategic understanding and a set of skills that will enhance their strategic actions. We want you to reflect on your understanding of the strategic processes, and understand the importance of:

■   context;
■   content;
■   processes;
■   strategy as learning;
■   dynamism and contestability.

Arnoldo Hax offers a useful typology, contrary to the long-established linear, deliberate and rational approaches. Thus strategy is characterized by:

- A coherent, unifying and integrative pattern of decisions.
- A means of establishing an organizational purpose and long term objectives.
- A definition of the competitive domain.
- A response to external opportunities and threats, and internal strengths and weaknesses.
- A logical system of differentiating managerial tasks at corporate, business and functional levels.
- A definition of the economic and non-economic contributions to and from stakeholders.

(Hax 1990)

CAN BUSINESS STRATEGY OFFER ANYTHING NEW TO REGENERATION?

The strategy literature developed from the world of business management, and there have been few specifically public sector strategy books. More recently Bovaird and Loeffler (2003) and Joyce (1999) have added to existing knowledge, and improved our understanding of the uniqueness of the public sector. As we show below, many of the existing tools, techniques and models of strategy offer useful starting points to understand how strategic decisions are made, but we would urge caution in wholesale adoption into very complex and disputed territories of contemporary regeneration.

The significance of the existing strategy literature lies in the attempts to foster systematic, linear and rational approaches to decision making, and we can see from its history that strategy as a discipline has evolved. However, in embracing rational models of strategy and attempting to impose these on complex systems we would agree with Southern that:

> Too much top-down managerialism can displace the social and political dynamics that operate locally and because regeneration is fertile ground for contestation and conflict as well as consensus building, regeneration managers must serve as enablers who assist in developing the understanding of the causes of deprivation and increase the social capital of communities.
>
> (Southern 2003: 1)

Indeed we argue that only in developing this understanding will strategists clarify the mechanisms needed to develop strategies and mechanisms to evaluate the effectiveness of initiatives. Arguably, without some understanding of the complexities of strategy:

- Interventions become badly designed, invented by regeneration managers on the basis of flawed assumptions and imposed on the community rather than implemented with its consent.
- Regeneration is often unsustainable, as communities which were never engaged in strategic decision making will defect once the money starts to dry up.
- Tools that regeneration managers use to 'understand' the community and to consult are inadequate. Rational and linear approaches and strategic tools, techniques and models, developed for use in the business world, are used, whose theoretical underpinnings are in a reductionist paradigm in a domain which is inherently complex.

We argue that strategy can be more effectively developed by appreciating the following:

- More appropriate tools and techniques may need to be adopted, ones that are better suited to the complex world of regeneration.
- That the current obsession with studying regeneration success stories is of limited value, because in the experimental world of regeneration it would be more appropriate to study failure.
- The relationship between regeneration and culture is not fully understood, and the socio-political and cultural elements of strategy are of equal validity.
- Too many regeneration success stories are only coherent in retrospect. As many existing business strategy success stories indicate, companies can be successful at a particular time in a firm's history and within given circumstances, but a change in circumstances can easily lead to failure.

It may be beneficial to move the analysis away from reductionist and deterministic perspectives that reduce holistic systems and isolate observable phenomena. Instead, we argue that seeing organizational forms, such as partnerships, as complex adaptable systems composed of a diversity of agents, interacting with each other, generating novel and innovative benefits for the whole system, is more understandable to regeneration managers whose activities are conducted in such arenas. Managers make long-term decisions that impact on the whole system, they need to co-ordinate the various elements of the system, and they encounter difficulties of working in networks, partnerships and collaborative arrangements to achieve objectives.

Regeneration managers work alongside other agencies to predict how:

- Clients, groups and other stakeholders will be affected by their decisions.
- Resources will be deployed.
- They will carry out contingency planning, evaluation and performance measurement.
- To be more imaginative, innovative and creative in delivering services differently.

We argue that many of the expectations of managers in regeneration are based on a false assumption of cause and effect, when in fact many activities take place in environments where smaller incremental decisions emerge rather than being based on grand designs or grand theories (Van Heijden 1999: 34). The experimentation needed in contemporary regeneration necessitates a reflective and learning process located in the context surrounding the change, the content of change, in other words what actions will bring about the change, and the processes that character-ize the change (De Wit and Meyer 2003).

STRATEGISING IN COMPLEX ARENAS

The dilemmas faced by regeneration managers as they seek to understand or 'sense make' the many diverse contexts within which they work are compounded, we attempt to show, by the plethora of existing strategic theory.

We provide a summary of some of the more well-known approaches, in order to illustrate how their inappropriate use can add confusion to an, at times, already contradictory setting. We also want to introduce you to some more recent attempts to construct and develop specifically public sector strategic models that provide more appropriate and adaptable ways to understand the ambiguous, messy and con-tradictory worlds you inhabit in your day-to-day professional lives.

Our main objective is to move you away from a reliance on 'off-the-shelf' or 'recipe book' approaches to the strategic process, and to facilitate a more reflective mode whereby you are able to see that there are no right or wrong answers to developing strategies, merely subjective and contestable views of how it should be approached. There are as many models of strategy as there are views on how it should best be carried out. But, seeking to draw upon the literature and draw the lessons that best fit your expertise requires confidence and a critical appreciation of the many variables that are present, though many strategic elements are non-negotiable.

In this chapter we want to challenge received strategic wisdom, and demon-strate that there are many ways of addressing strategic problems.

FUZZY WORLDS

Strategic planning can be seen as a fuzzy attempt to seek order and clarity. Unfortunately we agree with Grint (1997: introduction) that we cannot rationalize away paradoxes, chance, luck, errors, subjectivities, accidents and the sheer indeter-minacy of life through a prism of apparent control and rationality. Much strategy lit-erature is replete with buzzwords and fads, and what in our view is undeniable is the fact that while strategic management is complex, contradictory and ambiguous, it is at heart a political activity where value judgements, subjectivity and the correct and appropriate data on which to base right and wrong strategic decisions may prove elusive to you. The dynamic and changeable worlds that you inhabit daily are difficult to manage, and an acceptance of that key fact should liberate you, and allow you to recognize that you may make mistakes from time to time, and that those mistakes may be less to do with human error and more to do with factors outside of your control

Strategic management became the dominant paradigm in many public service agencies 25 years ago and its legitimacy and persistence can be explained by a powerful combination of academic literature on 'strategy' and a heavy investment by academic institutions in MBAs and strategic consultancy with senior public servants (Doherty and Horne 2002: 67).

To add to the complex literature, many writers limit their analysis of strategy by ignoring the importance of:

- The role of history, informality and linkages between individuals and institutions.
- Existing power relationships and traditional institutional forms of decision making.
- Socio-cultural and external aspects that impact on strategy.
- Clear categorization of state and non-state actors and institutions.
- Blurring of the boundaries between actors and sectors.
- Who has power, hidden or unobservable levels of power and influence, how it is distributed or how conflict/consensus are managed within the strategic process.
- The involvement of agencies previously regarded as auxiliary bodies, such as quangos, service interests, universities, sporting, arts and cultural agencies, trade unions, churches and the voluntary sector, now incorporated into strategic processes.

We show that the conceptual framework for studying strategy has developed from the existing private sector literature, though more recently writers have attempted to adapt such frameworks to public sector organizations (Bryson 1995; Nutt and Backoff 1992; Stoney 2001), or provide a wider picture (Bovaird and Loffler 2003; Doherty and Horne 2002; Hughes 2003; Joyce 2000).

Notwithstanding recent research, we argue that few writers have focused on the strategic dimensions of regeneration through the partnerships, though some recognized that 'regeneration requires a strategic overview' (Lawless 1996: 28) or that 'different partners understand the semantics of strategy in different ways, and see it as fulfilling a range of purposes' (Hutchinson 2001: 274).

Calls for a more 'strategic approach' to regeneration suggest that strategy at regional level can guide lower levels and act as a co-ordinated, coherent and responsive framework (Danson and Lloyd 1992: 46–54). Others highlighted the importance of regional strategies (Diamond and Liddle 2003; Elcock 2001; Roberts and Benneworth 2001), particular elements of urban regeneration (Carley 2002; Jacobs 2000), area committees (Coaffee and Healey 2003) or other locally based regeneration partnership strategies (Johnson and Osborne 2003; Liddle 2001; Liddle and Townsend 2003), but despite this growing literature in both private and public contexts it is generally recognized that there is no one best way to conceptualize strategy. We must, therefore, be cautious in adapting inappropriate business strategy models to unique public sector organizations (Goldsmith 1997) or those settings in which hybrid public/private/voluntary sector partnerships have developed or are evolving.

The words 'strategies', 'plans', 'policies' and 'objectives' are often used interchangeably in either public or private settings (Bennett 1996), but many strategies take place outside the normal boundaries of organizations, and are more akin to muddling through and successive limited comparisons (Lindblom 1959), groping along and experimentation (Behn 1988), logical incrementalism (Quinn 1980), emergent (Mintzberg 1997) or characterized by contradiction and fragmentation, as actors mutually adjust to each other's viewpoints (Simon *et al*. 1950).

We agree with Eden and Ackerman (1998: 4) in regarding strategy as an emergent journey and patterns of decision making, thinking and action derived from habits customs, culture and ways of working, but contingent on a number of factors (p. 7).

The benefits of strategy, we suggest, are:

- its holism (how decisions are likely to impact on the whole organization).
- long-termism (decisions taken with regard to long-term consequences).
- co-ordination of departments, units and other agencies (which is very difficult in a public sector setting).
- futuristic thinking on how stakeholder groups will be affected, how resources will be deployed, contingency plans developed, and evaluation and performance measured.

PROBLEMS IN ADAPTING BUSINESS STRATEGY MODELS TO REGENERATION

In summary we list below the major problems in attempting to bring business strategy approaches to bear on regeneration, and although this is not an exhaustive list, it does help to explain why problems persists:

- Visions and mission statements have many purposes.
- Stakeholders are difficult to identify, evaluate importance, or manage in the long term.
- Strategic techniques like SWOT, PEST or Porter's Five Forces are subjective, descriptive, arbitrary and biased. No weight or criteria are applied to relevant internal and external elements of strategy.

59

- Assumption of 'one best way' and that a recipe book approach will improve the strategic process.
- It is difficult to know which strategy fits the best conditions, and public managers must experiment with various initiatives to determine what works or does not work.
- Little empirical evidence to suggest that strategists or the environment are critical to strategic success.
- Hidden, unobservable or unintended aspects of strategy may be critical to success.
- Systematic control and synthesis are difficult owing to multi-faceted problems and dynamism of factors.
- Planning and formulating strategy are divorced from execution, implementation and evaluation.
- Power, values and negotiation on strategic content, context and process are vital to strategic change.
- Rational approaches are reductionist and isolate too few variables.
- Simplification does not deal with paradoxes, ambiguities, mess, chance, luck, errors, subjectivities, accidents or indeterminacy.

We would like to suggest, however, that in public or private sector organizations good results do not necessarily mean a strategy has worked, neither do poor results mean there was a poor strategy. This can be attributed to many variables, and good luck might be as important as having a good strategic fit between the objectives of the organizations and the internal strengths to the external opportunities. The missions and purposes of public sector organizations are not always easy to determine; indeed, because they are multi-purpose organizations, they have many objectives to achieve. We might ask what the purpose of a local authority or other public agency is, and countless answers might be revealed. Local authorities have a general competence to facilitate economic, social and environmental improvements (under the Local Government Act of 2000) but also satisfy many other objectives. It is therefore too simple to say that if the mission and objectives are clear a strategic direction will be taken.

Arguably, a strategic analysis helps to decide who the stakeholders are and each will have very divergent interests and expectations that need to be managed in different ways. The competitive domain in which strategists operate, and in which they look to place an organization in its industry sector to determine the power of competitors, new entrants, suppliers and buyers (Porter 1985), is not wholly appropriate for public sector organizations and partnerships. While many of them are now in a more competitive environment, many of their services need to be delivered in collaboration and consensually. Many public agencies do not face the same market pressures as private organizations, but they may have equally demanding pressures in other ways, such as being regulated or mandated to carry out certain activities

(Smith 1995) or there is public pressure to carry out activities, mainly through the political process. Indeed in most regeneration partnerships and forums (Primary Care Trusts (PCTs) and LSPs are good examples) citizens are actively encouraged to articulate their preferences. There is little choice for many public organizations in where they can be located, which market they can serve and what the clientele or stakeholders to be served are. PEST, SWOT, TEMPLES (Technological, Economic, Market, Political, Legal, Ethical and Social influences) are the preferred techniques for analysing the external and internal aspects of strategic analysis but are very subjective and, from a public sector perspective, flawed models (Doherty and Horne 2002; Goldsmith 1997).

To add to the problems, it is too simplistic to assume that public organizations have to favour either a planned, rational, linear and prescriptive approach to strategy based on how it should be carried out, or an emergent approach with an inbuilt view of how strategic change processes work in reality. Obviously, as mentioned above, managing strategic change is about experimentation, a reflective and a learning process located in the context surrounding the change, the content of change, in other words what actions will bring about the change, and the processes that characterize the change. This last aspect is vital to understanding the social, cultural and political change processes (Hax 1990). Hax recognized three strategic core processes: (i) cognitive, (ii) social and (iii) organizational – all necessary to build consensus on setting objectives and long-term change.

At the same time organizations have overarching missions, then broad goals and a strategic plan to attain objectives, then operational aims, objectives and detailed plans, with targets, timescales and personal and group responsibilities, but this hierarchical approach to strategy no longer holds true (Watson 2000: 4). While Whittington (2001) rejects this classical and rational approach, he introduced us to a biological evolutionary aspect where the law of the jungle prevails. His processual understanding of strategy has at core the belief that strategy is a pragmatic accommodation of imperfect organizations to imperfect and fallible markets. The final systemic approach sees the ends and means of strategy inextricably linked to culture, power and the social system in which they are embedded. However, the special circumstances of each public sector entity, especially the rules, regulations and mandates governing activities, make some actors powerless to act, and moreover they have to motivate fellow participants and maintain morale in the face of cuts to budgets, dramatic changes to the external environment and increased scrutiny and accountability (Watson 2000: 5). People who are charged with improving quality of services, increased consumer participation and ensuring strategic success are forced into a straitjacket of external audit, and this alters the strategic culture of the internal mechanics, with increased stress, job insecurity and other external pressures.

The key steps in strategy development on a rationalistic paradigm are: define mission, set strategic objectives, identify options, select maximum utility option, implement, appraise and control. However, because the realities of strategy mean

that strategists never know how to identify options, their intellectual and comput-
ing power are limited. They therefore choose the best or optimal choice of strategy. Therefore strategists must develop a series of scenarios that 'set reasonably
plausible, but structurally different futures' (Van Heijden 1999: 26). Rational
models assume a unitary organization, one best way of proceeding, that everyone
involved in strategy will arrive at similar conclusions and that implementation will
follow strategy. In reality strategy is an iterative and complex learning process with
many competing views of options and choices. Mintzberg (1987) observed that
strategists prefer verbal information rather than numeric, conversation rather
than reading, anecdotal information, smaller incremental decisions and are happy
to let decisions emerge rather than have grand designs or grand theories (Van
Heijden 1999: 34).

Nutt and Backoff (1992: 152) set out a six-point strategic plan, as shown in
Figure 3.1. As the figure shows, there is a need to:

- Depict an organization's historical context in terms of trends in its environments.
- Understand its overall direction and its normative ideals.
- Assess the immediate situation in terms of current strengths and weaknesses,
  future opportunities and threats.
- Develop an agenda of current strategic issues to be managed.

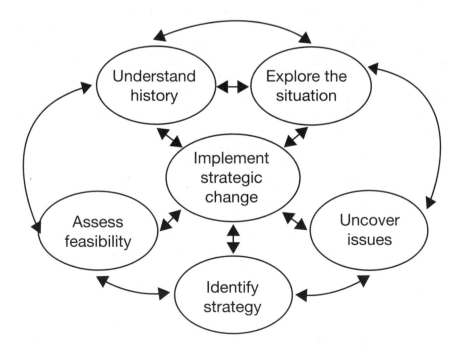

Figure 3.1 Nutt and Backoff's six-point strategic plan

■ Design strategic options to manage priority issues.
■ Assess strategic options in terms of stakeholders affected and resources required.
■ Implement priority strategies by mobilising resources and managing stakeholders.

You may wish to apply this approach to your own context or a partnership you are familiar with. What are the lessons you learnt from this approach?

Deciding a mission/purpose is difficult, and implies an enforced rigidity of plans, mainly because strategic processes are cyclical and iterative. Environmental scanning and strategy formulation must be ongoing, given the dynamism of environments, and rigid strategic planning frustrates creativity and innovation. This may be especially the case where vertical management processes at national levels frustrate the horizontal creativity necessary in partnerships and networks. In the public sector the content to which accountability mechanisms are applied has been reframed.

Political and constitutional constraints on strategy (Hughes 2003: 137) and organizational mandates, specified in legislation, allow organizations to re-examine what they are meant to do, what they are prevented from doing, and where they could possibly act more creatively (Smith 1995). But implementation is more difficult in a public sector setting as 'publicness brings with it constraints, political influence, authority limits, scrutiny and ubiquitous ownership' (Nutt and Backoff 1992: 201).

In highly centralized, bureaucratic and autocratic organizational forms strategies can be used to control, and allow little room for flexible thinking and action (p. 8). Many regeneration partnerships are constrained by higher levels of governance, financial control and accountability mechanisms. The extent to which they have space for flexibility may be limited.

Ring and Perry (1985) suggest that measuring public sector against private sector practice is unfair given the differences that tend to exist between the sectors, and suggest that strategy in the public sector is emergent rather than deliberate. Their propositions are given in Table 3.1.

The types of relationships organizations have with other organizations within a regeneration initiative will determine their approach to developing a framework which is qualitatively different from those developed within the private sector. While these can be competitive, antagonistic and based on rivalry and conflicting interests, or they can also be co-operative, collaborative and consensual and characterized by trust, commitment, reciprocity and mutual gain or win/win, organizations can reap benefits from surrendering part of their discrete organizational strategy by embedding their strategic approach into collaborative endeavours. Co-operative arrangements within a changing external environment can produce collaborative strategies (De Wit and Meyer 1999: 281). It is this latter model that we can see evolving in a number of initiatives: is it one that you would recognize?

Arguably, public sector strategists no longer manage by simple planning and controlling, but by developing the capacity of their organizations to manage resource issues, community issues and organizational issues within major environmental and organizational changes (Joyce 2000: 51). Traditionally managers were expected to carry out their duties, as exemplified by POSDCRB (Planning, Organising, Staffing, Directing, Communicating, Reporting and Budgeting) (Hughes 2003). They also have to articulate a vision agreed in consensus, and to meet public and social needs and the objectives of elected politicians to whom they are accountable (p. 71). Building the support of elected officials, public sector staff, the wider public and partnership organizations is essential to achieving these objectives, as is determining how well the organization's capabilities, resources and activities are aligned to overall goals (p. 71). However, it is important for organizations to carry out a mandate analysis to clarify the boundaries between what must be done, what could be done and what must not be done (Smith 1995). The work of state agencies is governed by statutes that stipulate certain duties and activities that must be undertaken.

In summary, for Bryson (1988), public sector managers need to carry out the following tasks to achieve a strategy:

- Initiating and agreeing a strategic process.
- Determining mandates, and developing and agreeing a mission or vision.
- Understanding the external environment.
- Understanding the political and public control, accountability, budget constraints.
- Assessing internal issues of staff, training, competences, politics and culture, vying for scarce resources.

Vertical approaches to strategy and service delivery which are characteristic of the UK governmental and administrative system present difficulties when complex issues of particular localities are being addressed and where problems do not neatly

Table 3.1 Ring and Perry's five propositions of public sector strategy

Proposition 1	Policy directives tend to be more ill-defined for public than for private organisations
Proposition 2	The relative openness of decision making creates greater constraints for public sector executives and managers than their private sector counterparts
Proposition 3	Public sector policy makers are generally subject to more direct and sustained influence from a greater number of interest groups than are executives or managers in the private sector
Proposition 4	Public sector management must cope with time constraints that are more artificial than those that confront private sector management
Proposition 5	Policy legitimating coalitions are less stable in the public sector and are more prone to disintegrate during policy implementation

coincide with the functional, hierarchical, organizational and territorial boundaries (Burgess *et al.* 2001: 13). The need to adopt integrated policy responses in increasingly overlapping contemporary policy making and implementation is the touchstone of the Labour government's stated commitment to solving complex problems. Dilemmas in moving from a vertical, functional, professional-led approach have arisen as strategic responses to deprived neighbourhoods, and there has been a preoccupation with area-based initiatives. According to Burgess *et al.* (2001: 14), it is within neighbourhood renewal where the challenges of joined-up policy making have been felt more acutely. Attwood *et al.* (2003: 9) advocate whole-system thinking to reconcile the challenges of top down versus bottom up, consumerism vs. citizens, treatment vs. prevention, consultation vs. involvement. They make the point that the role of civic leadership is found in the big picture or whole system. The role of leadership at local and sub-regional levels of governance is shaped by engagement and involvement, not hierarchy and domination (p. 17). Holistic government is about achieving substantially better outcomes across a wide range of policy areas (Wilkinson and Appelbee 1999: preface).

Regeneration managers occupy the 'space' where decisions are never clearly right or wrong, but at the heart of which is negotiation and compromise (Grint 1997: 204). Managerial theory (and within that strategic management) rationalizes away paradoxes, chance, luck, errors, subjectivities, accidents and the sheer indeterminacy of life through a prism of apparent control and rationality (Grint: introduction). We have a tendency to imagine away the fuzzy world and displace its occluded nature with a clarity of vision and control that becalms us (Grint: introduction).

Effective management is thought to be about taking the right as opposed to the wrong decision, analysing data correctly rather than incorrectly and considering both sides of arguments. This stems from Aristotelian binary logic where the world is divided into good and bad, right and wrong, truth and lies, life and death, and so on (Grint 1997: 10). Management (strategic or otherwise) is a complex, ambiguous and essentially political activity. It changes over time within a dynamic context.

Many of the partnerships evolving within regeneration are emergent and we feel they represent experimental forms of governance, characterized by multiple levels of intra- and inter-organizational negotiation and co-ordination that have developed within a complex and ambiguous external environment in attempts to deal with unmet economic, social and environmental needs. But this emergent form of governance, with many innovative and entrepreneurial individuals in public, private and other sectors, has arisen from a poorly institutionalized inter-organizational field of regeneration and the loosely coupled networks at national, regional, sub-regional and local levels.

Multi-agency partnerships are expected to work across boundaries, yet still operate within other forms of regional, sub-regional and local governance. Difficulties arise as members of the partnerships are required to work in collaboration with higher levels of governance: those existing bureaucracies underpinned

65

by deliberate, rational and managerialist organizational forms, not entirely democratic or open to public participation, but strategically contingent on global and central government constraints. As emergent and iterative forms of organization, these partnerships are based on a more inclusive approach to strategy, and as the embodiment of New Public Governance have to be set against the prevailing New Public Sector Management with its legacy of objective setting, targets and performance management.

To understand how UK regeneration policies are formulated, implemented and evaluated it is important to have cognizance of the way that the actors involved are embedded in the social system, how mechanisms are legitimated, and more importantly to examine the processes involved in strategic formulation and implementation. In theory at least, all strategic processes are open to debate, but fundamentally excluded groups rarely challenge decisions. Penetrating and accessing decision making to influence strategic choice and direction is difficult, mainly because regeneration partnerships are still at the emergent stage, and wider social influences have not yet impacted on their activities.

Existing forms of analysis on strategic decision making are limited, and those in existence, such as some of the urban regime theories, partnerships, networks and alliances, have many weaknesses. They are limited on the role of history, informality, linkages between individuals and institutions, existing power relationships and traditional institutional forms of decision making, as well as socio-cultural and external aspects. They are also weakened by having narrow categorizations of state and non-state actors and institutions, so are unable to explain how interests beyond the state are absorbed into decision forums. The blurring of boundaries within and between business, individual actors and institutions, state, civic and other interests has added to the confusion. Existing forms of analysis fail to account for micro decision making, especially the question of who has power, how it is distributed and how conflict/consensus is managed. Hidden levels of power are rarely considered, nor have the ways in which fragmented business, quango and service interests are incorporated into state agendas been explored systematically. Moreover, there are gaps in our understanding of the relationships between existing initiatives and other agencies, such as universities, sporting and artistic agencies, and trade unions.

Within regeneration partnerships there are dynamic relationships cutting across both inter- and intra-organizational fields and some very loosely coupled networks at various levels of governance. As the strategic, social context and space for collective action has become enlarged, there has been an increase in the potential for ambiguity on accountability, legitimacy and autonomy. The uncertainty of the environment coupled with the lack of mandatory guidance has created a situation in which individuals and agencies adjust to each other in more flexible and innovative ways to maintain, enhance and enlarge their power bases.

The problem, of course, is how much public support, legitimacy and autonomy regeneration partnerships can achieve, given that activities are still relatively ill-defined, and projects and initiatives appear to emerge in imprecise and largely unknown ways. The partnerships are rarely clearly specified in advance so excluded interests cannot subject them to debate or challenge. There is continued uncertainty on how solutions to regeneration problems will be evaluated, and for some, the overall mission to which all contributing agencies and actors adhere is ambiguous.

Once state organizations began to lose power and influence over locales, and could no longer engineer feasible solutions to social and economic problems, a much more complex field of intra- and inter-organizational negotiation and co-ordination emerged, strategically contingent on the varied constraints. This has encouraged multi-agency entrepreneurs to mobilize and co-ordinate advocacy coalitions that penetrate and shape policy networks and communities through which projects are formulated and realized. Empirical data on partnerships reveals iterative and emergent strategic processes, quite in contrast with those deliberate and rational approaches in evidence at higher levels of governance.

Regeneration managers need to:

■ Strike the right balance between structural constraints and collective agency.
■ Harmonize economic and socio-cultural activities by developing strategic contingencies.
■ Understand the dynamic institutional environment, inter-organizational politics and power relationships.
■ Manage and shape policy formulation and implementation.

There are many competing perspectives, and not much agreement on strategy. Thus strategy is about:

■ structural elements (Channon 1973);
■ strategic leadership (Leavy and Wilson 1994);
■ culture (Stacey 1993);
■ industry analysis (Porter 1990);
■ emergence and conditionality (Mintzberg 1987).

It has also been divided into various schools of thought, thus:

■ Design school;
■ Planning school;
■ Positioning school;
■ Entrepreneurial school;
■ Cognitive school;
■ Evolutionary school;
■ Classical School;
■ Learning school;
■ Power and cultural school;
■ Environmental and configuration schools.

(Mintzberg 1990)

67

Most regeneration partnerships reflect elements of all strategic schools of thought. The design school approach is shown in the drive to match partnership capabilities with external opportunities; the planning school emphasizes quantitative analysis; the entrepreneurial and cognitive schools provide interesting insights into the way agency representatives choose projects to engender change and improve social, economic and physical conditions. The evolutionary model informs some approaches, confirmed by continual reference to continuous learning, long-termism, sustainability and the need to transfer learning and policy between regeneration partnerships. Top-down and rational models of strategy offer partial explanations of some regeneration activities, but fail to explain micro-level power relationships, history, culture and informal networking. Nor do they show how environmental forces affect strategic choices, or how to deal with pluralism, political malaise, partnerships and networking (Brinkerhoff 1999; Lowndes *et al.* 1997), or emergence and incrementalism, both elements of Whittington's (2001) 'processualism'. Processualists concentrated on incremental adjustments and cultivation of core competences, whereas systemic theorists emphasized that the ends and means of strategy are inextricably linked into a prevailing social system. There has been a rejection of both the classical school as universalist, rational, detached and sequential, and the evolutionary school with a focus on the pace of environmental change (Mintzberg *et al.* 1998). More traditional approaches owe much to the rational, linear understandings of cause and effect. Achieving a strategic fit between an organization (or regeneration partnership) and the external world becomes paramount and this is based on a premise of uniqueness of organizations. In this respect, if an organization (or regeneration partnership) is able to establish the overall purpose, mission and vision, and distinguish itself from other similar organizations by following a unique tailor-made strategy then success will be forthcoming. Added to this design school of strategy there is normally a plethora of formal and systematic planning, and this can be seen very clearly in traditional local authority committee structures as decisions are made based on communicating corporate strategic decisions down to the operational or implementation levels. In positioning an organization (or partnership) in a competitive relationship with other organizations, the assumption is that the fittest will survive. However, much regeneration activity (if not all) must be conducted in collaboration and partnership, and these design school models are flawed and do not match with the realities of regeneration practice.

Cultural explanations help to explain collective action, and show that regeneration managers and other representatives act on behalf of civic society; what they fail to show is how excluded groups can penetrate decision making to influence direction. The informality and lack of transparency surrounding decision making means that decisions are rarely challenged. Added to this, strategies are rarely articulated in advance because of the continued uncertainty on missions or of finding correct solutions. When agency representatives claim to act on behalf of disadvantaged groups, such as the disabled, the poor, the ethnic minorities, they sincerely believe that they represent civic society, but in actuality legitimization of the mechanics and processes involved is never challenged. Access and control of relevant policy networks allow agency heads and selected regeneration representatives of the community (many of whom do not represent the entire views of the community) to maintain control of the regeneration agenda.

Nutt and Backoff (1993) emphasized the importance of leaders from multiple agencies who can instigate change management during periods of greater risk and uncertainty. Another view of strategy, what has been termed the entrepreneurial approach, has at core the notion of a visionary strategist whose experience and judgement allows him (or her) to know instinctively which future direction the organization should follow. Richard Branson and Anita Roddick from the business world or Peter Mandelson, former MP and now EuroCommissioner or many chief executives of public organizations would fit into this category; indeed large salaries are now paid to senior executives who display this entrepreneurial and strategic flair. Strategists who fit into this pattern are regarded as people who have the capacity to create mental maps of the external world and are able to develop strategies over time to bring about change. This evolutionary approach ensures continuous organizational learning, and may seem to be relevant in an organizationally bounded world; however, in the cross-boundary world of regeneration it has little resonance. Notwithstanding the fact that there is a crucial need for entrepreneurial flair and novel ways of looking at regeneration problems and greater risk taking, it is difficult to see how collectivities of strategists within regeneration are in a position to create the cognitive or mental maps of a dynamic and continuously changing policy environment. The requirement to work in partnership in solving regeneration problems usually leads to a collaborative strategic process, and this is contrary to the idea of a visionary individual using his (her) experience, judgement and instinct to solve issues. Much of the strategic process is based on individual or collective negotiation on issues, and what current models of strategy fail to acknowledge is the sometimes clandestine nature of alliance building, the hidden levels of power and influence and the ways in which strategic change can be aided and abetted or more critically, frustrated by a combination of internal power struggles. Many of the external forces beyond an organization (or regeneration partnership) can be so powerful as to usurp strategy completely, and this can effectively neutralize strong leadership, visions, internal analysis or understandings of the competitive world. Any change to the policy framework has massive implications for strategists in regeneration, no matter how good they are at carrying out a strategic analysis or attempting to forecast future plans. Moreover, the constant transformation and dynamism of the external world as organizations are configured and reconfigured over time means that multivariate elements cluster to effect strategic change. It is therefore very difficult to strategise in such circumstances.

Power, cultural, environmental and configuration perspectives on strategy are all critical to understanding how decisions are made within regeneration. Environmental forces have shaped the context in which decisions are made, and decision makers are forced into making strategic responses. They do this by manipulating symbols and continuously struggling for legitimacy and autonomy. By matching resources, knowledge and information to the challenges of the environment, they not only legitimize activities but also are able to adapt policies to local needs by choosing appropriate strategies. Decisions are made on future action, on behalf of the total population, and regeneration managers manage the complex interaction of informal and formal power relationship interactions over time. By striking the correct balance between structural constraints and collective agency, through contingent means they harmonize economic, social and cultural activities. Once the state began to lose power and influence and was incapable of engineering solutions, co-ordination of inter-agency power relationships became an important facet of adapting projects to achieve local aims. In the case of LSPs the state officials still have a role to play as funder, but the Government Office (GO) representatives occupy a number of ambiguous roles. It is still not clear whether they act in an advisory or guidance role, as a scrutineer of spending, or an accountable body. This may create spaces within which local managers are able to act in 'entrepreneurial' ways.

External forces, normally neglected in existing theories of urban/local and regional change, are critical to strategic analysis and regeneration managers recognize the need for benchmarking against other regeneration programmes/projects. To avoid duplication of effort, information is gathered at all levels of governance so that available resources are widely known.

Because regeneration partnerships are generally voluntaristic and there is little evidence to show how certain groups or individuals are invited to serve on them, and because of the lack of mandatory or democratic legitimacy, there is little room for others to challenge decisions.

Culture and shared stakeholder expectations are a crucial driving force in strategy, and these are reflected in supplementary coalitions that are created when specific projects, initiatives or events are used as regenerative activities. Some regeneration partnerships are organized by formally constituted forums supplemented by informal gatherings, with continuous interaction between the two. The interactions and linkages between formal and informal partnerships are crucial focal points between the external and internal worlds, as repositories of knowledge and information emanating from many different directions.

Rational approaches to strategy, exemplified in New Public Management, place the emphasis on target and objective setting, and managing resources. They have their origins in the scientific management school of thought, with an assumption that all tasks can be reduced to simple steps in a rational and linear fashion. However, strategic decision making in real regeneration settings is messy, ambiguous and leads to unintended actions and consequences.

Denhardt and Denhardt (2000) present a new public service (NPS) approach as a viable alternative for the dichotomy between the 'old' public administration and the 'new' public management (NPM). It seeks to balance the advantages of NPM with the emerging requirement for greater public participation in public service improvement. NPS theorists emphasize democratic citizenship and models of community and civil society, and postulate that rather than having traditional bureaucracies controlled from the top down and largely closed for citizens:

> The primary role of the public servant is to help citizens articulate and meet their shared interests rather than to attempt to control or steer society.
>
> (Denhardt and Denhardt 2000: 549)

NPS is intended as a viable alternative to both the traditional and the now-dominant managerialist models (Denhardt and Denhardt 2000). According to this approach, public sector organizations should be organized in such a way that public servants are not responsive to 'constituents and clients' (traditional public administration), nor to 'customers' (NPM), but to 'citizens'.

With citizens at the forefront, the emphasis in NPS should not be placed on either steering (NPM) or rowing (public administration) the governmental boat (Osborne and Gaebler 1992), but rather on building public institutions marked by integrity and responsiveness.

Denhardt and Denhardt (2000) suggest that NPS is built on the following six principles:

1   Serve rather than steer. Public policies are no longer simply the result of governmental decision-making processes. Government is just another, albeit important, player.
2   The public interest is the aim, not the by-product. It is necessary to establish shared interests and shared responsibilities based around a vision for the community and a single set of goals.
3   Think strategically, act democratically. Collective effort and collaborative processes should exist within open and accessible government.
4   Serve citizens, not customers, and have a concern for the larger community. Accountability is not simple and involves complex constellations of institutions and standards.
5   Value people, not just productivity. Processes of collaboration and shared leadership should be based on respect for people.
6   Value citizenship and public service above entrepreneurship.

We argue that the strategic process within regeneration is not a maximising activity in economic terms, but is one of satisfying (Simon *et al.* 1950). Decision making is therefore an evolutionary, dynamic process where 'partisan mutual adjustment' to all relevant views and as many circumstances as possible towards commonly agreed goals is more appropriate. Indeed as Grint (1997) confirms, much of the thinking in business schools has been influenced by economists who adopt a reductionist view of the world, when the realities are much more messy and unmeasurable. A political view of strategy would have to encapsulate the explicit and hidden aspects of power articulated by Lukes (1974) and Bacharach and Baratz (1962). The hidden aspects of the decision-making process are equally as valid as explicit and observable elements. Lukes refers to the three dimensions of power: the explicit decision which is clear to identify; the non-decision where an individual decided not to make a decision; but the most insidious level of power is structural power or hidden power, where the decisions made by individuals are conditioned by the context and underpinning societal power structures. Fulop and Linstead (1999) go further and add a fourth dimension of power, based on relationships beyond organizational boundaries.

Whereas rational models of strategic decision making are based on a top-down and managed approach, exemplified in the work of those writers who have influenced NPM, the realities of current regeneration show attempts at a more democratic, bottom-up, experimental, iterative and emergent strategic decision making in which broader cocktails of stakeholders are involved in reaching decisions. Friend *et al.* (1974) conceptualized 'action spaces' where planning decisions were made, where individuals learnt from each other about the consequences of actions, and where continuous improvements are experimented with.

Porter (1985), one of the foremost and well-referenced writers on strategy, has been influential in fostering a view of economic maximization and modelling, and later writers followed in the same vein. Johnson and Scholes (2003) developed a three-ringed model of strategic analysis, choice and implementation with an attempt to include stakeholders and power in strategic processes, but at every step of their strategic processes there are dilemmas and problems.

As Figure 3.2 shows, the strategic process consists of analysis, choice and implementation, but if we apply this model to the realities of regeneration it is clear that at every step of the way there are difficulties to be encountered. Moreover, making strategic choices and following options, based on analysis of the internal and external environments, are by far the easiest parts of the equation, but the most difficult part of strategy is the execution and implementation. This is the part of the process where contestation and managing the competing views take place. This is not to say that all elements of the strategic process are not fraught with difficulties, given the myriad expectations, varied values, competing external and internal forces and constraints on choosing specific options, the availability of budgets to commit to certain identified options, the clashes in cultures between agencies and how difficult it is to mainstream programmes, projects and budgets, the different planning mechanism, performance management and measurement regimes, and the rigidity of organizational structures. All militate against strategic success. Having strategic intent is one thing, carrying those intentions out is quite another thing. Once a strategic course is decided upon, then agencies have to commit resources, people and technology and may have to change the ways that their organizations conduct business.

Strategy is concerned with the long-term view whereas many of the agencies in regeneration making strategic decisions are fairly used to having short-term objectives. There is also a need to synthesize and bring together a disparate set of factors into a coherent whole plan, and again this presents difficulties when more than one agency is involved. Many of the actors in strategy do not possess complete information, may not be themselves strategists in their own organization, and cannot therefore commit adequate resources to the overall aims. If strategy is about having an overview and coherence it is clear that bringing together disparate organizations, with sometimes different representatives at different meetings, can create problems in achieving a coherent approach.

The role of resources as a foundation on which to build strategy is articulated in Grant's model in Figure 3.3. However, useful as it is, there are many problems when applying it to the public sector. First, it assumes that there is a competitive environment, when in fact many actors collaborate rather than compete. Second, the key success factors may be elusive, may be determined elsewhere, or may have to be negotiated with a range of different and competing stakeholders. The resources available to public sector agencies may be constrained (finite resources and infinite demands), or there may be incomplete data on all tangible, intangible and human or other resources. The scale of some organizations means that resources will be shared with other organizations. In some neighbouring local authorities cross-authority consortia or arm's-length agencies are being developed and staff are being seconded for short periods of time.

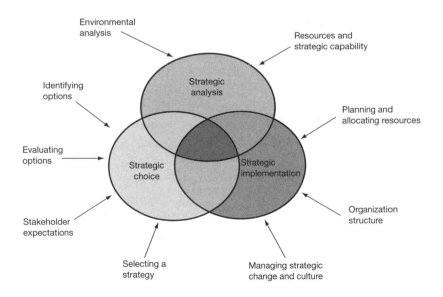

Figure 3.2 A realistic model of strategy process

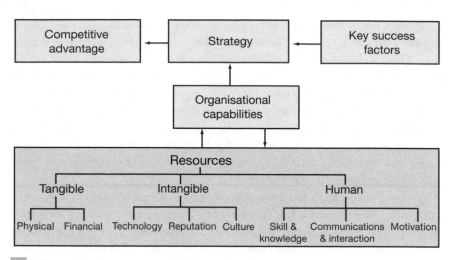

Figure 3.3 *Resources, capabilities and competitive advantage (after Grant, 1995)*

SUMMARY

Table 3.2 outlines the major differences between traditional and contemporary approaches to strategy, and illustrates the complexities of regeneration management.

Table 3.2 *Major differences between traditional and contemporary approaches to strategy*

Traditional approach to strategy	Contemporary approach to strategy
Rational and linear	Iterative and cyclical
Top down and hierarchical	Bottom up and more democratic
Objective setting and targets	Evolutionary and dynamic
Economic maximisation and modelling	Satisfying, incremental and mutual adjustment
One-off decisions	Continuous learning, ongoing decisions
No recognition of the realities of power relationships	Strategy as a political process
Models not grounded in socio-economic milieu	Accepts the messiness of political, social and economic worlds

Continued on next page

Table 3.2 (*cont.*)

Traditional approach to strategy	Contemporary approach to strategy
Assumes there are 'best ways' to make decisions	No one best way to reach decision
Bureaucratic	Flexible
Taken by a few key strategists	Citizen inclusion, democratic legitimacy
Defined membership	Ad hoc decision making, different people at different points in time
Public/private	Multi-agency, multi-professional and other inputs
Uni-organisational	Cross-boundary decision making
Clear boundaries of action	Indistinct boundaries
Stability of strategy group over time	Flexible, ad hoc and dynamic personnel
Formal arrangements	Informal aspects
No recognition of political/social aspects of power	Power relationships within strategic decision making and beyond at the core
Context seen as stable	Acceptance that context is dynamic and many forces shaping strategy
Mandates/legislation	Mix of mandatory and non-mandatory aspects
Deliberate	Emergent

DISCUSSION POINTS

■ What are the strengths/weaknesses of traditional or newer models of strategy?

■ Use traditional and newer strategic frameworks to reflect upon your own strategic experience, and identify the key external and internal aspects of strategic change.

■ What kind of a strategic thinker are you and what has shaped your strategic thinking?

■ How can strategic intent be realized within regeneration, and what measures and evaluation of strategic success need to be adopted?

Chapter 4

Leadership and stakeholder engagement

KEY THEMES

- History of the term 'stakeholder'.
- The importance of leadership in engaging stakeholders in strategy.
- Identification and prioritization of stakeholders: the key strategic role?
- Involving stakeholders and managing future relationships.
- Some barriers to involvement and how to overcome them.

LEARNING POINTS

By the end of this chapter we hope that you will be able to:

- Identify how and why stakeholders are important to strategic change.
- Understand that involving stakeholders demands new skills and competences.
- Appreciate the importance of leadership in the strategic process.
- Appreciate the structural, professional or other barriers to stakeholder involvement.
- Reflect upon the past, and identify some situations when you may not have managed stakeholder relationships appropriately.
- Reflect upon your own strategic approach to involving stakeholders and managing future relationships.
- Understand that strategic success depends on measures and evaluation developed in collaboration with stakeholders.

INTRODUCTION

Managing strategy is arguably one of the most important elements of regeneration, because it involves a thorough knowledge of the particular and present strengths and weaknesses or resources and capabilities of a partnership or network arrangements, as well as how to make choices on future actions and direction. An appropriate and feasible good strategic approach will facilitate analysis of the near and far environment, ensure intelligence and data collection, and allow strategists to achieve a good reputation and strategic positioning. To do this, as explained in Chapter 3, a strategy may be an expression of purpose and mission, but it must also help to gain the commitment of all stakeholders, if it is to be successful in the long term.

We contend that regeneration managers must be capable of harmonising and marrying a vast array of stakeholder demands, preferences and choices as they conduct the various elements contributing to strategic intent, but more importantly strategic success. To achieve a strategic positioning, and in appreciating the many conflicting agendas, you will require a high level of skill, experience and knowledge of the key issues. Moreover, it is essential that you understand some of the underpinning motives of those individuals and groups engaged in making strategy. In this chapter we will locate the myriad of stakeholders engaging in strategy, within complex and dynamic settings, to illustrate that your primary concern must be identification of key groups and individuals that can help to bring plans to fruition, but considerable problems arise in appreciating who should be included, or excluded from decision making, as well the basis for your choice. Once stakeholders are invited on to forums there is an additional question in determining which of those identified stakeholders may present barriers to your achievement of objectives, and if so what levels of power and influence they can wield to frustrate future plans.

One of the most essential skills that regeneration managers need is the capacity to manage stakeholder relationships both now and in the future. In this chapter we attempt to simplify a very complex process, and present some ideas and thoughts on how you can overcome some of the difficulties. Arguably a lot of your valuable time and efforts will be devoted to appeasing the demands of stakeholders at different levels of governance, and any strategic analysis must help you to decide who they are, and how best to manage their divergent and competing interests, preferences and expectations.

As stakeholders from wider agency backgrounds and experiences/histories begin to pool resources and work more collaboratively it becomes evident that managing and communicating between them will become increasingly difficult. In contrast with established mechanisms used in formal top-down hierarchies, we argue that these new relationships based on informal and continued relational interactions demand higher level skills to understand and appreciate how each partner is able to aid or frustrate strategic performance and success.

THE IMPORTANCE OF STAKEHOLDERS IN STRATEGY

The modernization agenda has created a clear desire to involve much wider stake-holder groupings in decision making, and to identify the correct processes to involve and consult with under-represented groups such as women, ethnic minorities, young people or the voluntary sector is a key part of the new regeneration process. However, there is little evidence to suggest this is being achieved, meaning that most 'consultation' is done through the traditional managerialist mechanisms. Indeed in an initial assessment of Regional Economic Strategies some RDAs were criticized for failing to deal with social exclusion or equal opportunities in a rigorous manner (Roberts and Benneworth 2001: 149).

As has already been explained earlier, regeneration managers need to balance the demands and expectations of communities of interest with what is appropriate, given the mandatory restrictions, what is feasible in budgetary constraints, and what is acceptable to all stakeholders. As was shown in Chapter 3, working with stakeholders to develop future strategies requires regeneration managers who are capable of continuous negotiation and dialogue, because what may be feasible, appropriate and acceptable to one group of stakeholders in a specific locale may be inadequate in another setting. The need to match what is required with what can be achieved is played out in partnership forums, and the entire process will be replete with constraints, frustrations and barriers to action. The scale of the problems facing you as you work alongside many competing stakeholders may result in satisfactory (but perhaps not totally adequate) solutions to given problems as you attempt to harness resources in efforts to address regeneration. The limitations on the level of discretion you have may hamper even the best efforts or ideas for transformation.

The involvement of communities and stakeholders needs closer examination because 'community' and 'stakeholder' are ambiguous, but literature emanating from the Social Exclusion Unit focuses on the 'community' as the primary means of driving neighbourhood renewal. As with many normative concepts it is not defined and Barnett (1998) argues that:

> Community can be defined as a commonality of interests but it is questionable whether this can be defined in relation to the geographic locality. In terms of service delivery people can be considered as a community for one purpose and not for other purposes. Communities can overlap geographically.

Communities are not homogeneous groups, as recent CVS consultation and awareness raising exercises reveal.[1]

NRSs imply that LSPs will use a stakeholder cocktail to determine community needs and this leads to extraordinary complexity. Communities are not easily identified, neither are the communities or stakeholder involvement clearly evident. The stakeholder concept has been common parlance for some time now, but the problems raised by the complex and fragmented institutional arrangements in local governance made the concept even more appealing. Stakeholding as it is now adopted stresses social inclusion, active participation, balancing rights and responsibilities and communitarianism. It has also been used to explain and reappraise institutional arrangements, but the number of stakeholders is large and their range is wide and each one has the potential to influence the future direction of LSPs.

Regeneration managers need to conduct analyses of stakeholders, to reflect and manage diversity. They also need to address the marginalization of those groups who may lose out by being disconnected from decision making. Moreover, in any future change process a series of complex relationships needs to be managed. Rhetorically at least, stakeholding is a prescriptive account that celebrates partnership and assumes that each partner has a level playing field in relation to their power and influence.

Strategy must also be suitable and feasible to all stakeholders and there are problems in identifying stakeholders, as well as managing their expectations. Moreover, the success of strategies depends on the measures used to evaluate, and who will be measuring the end results. As we move from representative forms to more consultative, deliberative and participative new forms of modern democracy (Pratchett 2000: 11), the cocktail of stakeholders continually changes, and people become active in regeneration at different times and on different issues as their views are sought or consultation is demanded.

HISTORY OF THE TERM 'STAKEHOLDER'

The stakeholder concept has had a lengthy and debatable evolution. It appears to have been used formally first within the Stanford Research Institute in the 1960s. However, by the 1970s, the concept (in its various forms) began to appear in a number of management journals. During this period the systems theory, social responsibility theories and organizational theory literature frequently referred to stakeholders, but the definitions and applications varied from case to case. Freeman then published a seminal work on the concept (1984), and he defined a stakeholder as follows:

> any group or individual who can affect, or is affected by the achievement
> of a corporation's objectives or purpose.

It became formally recognized in the 1980s that all organizations have multiple constituencies, and that executives needed to pay particular attention to groups that are critical to the success of a company or organization. A review of recent literature on the topic indicates that Freeman's (1984) definition is still considered by most scholars to be the classical norm.

But five important additional conceptual qualifications can be identified thus:

1   Stakeholder groups must have a legitimate claim on the organization (Alkhafaji 1989; Carroll 1989; Cornell and Shapiro 1987; Evan and Freeman 1988; Hill and Jones 1992).
2   Formal contracts must be in existence (Freeman and Evan 1990). Stakeholders must be directly and critically involved in the firm's economic interests and survival (Cornell and Shapiro 1987).
3   Stakeholders have a moral obligation to make decisions for fair distribution of harms and benefits of action by the organization (Carroll 1989; Donaldson and Preston 1995; Langtry 1994).
4   Stakeholders must be risk bearers, and commit to some form of capital, be it financial or human, and to assume the risk of loss or gain on behalf of an organization (Clarkson 1994).
5   Stakeholders must have the power or influence to affect organizational behaviour (G. T. Savage *et al.*, cited in Mitchell *et al.* 1997).

Clarkson (1995) differentiated between 'primary' and 'secondary' stakeholders as follows:

> a primary stakeholder group is one without whose continuing participation the corporation cannot survive as a going concern

and

> a secondary stakeholder group is one which has a direct relationship with the corporation but is not involved in regular daily transactions with the corporation: it may affect or influence, or be affected or influenced by the corporation, but it is not absolutely essential for the survival of the corporation as a going concern.

In accordance with this differentiation, it is therefore essential to identify the stakeholders (agencies and individuals) who are primary to achieving regeneration. Thus direct involvement and centrality to decision making, regularity of participation, ability to harness resources, be they tangible or intangible for partnership efforts, all make primary stakeholders powerful and the trick for mangers is to manage the inter-relationships both formally and informally. A secondary stakeholder will be any group or individual that has an 'arm's-length' and indirect relationship in decision making and can be called upon, as and when required, to provide tangible and intangible resources to fulfil objectives. Secondary stakeholders may be critical to achieving overall objectives, depending on the initiative in question, and may be absolutely essential to survival, but the regularity of participation and ability to harness resources will depend on many variables, not least mandatory or other obligations.

Donaldson and Preston (1995: 66–67), distinguishing between the descriptive, instrumental and normative aspects, suggest that:

> stakeholder theory does not presume that managers of a service are the only rightful locus of corporate control and governance

and

> it is the responsibility of managers to acknowledge the validity of diverse stakeholder interests and attempt to respond to them within a mutually supportive framework. This is a moral requirement.

Johnson and Scholes (1993) urge caution in identifying managers of a service as the honest brokers who can weigh up conflicting interests of groups, because practicalities and pragmatism are equally important in managing stakeholder relationships for overall survival.

The ambiguity and indeterminacy of the stakeholder concept has led to various definitions and interpretations of it. All organizations have multiple constituencies, and Freeman's definition is still considered by most scholars to be the classical norm, but six important additional conceptual qualifications have been added.[2]

Stakeholders need power or influence to affect organizational behaviour (G. T. Savage et al., cited in Mitchell et al. 1997) and mapping is a useful tool to identify groups and their expectations as well as how well they will accept or present a barrier to a certain issue. This can be done in relation to the relative power and interest they are able to exert (Johnson and Scholes 1993).

Stakeholder analysis provides a means of identifying power relations between individuals and groups, but it is clear that many stakeholders have little influence on the strategic direction or the ability to challenge decisions made.

Stakeholders are meant to have a 'stake' or interest and that level of interest can be direct or indirect. Primary stakeholders that have a direct and continued participation on decision-making forums, and have regular interactions, are concerned with maintaining partnership survival. Being in a senior position allows actors to harness tangible (finance, staff, premises, etc.) and intangible (knowledge, information, stakeholder management, capacity to lobby, etc.) resources. Secondary stakeholders will have an indirect or arm's-length role.

The balance of direct and indirect power/interest and influence changes over time and in line with specific events/initiatives. Some individual groups of stakeholders remain powerful in some circumstances but become less powerful at other

81

times. In assessing the cultural/political dimensions of strategy the unity, diversity, alliance or rifts that are evident will change depending on circumstances. The level, nature and frequency of communication between the various stakeholders also have an important impact on strategic direction.

Partnerships can maintain their role by excluding certain groups, achieving unity of purpose and being in frequent contact.

Stakeholder analysis is, according to Johnson and Scholes, 'the core of an assessment of the cultural and political dimensions of strategy' (2003: 165). In any regeneration partnership there are numerous internal and external stakeholders, operating within specific cultural contexts, each with their own conflicting expectations and each, perhaps, belonging to a number of stakeholding groups.

IDENTIFICATION AND PRIORITIZATION OF STAKEHOLDERS: THE KEY STRATEGIC ROLE?

Frost (1995) proposes stakeholder analysis as a strategic planning tool to explore ethical and moral issues by remembering less powerful stakeholders and continuously communicating and re-examining their relative position. He also believed that it was necessary to canvas support amongst stakeholders so that obstacles to progress can be avoided. Any strategic management process must therefore include the capacity to:

- Identify stakeholders.
- Prioritize according to relative importance/influence.
- Understand their expectations.
- Identify shared expectations.
- Evaluate consequential action of prioritising one stakeholder's expectations over those of another.

(Frost 1995)

As well as allowing the identification of direct or indirect levels of power and influence, stakeholder theory helps to prioritize:

- Relevant importance of stakeholders.
- Assessment of stakeholder expectations, particularly if they are shared.
- Their demands in relation to the demands of other stakeholders.

Specific events trigger off strategic formulation which can create unity, diversity, alliance or rifts between competing stakeholder groups, so it is important that level, nature and frequency of communication are understood. However, the balance of direct and indirect power/interest changes over time, and depends on any specific project. Some stakeholders are powerful in some circumstances or when certain issues arise on agendas, but become less powerful at other times. The use of rhetoric, symbolism and manipulation of language can be useful ways of removing obstacles to progress.

Johnson and Scholes (2003) propose a method of mapping stakeholder power to help strategists to balance and reconcile the competing demands; however, it is clear in regeneration that not only do stakeholders change from initiative to initiative, but also their power and influence change over time.

Regeneration partners are expected to adopt strategic processes, but these are firmly embedded in a particular political and cultural context, so representatives from multiple agencies interpret information from different perspectives and interests, as well as having diverse cultural frames of reference. This confirms the difficulties in identifying stakeholders, as relationships do not happen in a vacuum of dyadic ties, neither is the strategic process static. Rather the political and cultural milieu creates iterative processes in which dynamic influences affect others. These interactions between multiple influences constitute a 'stakeholder set'. Any organization is not necessarily the centre of a universe, but actors/agency representatives are part of other networks of differing importance. N. Rowley (quoted in Donaldson and Preston 1995) suggests that *network density* (the denser the number of relationships, the greater the diffusion of norms and the more effective the communication) means that a focal organization will have difficulty playing off well-informed and well-connected stakeholders who can constrain their actions. *Centrality* (closeness or level of dependency) and *betweenness* (degree of interaction between actors/agencies; the extent to which the agencies interact) also alter the balance of power.

Stakeholding, in its many forms, can be challenged because it is based on a pluralist premise that a multitude of actors with diverse and competing interests can be 'managed' in any given strategic process, by assessing, arbitrating and allocating resources. The very fact that the process of stakeholding needs to be managed creates an imbalance between those who are managing and those being managed. It implies a hierarchy and indicates inequality. The pluralist tendency to conceptualize organizations as constellations of competing stakeholders is extremely problematic too, and seen as naive and utopian by writers who assert that 'stakeholding is a political fantasy that cannot be a plan for getting from exclusion to inclusion, it does not confront the structural reality of redistributive conflict between stakeholders' (Froud *et al.* 1996: 120).

Pluralist explanations fail to show the contradictions, the unequal nature of differing interests, and assume that power can be observed, measured or negotiated only through democratic means. They fail to recognize the hidden or structural aspects of power, the historical and social forces shaping political action (Lukes 1974), and dominant interests who manage meaning (Fulop and Linstead 1999). Furthermore the quality of relationships between stakeholders will be

83

constrained to some degree by the roles assigned to each, by contextually specific practices, techniques, procedures and forms of knowledge routinely developed to shape the conduct of others (Fulop and Linstead 1999).

Interests/preferences are not always articulated or observable, and there is an assumption that all parties in decision making will be honest, outspoken and share their preferences/interests. Decision making in regeneration consists of many, varied and different relationships, some formal, others informal, so it is almost impossible to show how power/influence is distributed. Observable means of enquiry cannot always determine the many unwritten agendas and outcomes of decisions shared between actors. The strong desire to be cohesive means that rhetoric is used to lubricate the process.

BARRIERS TO INVOLVEMENT

Arguably, there are many barriers to overcome in facilitating community engagement. Although funds are available to lubricate the processes, the following challenges exist:

- What do we mean by 'communities'?
- Prioritising who needs training, how to select and on what basis.
- Has any training needs analysis been done?
- Hard-to-reach groups: how can they be trained?
- What are the expectations?
- Support mechanisms and ongoing support.
- Are training/learning experiences simply rubber stamping or box ticking to say they have been done?
- Knowing who does what on regeneration partnerships. How do they fit in?
- Knowing where to get funding/support and how.
- Mechanisms for involvement and for feeding back to communities, from those representing communities.
- Building trust and accepting different levels of training needs.
- How to do it? Forms of engagement? Who will do it?
- Communication between members of community, between community and regeneration partnerships, and between representatives of community and wider community needs to have a channel for engagement to be achieved.
- Incentives for training?
- Need measures of success/failures.
- Need for an independent broker.
- Short-termism; what about long-term needs?
- Communities need 'know-how', resource base, information and to know what works in other areas.

- Ownership of learning/training. Is it the partnership, community, Government Office?
- Will training be certificated?
- Tensions between levels of governance.

INVOLVING STAKEHOLDERS AND MANAGING FUTURE RELATIONSHIPS: THE NEED FOR LEADERSHIP

Leadership is critical to regeneration, but this presents problems for agencies working together, as there is generally no agreement on which body should take the lead, and which ideas will dominate regeneration agenda. To be creative, as regeneration demands, requires leaders who not only are themselves creative and have technical expertise, social and organizational skills, and the ability to 'sell' the message, but also provide inspirational motivation. This comes more from engaging people in a mission where they can make unique autonomous contributions and make sense of situations and contexts (Sosik *et al.* 1999: 227–257). The influence of leaders occurs through indirect mechanisms, such as providing resources, setting deadlines, identifying projects, but more importantly establishing an interactional climate, managing the context and providing a structure to support autonomous efforts (Mumford *et al.* 2003: 705–750).

Within the modernization agenda, we suggest that those in leadership positions must have the ability to inspire, communicate and operationalize their visions, and transforming leaders should create the conditions for others to transform realities and galvanize innovators (Maddock 2002), but while central and local government retain a high degree of control, this proves difficult.

Public bureaucracies do not possess information processing capacity, and cannot mimic market incentives, so public servants are often left in brokerage roles to ensure that socially just distribution would solve the ills created by markets (Jackson 2001: 5). Hybridized public/private sectors in the 1980 and 1990s created mosaics of flexible organizational forms and new architectures based on relational contracts and knowledge transfer (Jackson and Stainsby 2000: 14). The degree of vertical compartmentalism managers have at corporate levels means that managing other than top down is difficult. They have a vested interest in the continuation of risk-averse cultures.

Many local authorities are being forced into considering their traditional ways of conducting business, and the need to move away from professional or supplier-driven services to more empowering, facilitating, engaging or enabling consumer-driven approaches. Local authorities need to create the conditions of trust that allow citizens and consumers to talk freely and this requires heightened listening skills as well as skills to help individuals consider what the problems are. Facilitating discussions and allowing differences of opinion to emerge on what key problems there are needs managers who can understand the political and socio-economic context, the content and issues, and the processes in regeneration. If managers of services can suspend their own professional interpretations of required services and put themselves into the minds of users and citizens they may gain a deeper appreciation of exactly what the hopes and aspirations, as well as the barriers to achievement, might be. Many users of services are intimidated by the power of the local authority or are reluctant to engage in discussion with professionally trained people, for fear of looking foolish or being corrected on some point of detail, order or procedure, so it is understandable that there are barriers to be breached before reciprocal and trusting relationships can be built up. This process takes a long time to establish and cannot be done overnight.

For Taylor (2003: 86), policies for the socially excluded and involving partnerships are driven by the need to incorporate dissent and provide symbolic legitimacy, which becomes a zero-sum game with the dice loaded in favour of existing power structures. However, she believes that if we reject this zero-sum game and adversarial view of power, and instead think of it as energy flowing rather than being possessed by one group rather than another, disadvantaged groups could redefine the rules of the game. A more pragmatic approach to regeneration requires a more sophisticated understanding of the way communities work, the way power is distributed in society and how change agents (regeneration managers) can assess strategies available to them, given the many institutional dilemmas to be faced (Taylor 2003: 225).

One thing that communities cannot accept is when managers speak to them as token voices or because they are seen to be ticking boxes for some bureaucratic form-filling exercise; they prefer real and meaningful engagement. Quite often public engagement can degenerate into moaning and whinging sessions, but this is inevitable in the first instance as groups and individuals get pent up feelings out into the open, but once this has subsided there is a real opportunity for shared understandings and better working practices between professionals and communities.

Arguably committee structures and bureaucratic procedures can place limitations on engagement, so there is a need for managers to take their business 'to' the communities, rather than expecting communities to fit neatly into traditional practices and procedures. It requires great confidence for formerly disengaged or hard-to-reach people to fit automatically into preconceived mechanisms and some thought has to be put into having more innovative and creative forms of meeting or engaging with communities. There are many examples in the north-east of England where managers are meeting with young people in youth clubs, pubs, bars and other places where they congregate, or visiting old people's homes, health clubs, baby clinics, etc. Reducing bureaucracy can offer a sensible mechanism for greater levels of engagement. Unless managers are able to recognize the resource base and capacity in communities they are ill-equipped to address those fundamental deficiencies.

Communities are neither homogeneous nor harmonious groups and have inbuilt tensions, past histories and ongoing conflicts. Conflict resolution is essential (Diamond 2002b) but there must also be very careful management of expectations, because if communities are given the impression that they will have all their wants, desires and aspirations fulfilled, they will feel let down and deflated when the local council or managers responsible for regeneration cannot deliver on promises. Given the fact of shrinking resources and the need to mainstream from other funding pots, it is unwise to raise expectations beyond a reasonable and negotiated level. One of the problems for managers is working at the local level and asking the communities what they want, when in fact there are strategic priorities to be attended to. As an example, a senior police commander when speaking about the requirement for police to involve communities in determining priorities in the latest Home Office document *Policing: Building Safer Communities Together* (2003) commented:

> in every public meeting the same issue of bobbies on the beat comes up, and important though this is in preventing the fear of crime, the reality is that I, and my officers, also need to manage football hooliganism, theft, infiltration from the British National Front at elections, major incidents such as terrorism, and the like. You try telling that to Joe Bloggs in his village community when he's afraid of his back door being broken into in the middle of the night.
>
> (Interview with one of the authors, December 2003)

So it is important to be able to maintain a strategic focus at the same time as working at the operational level. As strategy is an iterative process of analysis, formulation, choices or options and implementation or execution, managers need to be aware of the differences.

Managers need detailed knowledge of communities, they need to build up trust, but above all they need the capacity to influence community discussions. This will require the ability to present a case, use verbal and non-verbal persuasive skills, communicate clearly and honestly to groups, and defuse tensions that might arise in public meetings. Chairing meetings and being able to allow all voices to be heard, and then summarising the mood of a meeting, are essential to ensure fair representation of all views. Professional skills are still as important as they have always been, but the generic management skills are useful. Far from needing the POSDCRB skills (Hughes 2003) managers now need to be

- Abstractors;
- Conceptualizers;

87

- Systems thinkers;
- Collaborators;
- Experimenters.

(Reich 1991)

and

- Imaginers.

(Morgan 1998)

as well as being

- Competent;
- Connection makers.

(Kanter 1994)

Community governance and community leadership emphasize a shift from managing and administering services, budgets and staff within local authorities or other public organizations towards taking the lead in the new governance systems beyond organizational boundaries within networks and partnerships. The local authority no longer has the sole responsibility to deliver services for the geographical population and govern its constituents. It now has to take on the role as community champion or community leader to assist local people and diverse groups in deterring overall needs and developing relevant capacities. Local authorities have always been the responsible and accountable body acting on behalf of locales, with the threat of political overthrow if plans did not have popular community approval or were outside of their mandated obligations. Local authorities not only have to lead their communities, as defined in the White Paper 'Strong Local Leadership-Quality Public Services' (Cmnd 5237, 2001), but have responsibility under the Local Government Acts of 2000 and 2003 for the overall social, economic and environmental well-being of the locale. Community leadership requires local authorities to:

- Shape and support grass root development of communities.
- Negotiate and mobilize effective partnerships with other public, private and voluntary agencies.
- Voice the needs and interests of the local community in regional, national, European and international arenas.
- Manage the local authority and give strategic direction on service development.

(Hartley 1998)

Specifically the NRU and ODPM (Office of the Deputy Prime Minister) have identified the need for different types of leadership:

Structural leadership: Those occupying a certain position in a group and who need to identify tasks to be carried out.

Informal leadership: Those who can influence attitudes and choices.

Transitory leadership: Leadership that moves around a group according to a stage in the process.

Transformative leadership: Capacity to transform settings.

Skills and knowledge leadership: Those who have special skills and knowledge to contribute to group efforts.

Enabling leadership: Leadership that encourages participation, identifies limits and calls on members to make decisions.

Consultative leadership: Those who present the situation, get input *but* make the decision.

Authoritarian leadership (for survival): Those who present decisions but invite questions for clarification.

The Smarter Partnership Toolkit (see http://www.lgpartnerships.com/howhealthy.asp?) is a check of healthy partnerships and shows how leadership, trust, learning and managing performance are integral to the success of partnership working.

SUMMARY

We suggested in this chapter that stakeholders are now central to regeneration, and that leadership is a shared process between competing and diverse groups and individuals. Leadership is crucial to engaging, communicating and managing the processes, and we have argued that it is still important for visionary individuals to inspire and motivate, but considerable problems arise when identifying which individuals and groups will enhance or frustrate strategic objectives.

Arguably the identification and prioritization of stakeholder demands is a vital role, perhaps *the* most important to future success, and regeneration managers must overcome many barriers to achieve success. Not only are there structural, professional and other barriers, but you must also appreciate many other competing demands. Leaders and other stakeholders are embedded in the social system, so there is a need to legitimize the types of mechanisms and processes used to bring about change in strategic formulation and implementation. Therefore, mobilization and co-ordination of stakeholder efforts to shape strategic change, and the realization of successful projects, programmes and plans, are vital.

The need to strike the correct balance and harmonize the inputs from a dynamic institutional environment, deal with powerful competing demands, and the capacity to shape the strategic processes are all essential ingredients to successful regeneration. In this chapter we have demonstrated some of the difficulties, problems and frustrations inherent in stakeholder engagement.

Arguably, managing and communicating with diverse and contradictory stakeholders, now and in the future, are two of the most crucial skills to success in bringing about regeneration of deprived locales. The need to understand competing, contradictory and diverse demands, preferences and expectations, and harmonize or balance these with other structural constraints, budgetary limitations and mandatory obligations, requires regeneration managers who can appreciate diverse elements of strategic processes.

DISCUSSION POINTS

- Is it always possible to identify, prioritize and determine the level of power and influence of all stakeholders?
- Is it possible to satisfy all stakeholder demands?
- What are the barriers to stakeholder engagement and future management of their needs, preferences and desires?
- What are the particular problems facing leaders in regeneration as they attempt to transform locales by engaging stakeholders? How different is this in comparison with those issues/problems facing leaders in the private sector?
- What type of leader are you?

NOTES

1 CVS (Council for Voluntary Services) is the preferred mechanism in most parts of England to ensure effective engagement, information flow, dialogue and empowerment, but success has been variable because in some areas the organization is not well developed.

2 Stakeholders may have legitimacy (Cornell and Shapiro 1987) and formal contracts (Freeman and Evan 1990), be directly or critically involved in economic interests and survival (Cornell and Shapiro 1987), have a moral obligation to decide on the fair distribution of harms and benefits (Carroll 1989), and commit financial or human capital, bear risks and take losses and gains on behalf of the organization (Clarkson 1994). Stakeholder power can also be assessed on urgency (Mitchell *et al.* 1997), ability to reward, how stakeholders

relate to others, knowledge and skills, status in hierarchy, reputation, claim on resources, size of budget, gaining or losing resources over time (Pfeffer 1981). There is also executive, reputational and cultural power (Clegg 1989) and to this we might add systemic power derived from socio-economic position, ability to mobilize resources, coalition, networking and lobbying, as well as local, regional and national linkages.

CASE STUDY

New forms of leadership within a Sure Start initiative

In 1999 the Labour government launched the Sure Start initiative by introducing 'Trailblazer' programmes to specific disadvantaged communities. The Trailblazers were expected to lead the way with innovative and creative service developments for pre-school children and their families in communities which had historically been disadvantaged, often as a consequence of being under-resourced and poorly serviced in terms of need as measured by the Index of Multiple Deprivation (IMD). Perhaps one of the most revolutionary aspects of the Sure Start approach was the funding mechanism with an intrinsic prerequisite for establishing multi-agency partnerships that incorporate equal parent representation in governance structures in order to secure government grant funding. It was an ambitious attempt to reshape and integrate existing mainstream early years learning/education, health and social care services at a community or micro level. It signified a departure from the insular 'silo' mentality of single agency service delivery, and exemplified the need for a different type of leadership to the more traditional top-down inspirational leadership.

The need for 'joined-up' integrated services in education, community health and the social care arena had been articulated as far back as 1998, but without real guidance on how to achieve this. In 2000, 18 Policy Action Teams (PATs) were established to fast-track policy initiatives in the most deprived neighbourhoods. It was clear that government had an expectation that mainstream and voluntary organizations involved in the delivery of child and family health, social care and education services would in some way simply unite strategically and operationally to plan integrated services to meet user needs more effectively. The actuality of this expectation on a national scale was disjointed and uncoordinated, with little real progress made by the agencies involved. Much of this disorganized response to the government's agenda was put down to agencies on the ground being too preoccupied with targets set by individual government departments and a lack of coordination at the centre. Bureaucratic and hierarchical command and control systems have been broken down centrally, but replaced by a new regulatory mechanism of audit, inspection, standard setting and review. As a result the relationship between (central) policy and local delivery remains problematic.

91

Sure Start was regarded as an innovative and key delivery mechanism for solving difficult social problems like social exclusion. The agency representatives involved in Sure Start have all struggled to understand, adapt and respond to the changing conditions in their internal and external environments, so there have been difficulties in failing to grasp the government's service integration agenda. This is because most organizations base their strategic approach on the causal, linear logic of mechanistic Taylorist sciences, by seeking to create order out of chaos. These organizational responses are only valid within given organizational boundaries and are counterproductive when boundaries become more fluid, as they are in multi-agency partnerships like Sure Start. Collaborating agencies within networked organizational forms are continuously learning and adapting, and leadership is essential for individuals from different professional backgrounds to work together to achieve common objectives. The Improvement and Development Agency (IDA) has recognized the shifting boundaries and introduced a self-sustaining improvement programme to support local government officers, as they move away from professional, supplier-driven services towards more empowering, facilitating, engaging and enabling consumer-driven approaches. Within this new form of community governance and community leadership, multi-agency leaders work across shifting boundaries with communities to help them to understand the causes of deprivation, to develop capacities to seek solutions in addressing the issues. An inclusive form of leadership is a significant factor in navigating organizations through the maze of shifting boundaries.

The government's intent to create new organizational boundaries presents new challenges to education, health and social care agencies, as manifest in the emerging Children's Centre and Children's Trust Initiatives. Much learning from micro service activities in initiatives like Sure Start, Children's Fund and Connexions has informed the debates. Sure Start programmes have been operating for three years, and multi-agency leaders have worked together in a highly reflexive and dynamic environment responding to the government agenda for change, as both direction and targets frequently shifted.

Sure Start embodies a newly emergent Service Domain, defined as:

A geographically specific integrated service base capable of delivering quality services to assess and meet need holistically through complementary working between professional disciplines.

Funding comes into the Service Domain programme from a commissioning body (in this case central government, but it could be an inter-agency partnership) thus creating a quasi-autonomous provider unit. Service design is built around integration and complementary working — that is, work of one service must add value to another service — therefore an analysis and understanding of service dynamics and inter-relationships is crucial. The experience of service users accessing services to meet their needs provided by a 'service domain' is one of a seamless transition between services, one not based on traditional hierarchies, but on strong, collaborative, co-operative and inclusive leadership. Complex networks such as Sure Start are illustrations of intricate inter-relationships that arise from the interaction of agents, who are able to adapt and evolve within a changing environment.

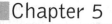

Chapter 5

Partnership

KEY THEMES

- Partnership working.
- Differences between collaboration and partnership.
- Recognising unstated conflict in partnership development.
- Local Strategic Partnerships.

LEARNING POINTS

By the end of this chapter we hope that you will be able to:

- Identify the central differences between local partnerships present in your area.
- Model a successful partnership and define its essential factors.
- Prioritise your learning needs and those of your staff team.
- Match your skills and those of your staff team to meet the needs of your local partnership(s).

INTRODUCTION

The history of regeneration initiatives in the UK has often been characterized by limited success. The criteria used to make these judgements will be familiar to practitioners. They include the following:

- Schemes were not clearly defined.
- Funding was short term.
- Initiatives were not well co-ordinated.
- Initiatives were not integrated into existing provision.
- Local people were not consulted or involved.
- Initiatives were not allowed to 'bed down'.
- Central government was too interventionist.
- Central government was not interventionist enough.
- The 'problem' was too large and multi-faceted to be addressed by the initiative.

(Dabinett *et al*. 2001; Rhodes *et al*. 2002; Robson *et al*. 2000)

In this chapter we want to explore the significance of the current emphasis on 'partnership' working. There are four main reasons why we think it is important and necessary to do this.

First, partnerships have come to be seen as *the* solution to the problems listed above. As we try to show in this chapter (and as you will be well aware) 'partnership working' is becoming the norm in regeneration activity. The existence of a partnership is now a pre-condition for most funding streams provided through central government or the European Union. This and the explicit commitment of the 'partners' to a specific initiative is seen by central government and the EU as evidence of an understanding of what needs to be done and why.

Second, partnerships are seen as a way of addressing the multi-faceted nature of regenerating areas and neighbourhoods. They hold out the potential of drawing together the diverse range of agencies and services present in a locality in order to tackle deep-rooted problems in a way which is beyond the capacity of one agency or one initiative.

Third, partnerships are seen to have the potential to act as 'change agents'. By bringing together different agencies and agreeing a common set of goals they can focus on particular needs and by so doing introduce new ways of working which become part of the legacy of the partnership.

Finally, we want to suggest that 'partnerships', also, can represent both a challenge and an opportunity to existing forms of governance and local management. As we show in this chapter, the creation of Local Strategic Partnerships (LSPs) as part of the Neighbourhood Renewal Strategy (NRS) represents a qualitative shift in thinking by the government. Hitherto local regeneration partnerships have been short term and temporary alliances between agencies, but LSPs have been about formalising and institutionalising relationships between agencies and local communities. We believe that this development is significant because it suggests that partnership working is not a temporary strategy but rather an attempt to remodel the institutions and structures of local government into something quite different, something that has long-term implications. To that extent this particular innovation can be traced back to a notion of 're-inventing government' (Osborne and Gaebler 1992) and draws upon those debates which highlight the concern over low election turnouts and alienation from the democratic process.

PARTNERSHIPS AS A QUICK FIX

In an important sense, 'partnerships' have come to be seen as the solution to the weaknesses and failure of previous regeneration initiatives, although this development is not itself without its own set of problems and difficulties. As you will know, putting together a partnership to address a particular set of problems may be the 'easy bit'. The more difficult part is to maintain the relationships and to manage the process so that positive change is experienced on the ground and local communities see (and welcome) the difference the partnership has made.

For practitioners who are involved in these initiatives the 'partnership' experience can be a frustrating experience as well as a positive one. We feel that there are a number of inherent tensions and contradictions present in the current partnership approach, and before we examine the detail of partnership working we want to rehearse them here. Our own experience suggests that a central difficulty lies in the underlying philosophy of current partnership working. This *assumes* that the bringing together of different agencies and/or services is possible without recognising (and addressing) the complexities this represents. For those involved in the management of partnership working (especially in developing and sustaining a multi-layered regeneration initiative) the task can be daunting. These complexities do not just involve bringing together different agencies with different histories and ways of working, different ways of allocating resources and priorities, but also involve drawing together the personal expectations and tensions present. In addition this involves liaison with local communities and identifying those local groups with whom the partnership must work. All of this is evidence of the need to support regeneration managers in this process through training and the development of their skills. Some managers may be unfamiliar with partnership working or find themselves in situations where they lack sufficient organizational or institutional power to effect change.

It might seem that we are focusing on the negative as you read the experiences of others or look at the case studies we have chosen. Of course, we have been quite deliberate in what we have selected. We believe that it is important to examine the difficulties present in partnership working. But our reasons for approaching it in this way is to avoid the conventional explication for partnership activity, which, though it offers a route to avoid some of the mistakes of the past, is not the *only* solution. It does, however, seem to us that this model will remain part of the landscape of regeneration activity for some time and, as a consequence, it is necessary to reflect upon all the aspects of such an approach.

We also want to highlight the longer-term implications this approach has for local institutions, forms of decision making and local accountability. The creation of LSPs represents a really important development. While we cannot anticipate how and in what ways they might develop (or indeed their life expectancy) they do sit within a pattern of change which has been evident for over 20 years. And while they are just *one* response to the 'problems' associated with the governance of local communities we expect them to be around for some time. Clearly, they will evolve (and their name may indeed change) but what they represent is significant and for those involved in the practice and process of regeneration management they are evolving institutions which have the potential to be a powerful presence at the local level.

In addition they represent a possible alternative model to the existing model of representative local democracy (Goss 2001). Defining and clarifying the relationship between the LSP and ward-based councillors remains an outstanding issue. For local managers it represents an additional dynamic in the relationship they have to contend with.

PARTNERSHIP WORKING

Part of the difficulty for those involved in regeneration management is to question the policy assumptions and, therefore, the practice response, which informs the current neighbourhood renewal and associated initiatives. A core policy assumption is the central role afforded to the local 'partnership'. Defining what is and is not a partnership is a task in itself. But it may be useful to begin by restating the basic premise which underpins the current fashion for partnership working.

Arguably the central claim for partnership working is the belief that it ensures *greater co-ordination* of existing provision and that it facilitates a *sharing of knowledge* between different agencies, which allows them to have a greater positive impact on a neighbourhood or client group than they would if they worked separately.

There is a further claim, which suggests that partnership working has the potential to *change the working policies or culture* both within and between participating agencies. This claim starts from the premise that such change is necessary and will have a positive effect on the working practices of the agencies involved.

There is a final set of claims, which advocates of partnership working make and which bases the promotion of this approach in the context of the *multi-faceted social and economic problems* experienced by local communities. Those so-called 'wicked issues' go beyond the capacity of any one agency or service and so partnerships are seen as the most effective way of addressing them.

These claims all focus on the ways in which the quality of services can be improved and the capacity of local agency decision making enhanced and refined.

97

As a consequence, it is argued, *resources*, both physical and human, *can be more effectively targeted*. A potential and often unstated by-product of this approach is that individuals working as part of a partnership experience an increase in their job satisfaction. In addition users of services do not recognize the different organizational and professional boundaries which separate services, and it is claimed that if partnerships are effective they too will experience positive benefits if the agencies act in a 'joined-up' way.

But, if it is difficult to question or to challenge those policy assumptions from first principles (because they have been 'normalized'), it has become even more difficult given the way the label of 'partnership' is used so indiscriminately. This is especially the case since the change in government after 1997. The Labour government has promoted partnership but in ways which make it difficult to discern one model of working. In fact, the term 'partnership' is used in so many ways that it is often unhelpful in terms of clarifying what is meant and what type of working practice is intended.

We want to agree with those (Carter 2000; Robinson *et al*. 2000) who suggest that there are different types of partnerships present within regeneration initiatives. It is important to define what they are in order to explore the implications they may have for your working practices and for the kind of alliances you might expect to form and what you might expect as a result.

We can categorize partnerships in the following way:

- Strategic partnerships (for a defined period and for a specific initiative).
- Strategic partnerships (unlimited time and covering many initiatives).
- Weak partnerships (with no resources/staff).
- Strong partnerships (with defined staff and budget).

But there are additional ways of defining and labelling partnerships and these might include:

- Neighbourhood based and established over a long time frame (10 years).
- Neighbourhood based in response to a short-term initiative.
- Issue based (short term) and sitting alongside existing partnerships.

These different labels or categories may help you to reflect upon your own experience. You might wish to place your own partnership against the typology identified above. But even adapting these definitions may not be sufficient for our purposes. The definitions above place the emphasis on the organizational relationship(s) between agencies and the ways in which strategic goals are set and resources allocated. The 'hidden' dynamics of partnership working (a change in organizational culture, the shift from identifying with the 'home' agency towards the needs of the 'host' partnership) are often unexplored within such definitions.

The implications of this are discussed below (see pages 106–110). In addition there are the significant changes which may be evident in the process of redefining the learning and training needs of the partnership which take place over time. Finally, there is the under-examined area of managing and sustaining change within the context of a partnership.

All of these 'hidden' dynamics will be present in any form of partnership working. The extent to which they are in the foreground will depend upon both the explicit and localized remit of the partnership and the quality of the interpersonal/ professional relationships of those involved.

We are suggesting that if the partnership is both explicit and local in terms of its terms of reference and/or priorities then it is more likely that the 'hidden' dynamics of the partnership will be revealed to all participants. For example, a neighbourhood management or regeneration initiative is more likely to find itself having to address the particular ways of working it adopts through a strategic (and more removed) partnership. In part this will be because neighbourhood staff (street-level officers) will be influenced by (and will influence) those living in the area and there will be more direct face-to-face contact with residents and other agencies.

As a result, the shortcomings of the partnership are more likely to be openly discussed and explored. It is likely that issues such as resourcing, the setting of priorities, and the ways of working adopted by agencies will be subject to scrutiny and questions. A more strategically focused partnership is less likely to have such day-to-day contact with either local residents/users or with front line staff. A possible outcome of this is that the more strategy-focused partnerships will address the 'hidden' dynamics of the partnership in a more detached and less open way. The approach to strategic partnership working is likely to be shaped by more formal models of discussion and decision making. It is likely to be more bureaucratic and rationalized in its ways of working. The 'spaces' for a more open and informed approach to discussing the needs of the partnership are likely to take place outside the formal, scheduled meetings in sub-groups, working parties and 'on the corridor'. As a result the strategic partnership is less likely to be able to respond quickly to issues raised by groups, which are not given the same status as those 'sitting at the table'. Access to information and to the processes of decision making are likely to be more carefully monitored and contained by those professionals who service the partnership. Or, alternatively (and dependent upon circumstances), this access may be contained by the agency that assumes (or who is given) the lead role in the partnership.

These difficulties and challenges are explored in the work of Bachrach and Baratz (1970) and Lukes (1974) who, in their different ways, have attempted to highlight the importance of formal and informal structures and organizational hierarchies in maintaining the power of key decision makers and the exclusion of less powerful interests.

Some of these issues were identified in the Annual Report of The National Evaluation (2002) on the New Deal for Communities initiative. In their executive summary the authors of the report make the following observations:

> Poorly performing Partnerships can become 'stuck' in cycles of blame or in continual crisis management. However, some, which the national evaluation team saw in scoping as being weak or struggling, are now performing reasonably well. While this provides hope that weak Partnerships can recover, equally so ostensibly more secure NDCs can still run into difficulties. The ultimate test will be the extent to which Partnerships can learn from conflicts and tensions in order to devise and implement effective programmes of long-term change which benefit all sectors of their local community.

> Areas of concern in relation to board membership include lack of clarity in relation to roles and responsibilities, adequacy of skills, and time commitments required of representatives. Many members appear to be left to their own devices rather than being properly inducted. This, together with the required steep learning curve, contributes to high turnover and burnout, particularly amongst resident members.

> Changes in membership and short term crises can distract boards from providing a strong and strategic lead. Some boards have become dysfunctional, due to conflicts between different groups and interests, and because of personality clashes.

> Partnership working is generally perceived by both NDCs and their stakeholder agencies as assisting delivery. However, some agencies, such as LSCs, are less involved in partnership working than might have been expected. Partner agencies are constrained in working with NDC Partnerships by the complexity of tasks and relationships, staffing problems and financial constraints.

> Relationships between NDCs and their local authorities remain complex, often dependent on the role of key individuals within both sets of organizations. In some cases tensions remain, although there is a sense that things are improving. Evidence points to numerous instances of close and effective working. It may be however that local authorities are according less importance to NDCs in a new policy landscape featuring LSPs and comprehensive performance assessments.
>
> (Neighbourhood Renewal Unit 2003)

100

Yet, partnership working is not new. In 1989 the Audit Commission and in 2001 the OECD issued discussion papers on the benefits of such an approach. They both set out what they considered to be the necessary pre-conditions for effective partnership working. They identified the following as key:

- to set out clearly their aims and objectives;
- to establish shared criteria;
- to identify agreed mechanisms to review and to monitor their work;
- to think through mechanisms for securing trust between agencies;
- to reflect upon ways of delegating tasks to specific groups;
- to address the issue of which staff (and why) will be involved.

All of these would enhance the quality and effectiveness of partnership working and, as the OECD noted, provide for better governance.

While these factors may be considered as 'the necessary pre-conditions' they do not of themselves convey the underlying assumptions upon which such work is based. Arguably, this lies in the perceived failure of welfare and state agencies to respond to the needs of local residents in deprived neighbourhoods.

Indeed, there are three assumptions in much of the official literature on partnership working. First, that successive governments have not addressed the long-term social and economic problems of particular communities and neighbourhoods; second, that the long-term decline is beyond the capacity of any one initiative and that as a result local communities themselves must enhance their capacity; and finally, that local agencies must themselves reform ('modernize') their working practices (Leach and Wilson 2000).

These assumptions do not separate the structural and political dimensions of the debate from the economic and organizational aspects. As we saw in Chapter 1, the competing stories of regeneration in the UK identify the ways in which structural and political change was not considered an area for debate and exploration, whereas physical redevelopment and/or investment in assumed labour market trends were considered priorities and necessities.

In a context where local partnerships exist it is more difficult perhaps for local practitioners to ignore or to escape the needs of local communities and the language which is used to define their needs. These issues are returned to in the next chapter. But, it is appropriate to remind ourselves that the current claims of partnerships that they are local and can be responsive to need can be traced back to the decentralization or 'going local' experiments of the 1980s (Burgess *et al.* 2001; Diamond 2002a; Pearce and Mawson 2003).

While these initiatives were mainly located in urban Labour-controlled authorities they were, in turn, influenced by the area-based committee structures introduced in the mid 1970s in a number of places as far afield as Stockport, Walsall and Newcastle. While the area committee model was largely about devolving some responsibility to ward councillors and officers the 'going local' model was much more radical and innovative. The reasons for its lack of success have been discussed elsewhere (Burns *et al.* 1994; Diamond 1990; Holden 2002) but the model itself contained the following features:

- One-stop shops for council-run services.
- An emphasis on community participation.
- A reform of separate service departments towards integrated multi-disciplinary teams.
- An attempt to change working practices in white-collar departments.
- A claim that such changes would enhance local democracy.
        (Boddy and Fudge 1984; Hambleton and Hoggett 1984)

There are a number of differences between the 'going local' experiments in the 1980s and the NRS and 'partnership' approach since 1997. The two essential differences can be summarized thus:

1 The 'going local' model was *explicitly* a political project and *implicitly* about managerial change.
2 The 'partnership' model is *explicitly* a managerialist development and *implicitly* about political change.

As we saw earlier, the claims for partnership working are based upon the assumption that welfare and public services need more effective co-ordination and, where necessary, integration as well as changing the 'culture' and working practices of highly professionalized services. Interestingly, each approach assumed that these two claims could be met in the models which were put forward. In both cases a core 'problem' had been identified, which was the negative effect of 'departmentalism', or in the current language, the 'silo' approach to the provision of services. The problem, as it was understood, was that departments developed their own internal systems, language and model of working. The development of separate identities at a local level was reinforced and mirrored by the departmentalism of central government. The government (through its separate funding streams) accentuated the differences and the reluctance (or opposition) to joint work and collaboration. As we saw in Chapter 1, the history of regeneration activity in the UK is littered with attempts to draw departments or services together to be replaced by new funding initiatives which pushed them apart.

   In the late 1970s/early 1980s some local authorities (through their experiments in decentralization or neighbourhood services) attempted to make welfare professionals in service departments work together. These initiatives were based upon the view that co-ordination (and possible integration) was a prerequisite to achieving a reform and improvement in the quality and effectiveness of service delivery.

Despite the uneven level of success, this period of experimentation laid the foundation of the reforms of the late 1990s. We can say that the legacy of 'going local' was the introduction of the NRS and, with it, a renewed emphasis on partnership, collaboration and integration.

The present system, therefore, uses a combination of approaches which run from the promotion of partnership working as 'good practice' to the formal establishment of partnerships as bodies with a clear remit accountable to external agencies at a regional level through to the centre. You will be familiar with some of the present initiatives and they include:

- Sure Start;
- Connexions;
- Adult Basic Skills;
- Policing and Community Safety;
- Health.

You will, also, have had some opportunity to reflect upon the advantages of such approaches. At a very basic level it is possible to rehearse the pre-conditions which are necessary for effective partnership working. While these are general they do point to the need for important and significant discussions to take place between different interest groups for them to be effective. We would suggest that the factors which can be considered influential for successful work are:

- commitment to the concept at senior, middle-management and operational levels as a prerequisite;
- clarity of roles and powers;
- clearly defined short-term aims;
- embedded changes in working practice;
- independent 'broker' to co-ordinate different agencies;
- successful co-ordination at operational level from good practitioner involvement.

We conclude that where these exist inter-agency working can:

- Lead to agencies being less reactive to local context.
- Focus the resources available more clearly.
- Be used to gain access to resources.
- Lead to changes in the management of partner organizations.

In summary we can say that partnership working is seen as having the potential to:

- Ensure greater co-ordination between different agencies.
- Facilitate the sharing of knowledge between agencies.

- Change the working practices and culture of agencies.
- Target resources more effectively.
- Address the multi-faceted problems of communities.

DIFFERENCES BETWEEN COLLABORATION AND PARTNERSHIP

The claims for partnership working discussed above only serve to identify some of the problems associated with using a generic label to describe quite different organizational structures, as well as quite different terms of reference and forms of accountability. While the term 'partnership' may imply some forms of joint working, it is too broad a term to convey adequately the more subtle nuances of change management claimed by the advocates of the partnership approach. Indeed the examples cited above only share the idea that 'joint work' is a necessary part of their approach, so that it may not be useful or desirable to assume that the 'hidden' yet important benefits of such joint working can be addressed. It may be necessary to develop a more nuanced language to express the complexity and difference present in such initiatives. In so doing it may be possible to develop a model which practitioners, like yourselves, can use to assist you in defining and clarifying both your expectations and your role in such activity.

An important starting point might be to recognize the limits (as well as the possibilities) of 'partnership' activity as agents of change within public and welfare agencies. Acknowledging such difficulties may then assist you in developing your own set of expectations or outcomes against which you can assess yourself and/or your agency. A helpful way of thinking about these differences might be to recognize that 'partnership working' is a 'fuzzy' concept (Regional Studies 2003) and that it is necessary to differentiate more clearly the internal organizational and governance structures which are in place in each specific area of activity.

The reason for adopting this particular approach is that it may tell us more about the potential for the local 'partnership' to effect change. In that sense it may point towards the specific elements of 'partnership' working which might be generalizable. We want to suggest that there are four critical aspects of 'partnership working' which need to be explored:

1   The context within which 'partnership' work is introduced.
2   The capacity of agencies to reflect upon change within their own organizational setting.
3   The differences in status and power between participants involved in joint working.
4   The concept of 'collaborative advantage' which may be more useful than the label of 'partnership'.

We go on to discuss each of these below.

The context within which 'partnership' work is introduced

Part of the difficulty (or challenge) for practitioners engaged in joint work is the multiplicity of 'local partnerships' with which they must function. From this we can conclude that the local (or sub-regional) context lacks a stable policy environment within which to plan and to allocate resources systematically. Local managers (for all public and voluntary sector agencies) find themselves having to respond to new initiatives without being confident that the current ones they are working on have 'bedded down' sufficiently or that they have taken steps to evaluate their impact and introduced changes to ensure that they meet their defined outcomes. In this relatively unstable policy context it is difficult for local managers or practitioners to sustain their own sense of what is important, nor is it possible sometimes to define clearly the gaps in staff training and development.

We can see these difficulties clearly by reference to the examples cited above. Some of the initiatives introduced by the Labour government have quite long-term goals (Sure Start, NRS and the Connexions strategy) and others are shaped by very short-term goals (anti-social behaviour, the Street Crime initiative). To add to the complexity, even those with a long-term strategy are informed by short-term targets which are expected to be met (adult basic skills and policing).

Some of these short-term goals may be subject to monitoring after a few months or a year or two. It is likely that this emphasis on short-term measurable outcomes is determined by a central government which is seeking to demonstrate a party political advantage over its opponents as well as claiming 'success' to its supporters and potential voters. None of this is new and we should not be surprised by it. What is different, perhaps, from previous administrations is the scale and pace of change and the degree of importance attached to joint work across public and welfare agencies in achieving these goals.

In one important respect the present Labour government is a clear champion of the 'partnership' approach in that it argues that many of the social and economic problems of local areas cannot be solved by agencies working in isolation from one another. However, the instability created by new initiatives and the 'target' culture has had the unintended consequence of making joint work more challenging than might have been expected by its advocates in government.

To add to these 'changes' at the local level, the demands which are placed upon local managers and practitioners are in addition to their work and usually require the creation of new teams and systems of monitoring and performance management. It is at the local level too that we can observe unevenness and instability in staff expertise, capacity and leadership to manage this process of change. This is in the policy context not only an unstable factor within which local managers have to operate, but also one in which there are likely to be gaps in experience and skill to undertake these new initiatives and ways of working. In order to achieve the necessary changes in delivery and outcome which the NRS, in particular, assumes, a significant change in professional development is also required. This was acknowledged in the Rogers Report on urban renaissance which prefigured the NRS (Rogers 1999). As both the Rogers Report and NRS-influenced Learning Curve (NRU 2002) noted, investment in the professional skills and knowledge of practitioners and local managers was necessary but not sufficient to ensure success. The real problem at the local level was how to put in place a new approach to local regeneration on top of or instead of the existing maze of initiatives which were:

- Not always co-ordinated effectively.
- Not geographically coterminous.
- Not funded on similar timescales.
- Not always inclusive of existing local agencies.
- Not always well managed and led.

Obviously, the experience of regeneration initiatives varied from locality to locality (or even within localities), but it is this unevenness which adds to the problems confronted by local managers. As we saw in Chapter 1, the experience of regeneration initiatives in the UK has been mixed and uneven. Even if we adopt a fairly wide measure of success by 1997 we can conclude that they had failed. We can also conclude that part of that failure was due, to a significant degree, to the lack of co-ordination between local agencies and professionals on the ground.

The capacity of agencies to reflect upon change within their own organizational setting

A potential barrier to change and to effective joint work may be found within the highly 'professionalized' ethos of welfare and public agencies. It may sometimes be that the completion of professional training and associated ethos may result in a process which is inimical to change. Indeed, we could argue that a consequence of the last 50 years of the welfare state has resulted in professionals who have become socialized into seeing the world through their particular lens and, as a result, represents the most significant barrier to innovation and changes in work practice. Before seeking to engage agencies in joint work and recognising the potential benefits of such an approach, it would be helpful to make the case for change within the different professional interest groups engaged in local regeneration initiatives.

If professional interests and ways of working have had the effect of precluding or resisting dialogue and joint work then this remains a real and profound challenge for the advocates of joint work.

It is important to hold on to the idea that most users of services do not see the invisible barriers between different professionals or even the barriers within organizations based upon notions of hierarchy and status. While this may be unfair to many individuals and agencies it is, we think, an important factor to be borne in mind. It may help to keep this difficulty at the front and centre of joint work because it is a useful reminder of the slow pace of reform. It is also useful because it may enable practitioners to think of routes around this barrier as a way of achieving particular goals.

Obviously the most important driver for change is the external one. As the government promotes specific initiatives or legislates for particular new structural and organizational arrangements, to make real policy decisions change (of a kind) will take place. As we discuss below, this is evident in the formation of LSPs. But new structures do not of themselves result in change in the way services are delivered or experienced by users and local communities.

Externally directed change accompanied by changes in funding or the way resources are allocated or achievements are measured does result in changes in the strategic management of services. What is not guaranteed is the way these changes are understood, accepted or reflected upon within organizations at different levels of the agency.

We want to suggest that the current fashion for 'partnership' working, while necessary and welcome, has (so far) failed to grasp the complexities involved in the process of the management of change. Some of the factors present in this observation will be well known to practitioners and local managers. It assumes that change is necessary because:

- Existing processes have failed.
- Existing practitioners lack sufficient skill.
- Existing managers have inadequate skills.
- Existing organizations lack sufficient flexibility.
- Existing arrangements and structures lack the capacity for self-reflection and innovation.

It is this catalogue of 'failure' which is presented as the justification for change and, as a consequence, many of those employed in these agencies may feel that they have been identified as the 'problem' rather than the 'solution'.

We want to argue that while some of these factors may be present in some agencies at some time, it is more productive to think about ways of enhancing the capacity of agencies to engage in self-reflection and continuous learning. As we pointed out in Chapter 2, this will involve a detailed assessment of the education and training needs of practitioners. But any such assessment has to be based upon a reflection of the persuasive influence of the ethos and culture of professionalization present in organizations. Before we identify specific training needs we have to acknowledge the presence of an organizational 'culture' which may inhibit changes in working practice and thinking.

For those engaged in the process of managing local regeneration initiatives this may feel like an additional burden which can be put to one side. On the contrary, arguably it is a necessary pre-condition to make effective change at the local and organizational levels.

There are a number of ways in which the process can be facilitated. Indeed many of the approaches advocated by those involved in this type of activity have been well rehearsed and will be familiar to many of you. They can include the following:

- Using external facilitators to help identify the barriers to change.
- Bringing in 'critical friends' for points of reference.
- Actively using the skills and expertise of evaluators to help influence strategic and operational management.
- Reducing the levels of decision making.
- Supporting and promoting the role of local managers.
- Enhancing the role and status of supervision.
- Promoting and supporting decision making at a local or team level.
- Deliberately setting out a policy and practice of staff development through external secondment and training.

You will be able to add to the list and may want to prioritize your own strategy with your staff group. Our basic point is that externally driven change is most likely to be matched against performance and funding. It does not, of itself, address the organizational culture *within* an agency or initiative. Indeed it may even re-inforce resistance to change. While the government is itself acknowledging the need to bring about organizational shifts in thinking and practice, the responsibility for changes in thinking does rest with practitioners. This is much more than paying lip service to 'thinking outside the box'. It is also about recognising that received ways of working or notions of professional status are socially constructed. They remain in place because we either actively or passively endorse them. On this issue there is no neutral position. If we do think about our ways of working and attitudes to other agencies then it is likely that we will question some of our own deeply held assumptions and expectations. Recognising this and then thinking about how we make the changes is a necessary part of the process. But, we do need to acknowledge how deeply held notions of hierarchy and status are. These are real and difficult challenges for all of those involved in the management of change.

The differences in status and power between participants involved in joint work

It is evident from both experience and the literature that successful joint work is predicated upon the expectation that senior managers from those participating agencies support and actively encourage the initiative under review. Most good practice guides make this point and most funding is dependent upon the signing up of key stakeholders in order to be successful.

Yet, our experience also tells us that such support, while necessary, does not question the perceived and real differences in status and power which are then present within any joint initiative. At a most superficial level the assumption appears to be that the mere presence of the signature of senior managers and/or political leaders or key community activists assures those involved in the delivery of an initiative that hierarchy, status and power do not matter or that they do not exist.

As many of you will be able to testify, this is not the case. Status, hierarchy and power differences remain and may undermine the initiative if they are not challenged or acknowledged. This can lead to explicit conflict or managed conflict as we discuss below.

At this point we want you to think about the issues and how they impact upon the work that you do. It may help if you think about a specific project you are involved in or refer to the case study in this chapter. We think that a fairly basic set of questions may help you in this. At meetings that you are involved in:

- Do participants identify themselves by their organizations and their role?
- Do participants defer to their line manager if decisions have to be taken?
- How are decisions made in your group?
- Are there 'key' individuals who lead the discussion?
- Who is involved in decision making or the decisions?
- Are gender and race issues made explicit?
- Do all those present contribute?
- Are some decisions made before or after the meeting rather than in the meeting?
- Is there a pattern to this?
- If there are local community representatives present, what is their role?
- Is there evidence of individuals deferring to particular participants or agencies in the meeting?
- Who sets the 'tone' to the meeting?

You will, doubtless, want to add your own, based upon your own experience. Even though this is really a 'rough guide' to the presence of differences in status and power it does point to the ways in which decisions can be made and to the absence of decision making based upon an explicit acknowledgement of differences in power.

As Bachrach and Baratz (1970) have argued, even non-decision making tells us something about the way 'power' is exercised within the process of deliberation and discussion. In other words, what is 'absent' from the agenda can tell us quite a bit about the ways in which agencies (and the individuals present) exercise their power. At a fairly superficial (and yet very important) level this can be found in the way meetings are conducted. The language used and the meeting process itself may inhibit some from participating. Those who attend meetings can reveal the attitudes and expectations of participating agencies. If agencies send relatively junior members of staff to meetings where other agencies send senior managers this may indicate the importance which both agencies attribute to the initiative under review.

Again we suggest that you reflect upon your own experience. In a very real sense what we are advocating is the idea that joint work and the arrangement for facilitating it may require a change in the way we have traditionally conducted our planning and strategy making approaches. As Mayo (1997) has very usefully pointed out:

> Elected representatives need education and training in community develop-
> ment, too, to enable them to maximize the opportunities and to see commu-
> nity development as a positive challenge, rather than a potential threat.

Her point is very telling. Much of the 'good practice' approaches to joint work and especially that which involves local residents argues in favour of enhancing the capacity of local communities to participate. Very often this has meant enabling local activists to learn the appropriate language and ways of conducting themselves. What has been absent is the reverse approach: that is, of thinking of ways in which the power differences can be reduced by enabling local practitioners to think differently about their language and their ways of working. We discuss this in more detail in the next chapter. But here we want you to think about the ways in which professionals themselves explicitly (or not) engage in the exercise of power differences derived from their own sense of their status and place in their 'home' hierarchies.

Can this process be managed differently? We suggest that, in part, it can but that an essential element in this may lie in changing our language. If 'partnership' has become redundant then maybe we need a new language which is less charged with expectations.

The concept of collaborative advantage which may be more useful than the label of partnership

Earlier in this chapter we suggested that the label of 'partnership' was not a useful term for local practitioners to work with. While it may retain a certain legitimacy for policy makers and politicians and a useful shorthand to convey a particular approach, it has ceased to mean very much at the local level. In part this is because of the multiplicity of 'partnerships', but, also, because of their diverse nature. For example, not all 'partnerships' are based in localities – some are organized at a regional/sub-regional basis. Not all 'partnerships' involve the presence of local residents. Not all 'partnerships' include different agencies – some are based within agencies and service providers. Not all partnerships are involved in direct service provision – some operate at a strategic level. Not all 'partnerships' are fixed term – some have an indefinite life expectancy (until the policy which set them up changes!).

In this chapter we are concerned with trying to explore the benefits of joint working. We have, also, tried to discuss some of the challenges and barriers to such joint working. It seems to us, therefore, that we need to think in slightly different terms when we both describe and anticipate the gains for practitioners of this joint approach to work.

We have, in this section, borrowed from and been influenced by the work of Huxham and Vangen (2000). They have described this process as 'collaborative advantage'. The advantage, it seems to us, of their label is that it conveys to practitioners (and possibly to those involved in the policy-making process) a much clearer sense of what can be gained by joint work and, indirectly, by what can be anticipated.

Despite the varieties of 'partnerships' the term itself conveys more than can be expected or, in the longer term, achieved with any degree of certainty. It also is rooted in an analysis of failure which we referred to earlier. 'Partnerships' are seen as the panacea for a variety of problems and are presented as offering *the solution*. Not only is this derived from a weak empirical base, but also it offers a poor prescription for change over the medium to long term. In part this is because most partnerships have ill-defined systems of accountability and governance, which we discuss in Chapter 7.

The benefit for all of us of the notion of 'collaborative advantage' is that it conveys, at its simplest, the idea that:

- Change can be achieved by clearly stated goals.
- Each participant has the potential to benefit.
- No one agency is responsible for success or failure.

In trying to match this idea with local experience we want you to think of the arrangements at a local level. In so doing we want you to reflect not just on those which have been externally formed (probably most), but also on how and in what ways local practitioners have attempted to direct, manage and to 'own' the process. In some places this may be few and far between. But if you were to think of these local arrangements for joint work (or these local partnerships) as opportunities for collaborative advantage, what differences might you expect?

As Vangen and Huxham (2002) argue, the usefulness of this term lies in the way in which:

> leadership is conceived of *as the act of shaping and implementing collaborative agendas*. This is a rather unique definition of leadership which emerged because the dominant theoretical developments in contingency, leader-member exchange and transformational approaches appear not easily translatable into collaborative settings. The primary reason being that they presume both a formal leader-follower relationship and some specified

111

goals that the leader sets out to achieve. Neither of these presumptions are valid in the context of collaborations, where there are generally no hierarchical relationships, whole organizations rather than just individuals to be influenced, ambiguity about who should be influenced and inherent difficulty in specifying collaborative goals. By contrast, research on leadership in collaboration emphasizes processes for inspiring, nurturing, supporting and communicating and the emergence of, and roles taken by informal leaders.

Just as we have argued above for a shift in our thinking about managing change and our practice we need to be more clear in stating what the gains are for joint work. In essence we think that they are the following:

- It has the potential to break down professional boundaries.
- It has the potential of increasing our capacity to reflect and our ability to change.
- It has the potential to improve the experience of users of our services.
- It creates a framework within which to work.
- It may encourage differences in our practice.
- It may facilitate 'risk taking'.

As you will have realized by now, we both feel that these are gains which are worth pushing at the spaces created by joint work. The concept of 'collaborative advantage' has the additional gain of being something which can be shared and understood by both strategic decision makers and front line staff. It is not the case that it poses no threats to practitioners, but rather that it offers a much more interesting and (potentially) productive way of reflecting upon the context within which we all work.

RECOGNISING UNSTATED CONFLICT IN PARTNERSHIP DEVELOPMENT

We want to suggest, in this section, that one of the most significant threats to 'partnership' work is not the unstable policy environment or the potential loss of funding, but rather the way in which conflict is managed within initiatives.

We start from the position that conflict is inevitable and is ever present within local regeneration initiatives. We take this view based upon the following propositions:

- All regeneration initiatives include areas and/or target specific groups and by definition exclude areas and/or groups.
- Joint working between agencies creates tension over resource allocation and the setting of priorities.

■ Within agencies there will be differences of views over methods of working.
■ Local community-based groups only acquire status and legitimacy by 'opting into' initiatives.
■ Local regeneration managers occupy a visible point of conflict between the initiative, the local community and their external reference points (GOR, LSP and so on).

These 'points of conflict' are in addition to other potential sites of conflict which are built into the processes of regeneration management and delivery. These are the ones which are most often acknowledged. They include differences in status, language, class, gender and race between the initiative and the local community. In effect they are expressions of the difference in power relations which are an integral and sometimes 'hidden' element in regeneration projects.

We are not suggesting that initiatives can be 'conflict free'. On the contrary we are arguing that it is necessary for managers to acknowledge both the potential for conflict and its underlying presence and then to reflect upon ways in which it can be managed.

What we want to explore in this section is the idea that while many local managers assume and anticipate the potential for conflict outlined in our five propositions, it is the latter sites of conflict which are often ignored. For many local managers the five propositions will reflect their own experience as well as their expectations. In a very real sense the inbuilt 'problem' of area-based (or neighbourhood-focused) initiatives is just that. They define, spatially, a location for the initiative and with it an externally set time frame within which the initiative will take place. The boundaries set (in both space and time) place a geographic limit on what can and cannot be included within the initiative. Not only does this raise the expectations of those who are 'lucky' to be caught within the boundaries of the initiative, but also it can alienate those who live on the other side of the boundary.

In addition to this all regeneration initiatives have their 'target' group. Usually these are in response to externally determined decisions and will be part of the measures against which the initiative will be judged. Of course, as you will know, many innovative managers seek to interpret these targets as flexibly as they can in order to maximize the impact of the initiative and to establish its credibility and legitimacy within the local area. But our experience tells us that this is difficult to maintain and as a result some excluded groups will feel marginalized by the initiative and not perceive what successes it has as being relevant to their lives and their experience.

The focus on specific targets can lead to misunderstandings (at best) or explicit conflict (at worst) with local initiatives. The investment in developing local/ neighbourhood groups or initiatives can be threatened by the need to meet externally decided targets. In the context of the NRS this has resulted in real debate over how mainstreaming is to be achieved, as we note below. But for local managers it feels sometimes like being a juggler who is in danger of dropping all of the balls.

Within agencies themselves there are likely to be competing and conflicting views about the nature of their work and the ways in which they work in 'partnership' or collaboration with other agencies. In part this can be explained by changes in working culture and the ways in which individuals identify themselves with their professional roles and responsibilities. It may also reflect significant differences in views over the nature of their role and the ways in which they define their professional role. It may not actually be about their wish to resist change because they feel threatened by it, but about something much more profound: a different definition of what their professional role and way of working should be. If this is the case then local managers (and those who have responsibility for a regeneration initiative) will need to be sensitive to these discussions and approach them carefully.

A different, but equally challenging, 'problem' is the way in which the NRS itself defines and legitimizes the presence of local community groups within an initiative. As we discuss in the next chapter, the issues of community involvement and the concept of community capacity building are controversial. But, at this stage, we need to reflect upon the way in which local groups acquire legitimization and how this may, in itself, present potential (or unacknowledged) conflict for local managers.

In framing the context for this discussion we need to separate the usual ingredients of the debate from this particular set of issues. The usual discussion points will be examined in the next chapter and they can, usefully, be summarized thus:

- Local groups and/or activists are unrepresentative of their community and communities.
- Such activists and groups can act as 'gatekeepers' to their communities and deny access to other interests.
- The 'usual suspects' provide a way into local communities for regeneration agencies and by so doing let agencies 'off the hook' from understanding themselves and the needs of those communities.
- Local activists become incorporated into the regeneration initiative and in so doing lose their independence.

The more subtle and important point is the way in which the NRS and local policy makers construct a notion of legitimacy which may predetermine who is involved and who is not. By making funds available to local groups contingent upon a formal relationship existing between groups and an initiative, it makes it very difficult (if not impossible) for local groups to 'opt out' of a process of participation. Put simply, we can argue that local groups have to 'sign up to' the aims and philosophy of an initiative in order to have a voice. This reduces their independence and their ability to offer an alternative perspective from outside the framework already defined by a local project or partnership.

This is not to say that those groups which do 'opt into' local regeneration initiatives are not vocal in their observations and expectations, nor that they feel less independent by being present. But, it is to point out that the NRS itself has a difficulty in seeking to accommodate local community interests where there is no single source of legitimacy which is uncontested.

This may be compounded by the differences in status, language, class, gender and race between the highly professionalized and bureaucratic world of the regeneration initiative and the less formally organized (in these terms) world of community groups.

For local managers this issue is one which is often ignored. When it is acknowledged it is usually to dismiss the legitimacy of those groups which have opted into the process rather than promoting the needs of a particular set of community interests and/or groups.

In seeking to explore strategies and approaches which local managers may adopt we suggest that managers borrow from the voluntary sector and be informed by those involved in social and/or youth and community work. While we do not assume that these groups have a monopoly of good practice or that they are always successful, there is much in their way of thinking and professional development which could shape a different approach.

In the broader context of dealing with conflict (both stated and unstated) we would suggest that their emphasis on reflective practice, and addressing issues of 'power' and being explicit about the ways in which structural inequality is played out, are essential here.

By utilising the skills, knowledge and approaches to training so evident in these sectors, local managers can be better prepared (and supported) to use the conflict present in initiatives in ways which have the potential to benefit the initiative rather than to weaken it. At its most basic we do not think that conflict can be avoided. It is, therefore, not just about being better prepared to face it, but rather to think about ways in which by drawing the conflict out and making it explicit more informed decisions can be made. Local managers and regeneration professionals can begin to address this by being:

- clear about what the aims of the initiative are;
- aware of their language use (jargon free);
- sensitive to and aware of differences in class, gender and race;
- open about their status and responsibilities;
- proactive in encouraging staff (and themselves) in using external support for independent advice and guidance;
- willing to meet local groups (on their terms) to answer questions;
- clear about what their relationship is to the local initiative and their external reference points.

This last point is especially important. As has been suggested elsewhere (Diamond 2001; North 2003) local regeneration managers can occupy a contradictory position. They clearly represent the visible and accountable face of the initiative to external agencies and individuals (GOR, LSPs, their own line manager). As a result they can and do 'represent' this world to the initiative rather than the other way around. In other words, they run the risk of anticipating the needs and demands of this external world and, as a consequence, they rule out certain choices at the level of the initiative.

You may want to reflect upon how far this is the case in your own experience and how you approach these choices and dilemmas. In anticipating the issues of conflict we suggest that local managers might reflect upon the following:

- Establish time for staff and local groups to develop an understanding of what the project is seeking to do.
- Understand the differing models of working utilized by the participating agencies.
- Develop the 'capacity' of local groups to participate.
- Ensure that agencies too develop their capacity to engage in community-based work.
- Clarify an evaluation strategy which is understood by all participants.
- Introduce innovative models of supervision for public sector agencies.
- Identify a 'critical friend' to the project known and accepted by the participants.
- Develop a conflict resolution strategy for the initiative.

LOCAL STRATEGIC PARTNERSHIPS

The creation of LSPs is an important part of the NRS introduced by the Labour government. We will discuss in Chapter 7 some of the implications this development has for governance and accountability. In this section we want to explore the relationships between LSPs, local regeneration initiatives and those who manage them. While we are at the very early stages in the development of LSPs and it is difficult to evaluate their significance to date, we can speculate on the implications they have for existing regeneration managers and we can begin to assess their impact on regeneration projects.

Whatever the stated intentions of LSPs as set out in the NRS and the way in which this remit has been both modified and interpreted subsequently, we can see that LSPs occupy a potentially significant role in determining local priorities and practice (McInroy 2001; Russell 2001). In particular, we can see that LSPs appear to combine five different (and competing) elements in the government's overall regeneration strategy:

1 An emphasis on collaboration across the public, private, voluntary and community sectors.
2 An enhanced role for local government as the lead agency in the process.
3 An emphasis on developing and monitoring the management of regeneration activity with neighbourhoods.

4   An attempt to depoliticize the process of regeneration.

5   An attempt to enhance the relationship between local projects and central government initiatives in centrally defined project areas.

While you may want to add to this list, it does seem to us that these particular aspects associated with the introduction of LSPs are competing and contradictory. Specifically, while LSPs are located for administrative and accountability reasons within local authorities, there remains an uneasy tension between the 'political' role and function of local government and the management and delivery function of local government. It is difficult to assess whether what we are seeing through the creation of LSPs is a deliberate policy choice to refashion local government into a more explicitly managerial and strategy-setting agency, or whether this is an unintended consequence of locating LSPs within the organizational and structural framework of local authorities (Liddle and Townsend 2003).

It seems to us that this is important to reflect upon. There are four reasons why we think this is necessary:

1   Regeneration management is essentially a political process.

2   LSPs are part of the external definition of what is needed and how it is to be provided.

3   LSPs narrow the space within which alternative views and narratives of experience can be heard.

4   LSPs represent new forms of decision making and may prefigure new institutions and structures.

Regeneration management is essentially a political process

As we have tried to demonstrate throughout this book, the relationships between social, economic and global change and their impact upon local neighbourhoods have been mediated through a variety of centrally determined initiatives. The active decision by the present government to introduce the NRS is, in some ways, no different from past initiatives introduced by previous administrations. They each have identified the need for change based upon a particular analysis of what constituted the 'problem' and, since 1991, have shared a view that redressing social and economic inequalities has to be accompanied by changed behaviour at a local and individual level.

Successive initiatives from City Challenge to NRS have stressed the necessity for intervention at the local or areas level to be sustained by changes in the way individuals and groups understand their relationship to the local and central state. This interpretation (which you may or may not accept) does lead to specific policies and approaches to defining what the 'problems' are and the extent to which their causes can be attributed to individual behaviour, ways of understanding the world and the limits (and scope) of state intervention in addressing them (Johnston and Percy-Smith 2003).

At the local level of a regeneration initiative this broad analysis will be played out through the targeting of resources and forms of intervention to specific groups which have, themselves, been defined according to a particular set of social constructs. We can see this process at work very clearly in the use of language and the categorization of particular groups.

Within (and as part of) this process sit a variety of professional agencies who have themselves defined the needs of a local area according to their norms, values and expertise. The role of the local regeneration manager is, therefore, to meet these already defined needs in a way which is also constrained by the availability of resources as well as to put in place particular organizational structures which are consistent with the policy objectives of the initiative.

The extent to which local managers are able (or willing) to look for creative spaces within which to innovate independently of the externally determined framework is itself a 'political' act. It will be dependent upon a series of variables (the manager's training, skill, knowledge, background, interpretation of the role, willingness to facilitate change and what services are driven by statutory imperatives) which means that we cannot assume that all initiatives will be managed in the same way. But, we can anticipate that in making choices between groups or in deciding to adopt a particular approach the 'politics' of the initiative will be present. In this process of change management the LSP now assumes a co-ordinating function and provides an additional tier of 'local' accountability. For the local manger it represents a new layer of governance which he (she) has to negotiate with and to be aware of the 'localized' differences of view which may be present.

LSPs are part of the external definition of what is needed and how it is to be provided

While we are at a relatively early stage in the development of the LSPs it is possible to assume that they will provide a significant contribution to the discussion on how to manage the processes associated with neighbourhood regeneration. In part we can make this observation because of their formal role within the NRS. But we could draw this conclusion in any event because, as part of the process of legitimization and justification for the LSP concept, those agencies/individuals present will want to be seen to be making a contribution and will want to define their role in terms of the influence they can exert within the NRS.

The extent to which this will happen and the time frame within which it will happen will vary. It will not be uniform. Indeed the experience of one LSP compared with another will vary significantly. However, the inevitability of the LSP acting as a key player within the process should not be in doubt. While there are obvious advantages to having key public agencies sharing information and having 'the conversation' the risk must be that this will reduce the opportunity for more localized and independent approaches to neighbourhood regeneration.

Instead what is more likely to happen (in the short term) is that agencies will wish to reserve their positions and/or further entrench the boundary divisions we discussed earlier. Over the medium to longer term they may become more interventionist and directive. Even so it is likely that they will provide an additional interpretation on what is needed and how it should be delivered to local managers.

We may expect that differences and divisions within the LSP will be reflected in the extent to which individuals and their agencies feel able to collaborate and this itself will be subject to and conditional on the way the LSP is managed and led.

LSPs narrow the space within which alternative views and narratives of experience can be heard

LSPs illustrate the present government's preference for inclusiveness in discussion and decision making. In a sense they illustrate New Labour's concern to legitimize pluralist forms of discussion as *the* method of seeking consensus. Yet, they are constrained in what they can debate and their primary role is to give oversight to the NRS at the local level. This has the effect of reducing the opportunities for a different perspective on the NRS and the priorities it addresses. As a consequence, debate and discussion is contained within a particular discourse and alternative views do not carry the same legitimacy as those agencies and interests which predominate at the LSP table. In much the same way as regeneration objectives are set externally, the remit of the LSP effectively 'rules out' interpretations which differ sharply from the received conventions. Local managers will be aware of this and this may influence what they feel able to say or propose.

LSPs represent new forms of decision making and may prefigure new institutions and structures

While we can observe the ways in which LSPs are establishing organizational arrangements to support their work, it is important to note that these arrangements may have long-term consequences for those engaged in neighbourhood regeneration. It is partly because LSPs have a direct responsibility for the Neighbourhood Renewal Fund (NRF), but also, and more significantly, they provide a model which could supplant existing structures at the local level. One possible outcome (over the longer term) is that LSPs replace local authorities as the key accountable body at the local level. By bringing together important and major agencies 'around the table' LSPs have the potential to become the commissioning and monitoring body at a local level for public services. This may not seem highly relevant at this stage in the development of LSPs for local managers. We include our observations here because through the use of the NRF we can already begin to see how LSPs might assume a greater strategic role in the development of policies and practices at the local level. We suggest that you watch this space!

SUMMARY

This chapter has focused upon the nature of partnership working. In reviewing the literature and by drawing upon conversations with local managers the key points we have highlighted are as follows:

- Partnership or joint working is the norm.
- Joint working is not without its difficulties.
- Organizational and cultural change are seen as the key priorities.
- Collaborative advantage may be a more useful concept to describe and to anticipate the benefits of joint working.
- Conflict is ever present within local regeneration initiatives.
- LSPs represent an important development in the social management of regeneration initiatives.

DISCUSSION POINTS

- Using the models discussed above, reflect upon your own experience (or reading) and try to identify the necessary conditions for success in partnership development.
- In the case study below how would you prioritize your learning needs and then the needs of your staff team?
- How can local partnerships involve local networks and retain professional autonomy in decision making? Is this possible?
- How do local partnerships address issues of difference and diversity?

FURTHER READING

Balloch, S. and Taylor, M. (eds) (2001) *Partnership Working*, Bristol: Policy Press

Newman, J. (2001) *Modernising Governance: New Labour, Policy and Society*, London: Sage

Rogers, R. (1999) *Towards an Urban Renaissance: Report of the Urban Task Force*, London: E & FN Spon

Social Exclusion Unit (2000) *National Strategy for Neighbourhood Renewal: A Framework for Consultation*, London: The Cabinet Office

CASE STUDY

Making partnerships work

Example: Communities That Care (CTC)

This model, which is supported by the Joseph Rowntree Trust (JRT) and other key agencies including the Youth Justice Board (YJB), is based upon four linked and crucial assumptions:

1   Initiatives need to plan over the long term (at least 10 years).
2   Collaboration and joint work between agencies and local community activists is a given and requires more than token support by key local leaders.
3   The potential successful future of local neighbourhoods rests upon the children and young people who live within those neighbourhoods.
4   Intervention needs to be targeted, closely monitored and provide demonstrable support to front line staff and local residents.

While the focus of the initiative may appear to be concentrated on crime, the reduction of offending and supporting children and young people 'at risk', the medium- to long-term benefits of this approach lie in the emphasis on neighbourhood regeneration. It might be that this model works best in areas which lack a regeneration initiative. But the principles of CTC are ones which apply in any context and provide a model for practitioners to reflect on (see Figure 5.1).

CHALLENGES, CHOICES AND DILEMMAS

■   If you work in an initiative that already contains a focus on reducing crime or intervening to support children and young people at risk how does this model help you?
■   What systems/forums do you need to have in place in order to avoid duplication or to identify new areas of work?
■   Given that this model is based upon the active support of local leaders, can you identify who might be involved in your locality? What barriers exist, if any, to secure their participation? How might they be overcome?
■   Can you see how you might be able to align the expectations of external groups to your initiative (LSP, GOR) to the needs and expectations of local groups present within your initiative?

121

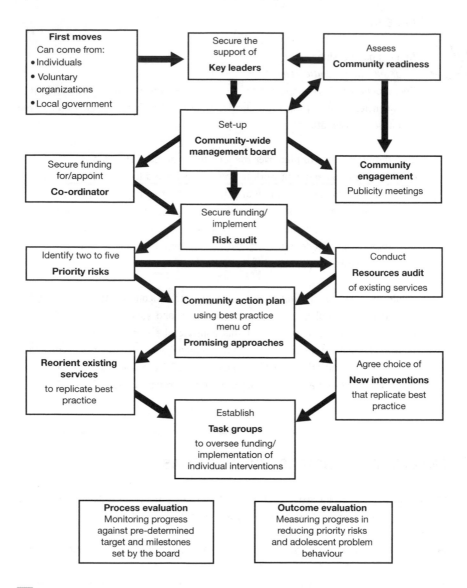

Figure 5.1 The partnership approach to decision making

Chapter 6

Capacity building

KEY THEMES

- Capacity building for whom and for what purpose?
- Capacity building and sustainability.
- Shifting decision making from the 'few' to the 'many' – a new pluralism at the neighbourhood?
- Managing resistance: are regeneration managers agents of change?

LEARNING POINTS

By the end of this chapter we hope that you will be able to:

- Identify the main themes in the literature in capacity building.
- Develop a model from your own experience on how you would manage the changes necessary.
- Prioritise your own professional development needs (and those of your staff team) to meet the expectations required by the NRS.
- Reflect upon your own experience (and reading) of how you might manage the relationship between a regeneration initiative and a range of diverse interest groups.

INTRODUCTION

By exploring the policy (and practice) implications raised by the emphasis upon 'capacity building' and the need for initiatives to have a 'sustainability' strategy we can see some of the real (and public) challenges faced by those involved in managing regeneration activity. In a very real sense they have become, we think, the new symbols of whether an initiative can be considered a 'success'. This is especially the case with 'capacity building'. As we discussed in the chapter on partnerships, 'capacity building' has become one of the criteria by which initiatives are judged. This is the case even though it is a concept which is open to interpretation and debate. And while it makes it difficult to devise a clear set of criteria by which progress can be measured, the concept of capacity building contains within it a set of expectations and assumptions which highlight the success (or failure) of many initiatives. The underlying assumptions contained within the term 'capacity building' will be explored and we will reflect upon the extent to which regeneration managers are best placed to meet those assumptions and expectations.

The concepts (and practice) of 'sustainability' and 'mainstreaming' will be approached in the same way. It is important to do this because there is a danger that the varied way in which these concepts are used will render them meaningless, and also because at their centre they encapsulate relevant and highly significant 'trends' of the progress of any regeneration initiative. They have come to be *symbols* of the success factors associated with change within a locality or neighbourhood. They are charged with meanings for different interest groups, and for those who are responsible for managing the process and delivery of change it is important to be aware of these meanings.

CAPACITY BUILDING –DEVELOPING A DEFINITION

A starting point in the discussion about 'capacity building' is to be clear about who is involved and why. A recurrent theme, so far, which we have developed is the need for clarity in setting strategic objectives, articulating an approach to the work and defining the way in which progress is to be assessed. It seems to us that one of the difficulties in framing the discussion around 'capacity building' is the lack of clarity and the way its meaning is assumed rather than explicitly discussed and, if possible, agreed by 'partners'.

Before we explore the debate in detail it may be useful to illustrate these concerns by pointing to different, but related, assumptions present in the policy literature on the NRS:

■ Capacity building is about enabling the local communities to participate, as active and equal partners, in the decision-making process associated with the regeneration of neighbourhoods.

124

■ Capacity building is about enhancing and developing the educational achievement, training and employment level of local communities in order that they have the necessary skills to take advantage of the changes in the economy and labour market potential offered by the regeneration of their locality.

While these two are not mutually exclusive they do suggest quite different strategies and approaches if they are to be successful, and they assume a quite different time frame by which they might be judged. More significantly (and this is the controversial observation) they suggest a particular social relationship between the regeneration initiative and the local community. We believe that this relationship is, essentially, a passive or dependent one. We discuss, below, in more detail why we think this is the case, but what these definitions *assume* is that the regeneration initiative itself has the capacity to work with local communities as partners. So, in addition to the assumptions above we would identify the following:

■ Capacity building is about the local regeneration initiative itself identifying and reflecting upon its strengths and weaknesses in relation to how it will collaborate with local communities in setting objectives.
■ Capacity building for regeneration professionals involves thinking about and then changing their work practices if they exclude the active participation of local residents.

We develop these ideas in the rest of this chapter.

At the centre of this discussion is a debate about the terms and limits of the social relationship between the initiative and the local community. It is about whether this relationship is one which is defined by developing an approach which encourages the active involvement of local people or is one which has the effect (intentional or not) of limiting the relationship by keeping local interest groups at a distance and so enhancing their passivity and dependence.

Some of those reading this may feel that this is too stark or too simplistic a way of expressing the dynamics present in any regeneration initiative. We accept that regeneration initiatives are themselves complex and uneven in their approaches and ways of working. Indeed, it is one of their strengths that by bringing together different agencies and, as a result, different ways of working, some projects within the larger initiative will be experienced and more open to participation and dialogue than others. But we express the points of differences starkly so as to identify the issues they represent. Put at it simplest, the questions are these:

■ At what point in the 'life' of a regeneration initiative do local people get involved as equal partners?
■ How do initiatives ensure this principle of equality?

125

- What changes can we expect (or demand) of regeneration professionals and their partner agencies in this process?
- More significantly, how do we prepare and support regeneration managers in the process of change?

These concerns are important to acknowledge and we do explore them below. They are important for another very good reason which all regeneration managers will recognize. Regeneration initiatives do not take place in isolation from the wider political and managerial concerns of those framing local, regional and national policy. Local managers are answerable to a wider (but often invisible) world of governmental agencies and evaluators. The progress made by local managers is subject to external financial scrutiny and monitoring. Quite often local managers find themselves 'caught' between the competing demands of their local communities, their local partnership board and agencies, and the expectations of regional agencies and national interests.

We are suggesting below that by exploring the tensions inherent in the concept and practice of 'capacity building' it may be possible to define (and therefore address) what is meant by a policy of capacity building, one which takes account of the limitations as well as the possibilities of such an approach.

We start from the presumption that there is a real challenge for local managers to balance the competing demands of the external world with the expectations of local communities. If we are right, then local professionals need to share this with the local board and the local community. We are, also, aware that this may be difficult to achieve. But, as we try to demonstrate in the examples below, the potential gains for local initiatives are significant and the scope for developing an *active* relationship with locally based organizations may be greater than is first assumed.

CAPACITY BUILDING FOR WHOM AND FOR WHAT PURPOSE?

In seeking to reflect the wide literature on capacity building it is perhaps useful to refer to the two assumptions we highlighted above. We suggested that:

- Capacity building is about enabling the local communities to participate, as active and equal partners, in the decision-making process associated with the regeneration of neighbourhoods.
- Capacity building is about enhancing and developing the educational achievement, training and employment level of local communities in order that they have the necessary skills to take advantage of the changes in the economy and labour market potential offered by the regeneration of their locality.

In terms of the NRS both those two assumptions are compatible and desirable. Indeed, as you will know, they often form one of the benchmarks of outcomes against which a particular initiative will be measured. We want to suggest that it is possible that, while both may be desirable, it does not follow that they are, by definition, compatible. Indeed, we will suggest that if the first is achieved the second may be called into question by the local community as a legitimate outcome.

The primary focus of this section is to explore and to reflect upon the meaning(s) ascribed to the term 'capacity building' and to examine the extent to which there is a shared definition amongst practitioners and policy makers. This is not some irrelevant exercise. As managers of regeneration initiatives have told us, seeking to clarify the meaning of 'capacity building' and then to think through how it can be achieved is a difficult (and sometimes frustrating) task. In particular, local managers have to balance this policy objective alongside a variety of others which, in the short term, may receive more attention and achieve greater significance. In part this may reflect a lack of professional knowledge by local managers. It may also illustrate the difficulty in framing a model of practice which addresses complex social, educational and organizational issues. It may even reflect a sense of disengagement by local people in the process itself and managers may think they have to pursue a strategy which is about 'winning over' local residents to the initiative. And, of course, it may not be what local residents want. One of the interesting aspects of the NRS is that local residents and local community groups are going to 'get' their capacity built whether they want it or not! While some may regard this latter observation as a trivial point, it is important to remember that the NRS is quite explicit in terms of its diagnosis and prescription. As we discussed in the previous chapter, 'opting out' is not an option.

These dilemmas for local managers raise a number of points:

- Do they have sufficient skills and knowledge to embark on a policy of 'capacity building'?
- How do they identify those groups/individuals which will be included?
- Do they explain/negotiate (and agree) what such a process will entail?
- How do they assess the success of a policy to promote capacity building?
- How do they reflect upon the experience to inform the broader work of the initiative?

And there is, perhaps, a more fundamental dilemma for local managers when addressing the second assumption set out above. It is this:

- If the primary purpose of the initiative is to 'regenerate' the area over the long term and at the same time a number of local people become more economically active and leave the area, how does that assist a broader policy objective of sustainability?

127

These are real dilemmas not only for local regeneration professionals but also for policy and decision makers at the centre. Even if this issue is not addressed explicitly it may, nonetheless, inform the type of economic and social strategy adopted by the initiative. It may encourage a training and education approach which attracts investment in jobs which do not facilitate the outward migration of labour from the area, but rather increase the dependency of local people on semi-skilled or low-paid employment.

As well as thinking about what 'capacity building' means and thinking about the contested nature of it, we also want you to locate your approach alongside the type of employment, training and education strategies you might adopt within an initiative. It seems to us that these twin concerns need to be thought about alongside one another.

The primary focus of 'capacity building' in the context of the NRS is that which centres on the involvement of local community groups as members of a local partnership board (Neighbourhood Renewal Unit 2003; Pearce and Mawson 2003). It is assumed that such involvement is a necessary pre-condition for the longer-term success of any initiative once the period for funding has ended. This particular focus, also, implies that a local initiative has the 'capacity' itself to identify, co-opt and sustain the participation of local residents in the work of the initiative. The NRS, in this respect, sees the presence of local residents as an indicator of the legitimacy of the initiative within the local community (Social Exclusion Unit 2000a).

As we indicated in the previous chapter, we need to draw a distinction between:

- How local residents are identified and selected by local initiatives.
- The presence of local residents as members of a partnership board.
- The concept of 'active' rather than 'passive' involvement in such a board.
- Whether local residents are seen by the initiative as representative of the local community.
- Whether the local community is involved in the identification and appointment of such local members.
- The experience of local residents as members of boards.
- The experience of local managers and other agencies in such a process.

We would suggest that the stages listed above may provide a useful reference point against which you can begin to assess your own experience. There is a secondary set of issues for us to reflect upon and that is the differences between the perceptions of local managers and why (and which) local activists are encouraged to join local boards and the perceptions of local activists themselves. We can summarize these differences thus:

- Local activists may be seen by agencies as local leaders because they:
    - have particular knowledge of the area;
    - provide direct access to local groups;

- are sponsored by other agencies;
- articulate the needs of the area which 'match' those of the initiative;
- demonstrate a willingness to become involved;
- have the time to attend meetings;
- provide legitimacy for the initiative.
- Local activists may, on the other hand, become involved because they:
  - are concerned about specific issues in their locality;
  - have criticized the local authority in the past;
  - represent a number of community-based organizations;
  - have the time to attend meetings;
  - articulate the needs of the area which may not match those of the initiative;
  - have a specific interest in one particular set of issues;
  - have a base of support in the area.

As you can see, there is no clear 'match' between these differences. From the perspective of the local manager it is likely that the main concern will be to seek out and recruit local people who have both time and are considered 'safe'. Both these factors are perfectly understandable in the highly pressured environment of a local regeneration initiative. In particular, if local managers are looking for individuals to join a local regeneration partnership board it follows that they are anticipating that the individuals *will* have the time to attend meetings and that, given the external constraints on the initiative, they will sign up to the aims and objectives of the project.

While local managers may anticipate such a relationship between local activists and the initiative, we are suggesting that it cannot be as given. On the contrary it is more likely that local activists will (because of their history(ies)) come to the local partnership board with their own set of expectations and wish to see changes achieved which may not be congruent with the aims of the initiative. One issue which flows from this assessment is to observe the processes whereby local activists do or do not take on the values and expectations of the initiative. Experience suggests neither that this will be uniform nor that we can clearly predict in what circumstances such an identification will or will not be successful. We can assume, however, that the values and objectives of the partnership will remain constant and that local residents who are members of the partnership board will:

- accommodate to these values, or
- adopt an oppositional role, or
- reject them and leave.

There are, of course, other factors which may explain why local activists either accept the values of the partnership or reject them. As Purdue *et al.* (2000) have suggested, local activists who see themselves as 'local leaders' or who are defined as such by local agencies may be involved because it enhances their status within their communities and/or it enables them to gain access to resources for their groups or puts them in perceived sites of influence. Additionally, we do know that some of the reasons cited for local residents disengaging from local initiatives can be attributed to being 'overworked' by the initiative and experiencing 'burnout' as a consequence (Taylor 1995).

As the NRU (2003) Evaluation Report itself notes:

> Partnerships have generally seen community engagement as one of their key objectives. Many Partnerships have introduced imaginative schemes designed to engage with those groups which have tended to be marginalized in previous Area-Based Initiatives (ABIs).

A number of factors appear to ease the process of community engagement:

- Existing, and dense, community and voluntary networks.
- A strong sense of local identity.
- The existence of community facilities.
- The appointment by the Partnership of community development staff.
- Recruiting local residents to link with the community.

However problems remain:

- The 'local community' is often taken to mean local residents; other potential constituencies such as local business and the voluntary sector can still be relatively marginalized.
- Partnerships have not always considered as much as they might have done issues of gender or disability and their implications for community engagement.
- Many NDC areas consist of more than one distinct community.
- Several NDCs report problems of territorialism and community conflict which have contributed to serious local tensions in a small number of instances.

Challenges for community engagement include:

- Mainstreaming commitment and initial support from the community and bringing in 'fresh blood' to counter problems of burnout.
- Ensuring representativeness: involvement can be dominated by small groups or cliques.
- Raising the profile of the Partnership: limited delivery and poor marketing may contribute to apathy and disillusionment on the part of the community.

130

■ Making sure the organization, frequency, chairing and operation of boards and other meetings does not militate against the involvement of resident representatives.

We do not underestimate these factors and they are significant concerns which local managers should be aware of and take account of when recruiting local people to partnership boards. They also highlight the underlying theme of this chapter. If 'capacity building' is about enabling local people to participate as equals within the management of a local initiative what support, guidance and training should be made available?

There are a number of very useful guides available to local practitioners and managers to assist them in addressing these issues. They include:

■ Pete Duncan and Sally Thomas (2000) *Neighbourhood Regeneration: Resourcing Community Involvement.*
■ Danny Burns and Marilyn Taylor (2000) *Auditing Community Participation.*
■ Steve Skinner and Mandy Wilson (2002) *Accessing Community Strengths.*
■ Peter Dale (2002) *At the Starting Blocks.*

Their strength lies in the way in which they provide a 'benchmark' against which local managers can assess their own initiative. In addition they provide a framework within which local boards can, themselves, reflect upon their own practice and make an informed judgement on the progress they are making. Such 'toolkits' provide a valuable resource for local managers and can lend to a critical reflection on their attitudes, expectations and experience of engaging local activists within the processes of decision making in a local regeneration initiative.

However, their weakness is, in our view, a much more basic and conceptual one. It is that such approaches do not always allow for the complexity and dynamism which are common to regeneration initiatives. They tend to present a uni-dimensional view of regeneration experience rather than a multi-dimensional view. So, it will be possible within a particular project or set of projects to assume that local residents are active participants in the process. We have seen evidence of such experience and listened to local residents describe their experience in very positive terms. They are able to identify ways in which they have contributed to and informed the shape and style of a specific project. It is evident, too, from listening to local practitioners that the inside knowledge which these residents have brought has been valued, respected and acted upon. But the overall framework of the partnership, its expectations, its assumptions and the power relationship within remain unchanged.

The models of capacity building/empowerment which suggest an alternative outcome is possible (Arnstein 1969; Burns 1991; Banks and Shenton 2001) need to be contrasted with their approaches (Byrne 2001; Mayo 1997; North 2001).

131

These models of capacity building provide us with rich descriptive accounts of particular places at particular times and they offer us a 'snapshot' of what is happening. They also provide a critical reflection upon the nature of the power relationship which exists within a partnership or between a formal partnership and local community groups.

'Partnerships' are not, of course, fixed. We are not suggesting that we can read off or anticipate a particular outcome on the assumption that change is not possible. But, without exploring the nature of power within local partnerships and between partnerships and local groups, we will either miss significant changes or expect too much (or too little) from regeneration projects (Mayo and Taylor 2001).

In the work of Schuftan (1996) we can see a different approach which attempts to present the multi-layered nature of partnership work and the building of the capacity of local people to engage and to question the dominant professional discourse.

Schuftan's approach is one in which the dynamism of the language and the categories identified adds both complexity and clarity to this process. In particular, it helps us to chart the ways change can come from *within* a local community at all levels (individual, group, organizational). In a way it offers a three-dimensional perspective which others lack. Arnstein's 'Ladders of Participation' still provides a useful starting point but lacks insight into the 'to-ing' and 'fro-ing' of community-based activity.

Perhaps the 'gap' in the Schuftan approach is its inability to record the process of incorporation/co-option inherent in many regeneration projects. Nor does it help us understand the dynamics of power which are present in the 'networking' experience which is implicit in partnerships or multi-agency initiatives (Huxham and Vangen 2000). Nevertheless its value is in establishing a dialogue with community-based organizations and with regeneration agencies to explore the extent to which the needs of local groups (as *they* define them) are being addressed.

Power differences will still remain and they will exist on several levels. They can be identified as follows:

- Between organizations as well as within organizations and agencies.
- Competing conceptions of what is needed.
- Differing professional discourses.
- How individuals exercise their 'power' through their status (real or perceived).
- How that 'power' is shared or negotiated.

The potential offered by this approach is that it enables all those engaged in 'capacity building' to reflect on the process and to examine the level of change created. Even these steps are likely to be 'contested', but nevertheless it does allow an exploration of change at a deeper level.

So far we have discussed:

■ The difficulty in defining the concept of capacity building.
■ The possible conflict between the needs of partnerships to have community representatives and the expectations of such representatives.
■ The use of different 'toolkits' in assessing local involvement.
■ The contested nature of community involvement.

The next section looks at the particular skills and knowledge base which many practitioners consider a necessary part of any 'capacity-building' approach. In identifying both the skills and the perceived knowledge base it is important to remember that these two are externally defined. We are suggesting that part of the problem in defining with clarity the exact scope and purpose of 'capacity building' is that it is based upon a 'deficit' model of local communities. In other words, many external agencies and professionals underestimate the capacity present in local communities because they are seeking to 'fit' the experience and knowledge of local communities to their analysis and perception of a local neighbourhood. While there will be many skilled and informed local practitioners who are aware of the depth of skills present in the locality, the 'regeneration partnership' has a particular model which it is promoting.

Thus, many local capacity-building initiatives are informed by a need to enable local residents to meet the organizational, legal and structural requirements of the initiative rather than the other way around, or indeed a combination of the two.

There is a broad consensus (Banks *et al.* 2003; Stewart and Taylor 1995) on what skills and knowledge local residents are assumed to require in order that they can 'fit into' a local partnership. It is relatively straightforward to identify what these are:

■ Understanding of the partnership objectives.
■ Understanding of the management function of the partnership.
■ Knowledge and understanding of the financial and legal status of the partnership.
■ Skills in participating in meetings, in particular the formal processes of meetings including the recording of decisions.
■ Knowledge of meeting procedures.
■ Understanding the structure of the partnership and its relationship to other agencies and initiatives.
■ Knowledge and understanding of government policy.
■ Knowledge and understanding of the relationship between the partnership and local and regional structures.

You may wish to add others to the list. From this initial summary of what is considered essential it is evident that the focus is on local residents 'fitting into' the needs and expectations of the local partnership. We would maintain that these skills are necessary but not sufficient. The real test is the extent to which local partnerships and professionals are willing (or able) to engage in a similar exercise in which local activists act as the facilitators/trainers and provide a course in extending the skills and knowledge base of local professionals. At a very basic level what the existing model of training implies is that local residents are lacking sufficient skills and knowledge to participate in the work of the initiative, whereas local professionals and local agencies do not have to rethink their approaches when working in and with local communities.

A number of regeneration initiatives have acknowledged their lack of sufficient knowledge and have adopted strategies to resolve this. These initiatives have included the following:

- Explicit attempts to explain the work of the initiative through public meetings, workshops and attending local groups.
- Use of 'planning for real' events involving local residents, children and local agencies.
- Appointment of local community development workers to liaise with and support the work of local groups.
- Deliberately appointing local residents as development workers.
- Joining local pub quiz teams and promoting social events which include local residents/members of partnership boards.

There is no doubt that such approaches can enhance and develop strong personal bonds and provide local practitioners with greater knowledge (and perhaps understanding) of the 'private' worlds of local activists. But social networks do not guarantee that local professionals will be willing to alter the inherent inequality in the power relationships between themselves and local residents. Perhaps the most important conclusion we can draw from this is that such an unequal distribution of power cannot be redressed easily and that local professionals should not confuse the development of social networks with a sharing of power.

The unequal distribution of power, status and access to resources is reflected in the second assumption about capacity building:

- Capacity building is about enhancing and developing the educational achievement, training and employment level of local communities in order that they have the necessary skills to take advantage of the changes in the economy and labour market potential offered by the regeneration of their locality.

A number of studies (Banks *et al.* 2003; Hastings *et al.* 1996; Schaecter and Loftman 1997) have argued for a change in policy and practice in this area. In particular, Henderson and Mayo (1998) make the point that in seeking to frame the education, training and employment needs of a local area there needs to be a qualitative shift in thinking and practice.

In particular, as Pearce and Mawson (2003) observe, there needs to be:

- Greater emphasis on the inter-exchange between front line staff and policy makers.
- Flexibility and discretion over funding at the 'local' level.
- Improved use of local resource allocation knowledge to inform 'local' policy.
- Support for risk taking and innovative practice.
- Support for community engagement in decision making.
- Better benchmark data to inform strategic decision making.

If we combine this approach with those discussed earlier it is likely that a different 'conversation' with local communities will take place. It will be more complex and difficult, but it will have the advantage of providing a regeneration initiative with a longer lead time. As a consequence we will need to acknowledge that the present approach needs to be reformed and that greater use of a pre-planning phase is necessary.

You may want to reflect upon the implications this has for your practice.

CAPACITY BUILDING AND SUSTAINABILITY

The associated problems with reaching a clear consensus on the meaning and implications of 'capacity building' become more complex when this discussion is joined with the notion of 'sustainability'.

We can identify a number of shared assumptions inherent in regeneration thinking over the past decade. These assumptions can be summarized as follows. There is a need:

- to co-ordinate service delivery within localities in order that social and welfare services are more effectively and efficiently provided;
- to ensure greater flexibility in the local management and delivery of services at the local level;
- to break down bureaucratic and 'professional' barriers to such flexibility;
- to establish partnership working at a local level which draws together relevant agencies and the voluntary and community sectors;
- to develop a planned and 'sustainable' succession strategy after the funding period ends, which includes the active involvement of local people in the decision-making process.

(Atkinson 1998; Burgess *et al.* 2001; Chanan 1997;
Duncan and Thomas 2000; Jacobs and Dutton 2000;
Joseph Rowntree Foundation 2002; ROOM 2001;
Wolman and Page 2000)

135

What is missing (though implied) from these policy assumptions is the recognition that such changes are contingent upon a change in the decision-making processes, resource allocation and power relationships at a local or city level. In the 'received' model of neighbourhood regeneration the first two of these necessary changes are assumed but the last is not. It is rarely addressed or even acknowledged.

Both partnership working and capacity building can be seen as the panacea for addressing structural and systemic weaknesses in contemporary urban society. As Leach and Percy-Smith (2001) have noted, they offer a route to tackle the so-called 'wicked issues' of economically poor and low-skilled communities in the UK today. Yet, creating new localized forms of delivering social and welfare services under the label of the 'local partnership' does not, of itself, ensure that the services provided or the resources allocated will meet the needs and aspiration of the local community.

In this section we need to rehearse the policy and practice assumptions contained with this objective. In particular, we will need to clarify what is meant by both:

- a sustainable succession strategy and;
- the active involvement of local people in the decision-making process.

We need to note that both of these objectives derive, in part, from well-documented critiques of regeneration initiatives over the past 30 years. A number of studies (Dabinett *et al.* 2001; Rhodes *et al.* 2002) have argued that previous attempts at area-based regeneration have failed precisely because they:

- Lacked co-ordination.
- Failed to engage with local communities.
- Suffered from short-term funding.
- Did not address the consequences of withdrawing additional funding.
- Did not think through the reallocation of staff to other projects.
- Did not prepare local communities for the ending of the initiative.
- Had no follow-up strategy after the 'lifetime' of the project.

MAINSTREAMING

The NRS aims to address the particular concerns outlined above. Specifically, the NRS requires LSPs and other relevant agencies not only to address specific targets in improving education, educational attainment, reducing and redressing crime and health inequalities, but also to consider how existing NRS-based work can be 'mainstreamed'.

'Mainstreaming' has become another example of the lexicon of the NRS which lacks a specific definition (like 'partnership' and 'empowerment') but has the advantage of giving an *indication* of what is intended. We can argue that 'main-streaming' represents a real shift in thinking by the central state. It is an acknowledgement that short-term measures can only act as a stimulus to change and that by itself such fixed funding can achieve little over the medium to long term. This shift in thinking has the potential to stimulate change beyond the geographic boundaries of any one regeneration project. At the level of the local authority and other relevant public agencies there is an expectation that through the effective working of the LSP a longer-term strategy will be developed further than the progress achieved through the NRS and its associated initiatives. Such a longer-term strategy requires greater collaboration between local agencies to ensure that neighbourhood-based interventions can be supported after the NRF has come to an end.

However, as the Neighbourhood Renewal Unit (2003) evaluation notes barriers to mainstreaming include:

■ Mainstream service providers claim they are constrained by lack of resources.
■ Some mainstream agencies are reluctant to allocate further resources to NDC areas, because of the competing needs of other priority neighbourhoods.
■ The widening neighbourhood renewal agenda has sometimes diverted attention from NDC areas to all disadvantaged neighbourhoods in the locality.
■ The potential role for LSPs in planning and enforcing changes in mainstream services is currently unclear.
■ For some agencies, the small size of NDC areas militates against NDC pilot activities being taken up by the mainstream.
■ Not all NDCs, and certainly not all community representatives, are committed to mainstreaming.

The existence and nature of mainstreaming varies widely, and is dependent on individual agency culture, commitment and capacity. There is evidence of a commitment to mainstreaming and a recognition of its importance, but its implementation in practice remains fragile. Current practice in relation to mainstreaming is widely seen as one of the main constraints to delivery.

There is lack of clarity about exactly what 'mainstreaming' means and what should be done to enhance it. This evaluation has used a fourfold definition:

■ Changing policies to deploy resources more effectively in deprived areas.
■ Redistributing or 'bending' resources.

137

- Reshaping services to make them more responsive and accessible to local communities.
- Incorporating innovations and lessons from special initiatives into mainstream practice.

An additional expectation is that the LSP will seek to encourage and/or facilitate the policy and practice transfer of the lessons learnt through the NRS to other areas within the local authority. This transfer assumes that these initiatives will have experienced the 'learning curve' of the NRS and so will be able to demonstrate their impact over a shorter period of time.

NRF is, therefore, intended as a means of 'pump priming' change and is not intended to become the normal means of supporting innovation and intervention. The responsibility for maintaining change is to be the primary function of local agencies.

We could also interpret the difficulty in defining what is meant by 'mainstreaming' as another example of deliberate ambiguity in the formation of public policy. It points to a particular direction but is vague about how movement towards it is to be achieved. It follows that:

- It does not inspire confidence by practitioners and local community activists that change will take place.
- It provides local agencies with an excuse to do little or nothing until the policy is clarified.
- It weakens the ability of local managers to make the case for specific projects they believe are of value.
- It does not guarantee that local agencies will receive additional funding to support their work.
- It can lead to policy and practice stagnation at the local level in framing a succession strategy.
- It does not appear to represent any change at all.

Even if we note the potential policy vacuum we still need to reflect upon how our contribution to the work of an initiative may (or may not) enhance the promotion of 'mainstreaming' and/or 'sustainability'. This dilemma for many regeneration managers illustrates the pivotal role they occupy within an initiative and the pressures they experience. In seeking to model possible strategies to adopt it, it is important to acknowledge how this set of specific issues underlines the competing audiences regeneration managers need to address. In summary, managers have to take account of different audiences with different agendas:

- European, regional and local interest groups to whom they have to report progress on meeting externally monitored targets.

- The regeneration partnership board to whom they need to present a succession or exit strategy.
- The regeneration workers whom they need to encourage to stay to complete their work and, if necessary, facilitate their transfer elsewhere.
- The local community represented by local residents as well as the voluntary and community sectors which may be expected to 'fill the gaps' after the formal funding period.

These interest groups have quite different needs and expectations. Separately (and together) they will seek to exert influence on the priorities set by the local manager. He (she) will need to balance these interests as well as attempting to shape policy and practice at the local level. This illustrates quite well the complexity of attempting to develop a model of accountability which can embrace quite different interests with very different ways of articulating their needs, over quite different time frames and with varying access to power and influence.

In most cases we can assume that most managers will be sensitive and responsive to the needs of the regional and local elites and the partnership board. They have formal and direct lines of management and supervision to local managers. They are most likely to experience their needs as having a priority over the needs of the other two.

However, at certain times and in some places the regional/local elites may find themselves in alliance with the local community interest groups. This will be most evident if there is a clearer notion of what mainstreaming and/or sustainability means. It is more likely that both these concepts will be 'fudged' at a regional and local level. What we can anticipate is that such alliances will be temporary, with the expectation from the region that the voluntary/community sector will move in once the funding has ceased.

It is this replacement of the local state agencies by the voluntary sector and/or not-for-profit organizations which is likely to increase and to expand over the next 5–10 years. While it is part of a transformation of this sector (and many welcome it), it brings with it an additional set of concerns over accountability, decision making and governance some of which we discuss in Chapter 7.

SHIFTING DECISION MAKING FROM THE FEW TO THE MANY –A NEW PLURALISM AT THE NEIGHBOURHOOD LEVEL

As we have discussed earlier (see Chapter 5), the introduction of the NRS has resulted in the formation of LSPs. LSPs provide not only an important place within which the local neighbourhood renewal strategy can be discussed, but also a forum within which local agencies and providers together with locally elected community representatives can meet and deliberate on local initiatives.

We can interpret this particular development as evidence of New Labour's concept of a new pluralism at the local level. In part, the desire to establish additional structures to facilitate such debates and to create, in some senses, parallel structures to existing processes can be understood by reference to the need to address the perceived failure of past regeneration policies. As we have suggested, this failure is partly attributable to the reluctance on the part of public agencies to co-operate with each other and to approach the needs of deprived neighbourhoods in a holistic way. In establishing LSPs whose membership includes local community representatives as well as local political leaders and relevant agencies, the expectation is that this model will provide an appropriate context within which strategic planning and co-operation can take place.

We cannot know how successful LSPs will be as a means of achieving the required change; they do represent a potentially significant forum for local debates and an alternative model of the governance of local authorities. In theory they also place local community representatives on a par with senior managers in public agencies and the locally elected (council) leadership of communities.

These changes can also be seen as part of a strategy to reform the decision-making processes at a local level. These changes include:

- Local regeneration partnership boards.
- Neighbourhood-based initiatives which include local residents on management committees.
- Direct funding to establish Community Empowerment Networks (CENs) as part of the NRS.
- Resident involvement in housing initiatives.
- Direct resident participation in local regeneration projects.

We can view these developments as an essential part of investing in the capacity building of local communities. The presence of active residents' groups, the voluntary sector and the CEN initiative within local neighbourhoods clearly adds to the skill base from which local communities can draw. Within a relatively short time frame (say five years) the number of active local residents who can engage with local initiatives and can represent different views from the initiative or can publicly endorse the aims of a project will increase. The 'pool' of expertise and knowledge can add to the existing 'pool' of existing professional community development workers. Assuming a 'best case' scenario we can anticipate a growing number of self-confident, articulate and informed local residents who could act as a counterweight to the domination of local initiatives by welfare and social professionals (Thompson 2002a; 2002b).

As we have indicated in this chapter, we should also anticipate that such initiatives are not without their problems. From the perspective of those who have formulated policies there are a number of potential unintended outcomes. A number of possibilities exist:

- Local forums may be dominated by 'unrepresentative' resident interests.
- Local forums may become the sites of conflict between 'establishment' agencies and local communities.
- Local residents may withdraw from partnership boards because they have become alienated from them.
- CENs may be a training ground for dissident groups and individuals.
- The regeneration initiative may become 'politicized' and fail to meet its objectives.

There is already evidence that some local political interests are reluctant to engage significantly with LSPs. The concerns expressed in this survey indicate areas of concern which could have been anticipated. They include:

- The marginalization of the role of local authorities.
- The decline in the political authority of local councils.
- The low ability of the local authority to set strategic and political goals at the local level.
- The 'unrepresentativeness' of local residents.

While these concerns are legitimate and pose important issues to be discussed and resolved, they may also point to a reluctance of local authorities (at a political level) to engage with the LSP concept.

We need to place these developments in the context of New Labour's desire to 'modernize' local government (Social Exclusion Unit 1998). These were set out as aspirations by the government quite early in its first term, and are part of a broader set of constitutional changes introduced by the government. This 'package' of reforms included:

- A Scottish Parliament.
- A Welsh Assembly.
- An Assembly for Northern Ireland.
- An Assembly and directly elected Mayor for London.
- Regional Assemblies in the English Regions.
- Proposals for directly elected English Regional Assemblies.
- Reform of the decision-making structures at a local level.
- Provision for directing mayors at a local level.
- Introduction of proportional representation (PR) for elections to the Scottish, Welsh, London assemblies and the European electors.
- PR for the election of a London Mayor.
- Resident elections for the Urban Development Companies set up by the NDC initiative.

All of these changes illustrate the commitment of the government to create not only new structures but also new ways of securing representatives to sit on some of these new structures. From the perspective and experience of local regeneration managers we need to explore what impact these new structures and processes have on the ability of managers to develop initiatives and to take decisions. We also have to take account of the fact that change is an inevitable part of the process. While the above list illustrates some of the reforms introduced since 1997, we will all be aware of the continual reforms in health and social care, housing, the police, the youth justice and prison systems. These changes have (and will) create new systems and structures and will impact upon the delivery of services at the local level.

You may want to reflect upon your experience and/or to anticipate the ways in which decision making at the local level will be enhanced or weakened by these changes.

It is possible to identify potential gains for decision makers. We can sketch out some of them and you may wish to add others. The gains may include the following:

- Decisions can be made which draw upon a greater diversity of experience.
- Decisions can be 'owned' by those involved, which shares the responsibility for actions taken.
- Priorities which are set reflect the knowledge of the neighbourhood.
- The concept of 'knowledge' is reformed to include local resident as well as professional forms of knowledge.
- 'Community' knowledge and experience can inform and be informed by 'professional' knowledge and experience.
- Local residents can 'see' evidence of their contribution.

Despite these potential gains, new organizational and institutional structures may inhibit the decision-making process. In particular, the negative aspects of this approach may include:

- Conflict between 'decision makers' and local community interests.
- A sense that 'nothing gets done' because it takes too long.
- Community boards and/or panels are seen as 'talking shops'.
- Local politicians feeling 'resentful' of the role of community interests.
- Local managers being 'caught in the middle'.
- Local projects are seen as 'inactive'.

You will be able to add to these and see how the complexity of the process is much more than defining systems and devising organizational flow charts, important though these are. We want to suggest that in this new and evolving context it is important to restate some basic principles for local managers:

- There needs to be clarity in the decision-making process.
- Your responsibility needs to be defined.
- There should be a time limit for the decision-making process which all parties understand and agree.
- An important distinction needs to be made at each stage between information giving, clarity on what is open to consultation and change and clarity over who is responsible for delivery.
- There should be open and agreed systems for monitoring and evaluation.

Conflict cannot, as we have suggested, be avoided. But often conflict takes place where there is ambiguity. If local groups sense that they have been excluded or are there to give an initiative respectability they are likely to protest. But if there is a clear sense of why they are 'at the table' then the role of the local manager can be facilitative rather than defensive and controlling.

Inevitably, as a result, local managers should expect a degree of conflict within their initiatives. These new forms of decision making (while inviting the presence of a diverse set of professional and community interests) are likely sites of such conflict.

As a consequence they bring us back to the role of the local manager and how he (she) is positioned.

MANAGING RESISTANCE: ARE REGENERATION MANAGERS AGENTS OF CHANGE?

On the face of it local managers occupy an unenviable position. They are appointed to local regeneration projects often after funding has been secured and the targets/measurements set. They are accountable to a variety of different individuals representing quite different perspectives and they exercise different level of influence and power. They are expected to work 'in partnership' with individuals who themselves may not have been involved in the design of the programme. And they are judged against the actions and interventions of a multiplicity of agencies within the context of neighbourhoods and communities experiencing high levels of deprivation.

As Southern (2002) has usefully suggested, the 'ideal' or 'successful' manager needs to embrace a wide range of interpersonal, technical and financial skills as well as a sufficient knowledge base both to understand the scale of the task and to engage with a variety of interest groups. Southern (2002) identifies the skill base as including:

- organizational and financial planning;
- human resource management;
- strategic management;
- performance management;
- marketing management;

- relationship management;
- technology management;
- risk management.

We would add to this list three additional, but in our view critically significant, skills or understanding of:

- managing change;
- negotiation/conflict resolution;
- local 'political' awareness.

While these are implied in the typology discussed by Southern we think they need to be explicitly named and discussed. This is important because they are illustrative of the 'dynamic' nature of regeneration initiatives. They also point to an important, but sometimes underestimated, feature of regeneration management, that is the highly charged and intense set of experiences associated with change. In particular, the discussion of regeneration management shifts from an identification of specific skills to one which explores the challenges confronting many managers in seeking to bring about change within neighbourhoods.

While the need for change may be self-evident, the ability of a small number of key individuals is confronted by a culture which is resistant to such change. Regeneration managers are, by definition, 'change agents' in the process of regenerating neighbourhoods.

Yet they themselves will be imbued with a set of professional assumptions expressed in a particular language or discourse which may inhibit their potential to make the changes which are expected. At the same time they will be functioning within an externally defined environment which may limit the scope for change.

The evaluation of the NDC initiative (Neighbourhood Renewal Unit 2003) provides an indication of these limits:

> Many Partnerships have up to now concentrated on establishing internal structures and implementing relatively small scale 'quick win' projects. Many are now moving into the delivery phase. It may be difficult for some to balance achieving annual expenditure targets, keeping up the momentum of their programme, while maintaining a strategic focus.
>
> The main factors assisting Partnerships in delivering their programmes are:
>
> - Support from Government Offices and the NRU.
> - Community involvement in planning and delivery.
> - Partnership working.

144

The main constraints are:

- Staff turnover and human resource issues.
- The design and implementation of projects – capital projects, particularly in housing, seem to be most subject to delay.
- Problems associated with mainstreaming.
- Internal management and financial systems, particularly in relation to monitoring project progress and risk assessment.

The potential (or real) barriers to change may be seen by some to rest with individuals who are regarded as acting as 'gatekeepers' or who actively undermine the progressive nature of regeneration initiatives. We do not want to assume that individuals through their action or inaction are not significant. Indeed, it seems to us that individuals can make a difference within these processes. We would want to draw upon our own experience of listening to and observing many individuals across the country who within their own projects are able to and positively want to effect change. There will be a variety of reasons for this:

- They occupy a significant role within their own agencies/organizations and use this role to support, to introduce and to manage change.
- They have the support of senior staff who facilitate their work.
- They have established a close network of workers across different agencies which is mutually supportive and share a particular set of ideas/goals.
- They have well-established links with local community activists and have a deep knowledge of the specific needs of local communities.
- They have become skilled in anticipating policy initiatives and in resource procurement.
- Over time they have established a record which gives them legitimacy within and across organizations and which gives them 'space' to be innovative.

The factors which shape these individuals may be found in their personal/professional biographies and the ways in which they have developed a sense of their own personal narrative and sense of identity and the extent to which this gives them a focus to their work. They are likely to have a range of additional personal skills:

- An ability to listen and to learn from others.
- A well-developed ability to be self-reflective.
- An ability to demonstrate empathy.
- An understanding of their own organization, how it functions and its sense of purpose.
- An ability to be self-critical.

- A willingness to take risks.
- A high level of flexibility in their thinking and practice.

While these cannot be 'learnt' in a series of courses, some of them can be developed over time. But we would suggest that all of the above need to be located in an understanding of the organizational culture, place and structure of regeneration initiatives in a social and political context.

In summary we are suggesting that individuals do matter and can make a difference. We need to understand the particular organizational, cultural and political constraints which may define or limit that ability to effect change. Regeneration managers may wish to be 'agents of change' but find themselves maintaining a status quo. Why might this be the case?

As we have discussed earlier in this chapter and in the previous chapters, local regeneration initiatives are externally defined and assessed. They are a 'product' of the social and political assumptions of their time. Those who manage such initiatives occupy contradictory roles. They are the 'public' face of the external world of central government within local communities. But they are also the accountable face of such initiatives to regional agencies and policy makers. In navigating their way through these relationships some managers may look for the 'unclaimed spaces' within which they can seek to be innovative and to take risks. They may wish to develop ways of bringing local groups into the inner world of the initiative to support them in their attempts to introduce and to sustain change.

It is in these 'spaces' that managers may be at their most vulnerable. The process of managing change and seeking to effect cultural/organizational change within highly professionalized and resistant organizations is not without risk.

But we can anticipate that at the points of conflict either within the partnership or between the external world and the local community local managers are likely to take the external world as their references points too. It is here that we might observe ways in which change is limited and contained.

You may recognize some of these experiences. We want you to reflect upon your own experiences when thinking about these ideas. What are the possibilities of local managers acting as change agents?

SUMMARY

In this section we have explored the possibilities and restrictions on 'capacity building'. We have suggested that the key ideas to consider are:

- Clarifying what we mean by 'capacity building'.
- Reflecting on the ways in which public sector agencies need to have their 'capacity' built.

- Identifying what the tensions are in framing and implementing an existing strategy for a local initiative.
- Locating local managers as key agents for change.
- Thinking about ways in which the skills and knowledge base of local managers needs to be developed and supported.

DISCUSSION POINTS

- What are the managerial skills necessary to support you in working with local community groups?
- How do you develop a 'succession strategy' in a 'failing' initiative?
- How do you develop a 'succession strategy' in a successful regeneration initiative?
- Is local conflict between regeneration initiatives and local residents inevitable or can it be avoided?
- How can 'capacity building' assist in sustaining work in difference and diversity?

SUGGESTED READING

Banks, S., Butcher, H., Henderson, P. and Robertson, J. (eds) (2003) *Managing Community Practice*, Bristol: Policy Press

Burgess, P., Hall, S., Mawson, J. and Pearce, G. (2001) *Devolved approaches to local governance*, York : Joseph Rowntree Foundation

Burns, D. and Taylor, M. (2000) *Auditing Community Participation*, Bristol: Policy Press

Schuftan, C. (1996) 'The Community Development Dilemma: What is really empowering?', *Community Development Journal* 31(3): 260–264

CASE STUDY

A model for capacity building

The present government's proposals (out for consultation) on capacity building identify a number of potential benefits for the community and voluntary sector. These are itemized in Figure 6.1. Within the NRS an important feature has been the funding and setting up of Community Empowerment Networks (CENs). In one CEN (in South London) the experience suggests that they do have the potential to meet the 'ideal' model outlined above. The issues below were identified following an external evaluation conducted by one of the authors.

147

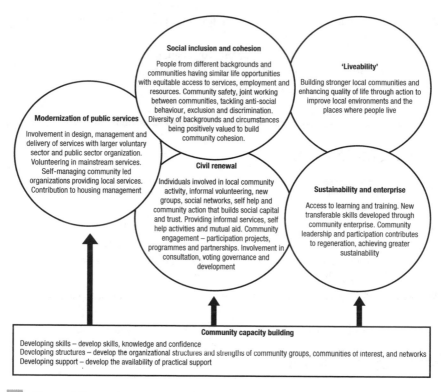

Figure 6.1 *A sustainable and effective community*

The strengths of this CEN are:

- High levels of personal and professional commitment by the paid staff attached to the CEN.
- High level of personal commitment by members of the CEN.
- Evident ability to generate interest in the CEN through the open days with high levels of attendance.
- Willingness to explore alternative/creative ways of engaging with local groups.
- Real attempt to ensure broad representation in the CEN in terms of race and gender.
- Real attempt to ensure that the CEN is serviced/supported by the professional staff.
- Real attempts by the staff to network outside of South London.
- Real attempts to keep CEN informed about practice and policy debates both within and outside the local authority.
- Real attempt to 'translate' the language and practice of the NRS and the LSP to ensure greater participation in exploring its implications for voluntary and community groups.

The opportunities for this CEN are:

- Potential to use the 'critical mass' of CEN members on the LSP.
- Real potential to have a 'conversation' with members of the LSP.
- Potential to develop lines of communication/dialogue outside the LSP and the Council.
- Potential to develop the CEN as a model within the NRS.
- Rich/diverse histories of voluntary sector in South London to frame the debate within the region and nationally.
- Potential to develop alternative(s) perspective(s) of the NRS and community development.
- Potential to develop new alliances across the authority.

CHALLENGES, CHOICES AND DILEMMAS

For local managers the real challenge lies in how to facilitate (and mainstream) a conversation with the CEN which acknowledges differences and attempts to arrive at agreement (where that is possible):

- Given the challenge for local managers in balancing competing interests what strategies might you adopt?
- Local CENs have their own particular needs and local agendas. How do you reconcile those if they are in conflict with yours?
- CENs provide a rich source of different perspectives on the needs of local communities. But their reference point is the LSP. As a local neighbourhood manager how do you bring them 'in' to support, advise or contribute to your work?

Chapter 7

Governance, scrutiny and accountability

INTRODUCTION

In this chapter we illustrate how the social context and space for collective action has become enlarged, with a concomitant increase in the potential for ambiguity on accountability, legitimacy and autonomy. The uncertainty of the environment coupled with the lack of mandatory guidance has created a situation in which individuals and agencies within regeneration adjust to each other in more flexible and innovative ways to maintain, enhance and enlarge their power bases. This has massive implications for the governance of local areas, and drawing from some current literature on governance we show how the changing policy context has altered the balance of accountability and scrutiny.

As we have already explained in the preceding chapters, the new choices, challenges and dilemmas within regeneration are very evident when considering the accountabilities underpinning the work of managers. Not only does this alter behaviour, but also it requires some clearer understanding of the accountability mechanisms governing the work of managers in partner organizations.

Drawing upon a number of explicit themes from earlier chapters to focus on the issues of governance and accountability we show that current arrangements are in the transformative phase of an emerging and contested form of new public governance. Regeneration managers must be in a position to distinguish between their implicit forms of accountability and more explicit requirements to account for their actions. In your experience of working in new organizational forms across boundaries you will see some of the difficulties in disentangling the lines of accountability. It is hoped that you will reflect on your own experience to identify where issues of accountability and governance lie.

In this period of change and transformation, new forms of governance are blurring the traditional lines of accountability. In this chapter we set out to identify why we believe that new governance arrangements are significant and to indicate how we want to explore the problems being created. The starting point for the discussion is that, while accountability is still core to the work of public managers, the traditional lines of responsibility and accountability are becoming blurred and ever more difficult to distinguish, and practitioners are grappling with the new changes as they seek to deal with a multitude of stakeholders requiring explanations and an account to be made.

ACCOUNTABILITY: A DEFINITION

Accountability is a concept that has lost some of its former straightforwardness, and has come to require constant clarification and increasingly complex categorization (Mulgan 2000: 555). Relationships of accountability in the public sector are themselves complex, with public managers expected to be responsive and accountable to a wide range of actors. The terms scrutiny, legitimacy and accountability are surrounded by much jargon and to add to definitional problems the last is often confused with notions of responsibility. It is therefore more appropriate to adopt a multi-perspective conceptual framework to examine these concepts and their validity in a UK public management context. We must also locate our examination within some of the debates surrounding changing governance structures resulting from the realignment between government, the private sector and civil society (Geddes 1997). There is general agreement that accountability is associated with the process of being called to account to some authority for one's actions (Jones 1992: 73), and that public accountability rests both on giving an account and being held to account (Stewart 1992: 2). However, the present crisis in accountability is due to emerging patterns of governance which place an ever increasing burden on a single line of accountability. The reality for many public servants is that they are pulled in different directions by varied mechanisms of accountability. Tensions mount as they seek to explain who does what, and more significantly who is responsible for how the 'rules of the game' have altered.

THE MODERNISING GOVERNMENT AGENDA AND ACCOUNTABILITY

As we have already explained in preceding chapters, the drive to modernize government and involve variegated communities of interest in decision making is central to understanding the national state's Modernising Government agenda. This focused on achieving the twin aims of efficient public services and equity of distribution (Maddock 2002: 13–44). Indeed the 1997 Blair government's three key aims for improving the quality of public services were:

1   Modernization and innovation of services.
2   Renewed social democracy with an emphasis on welfare, and because big government is dead.
3   Partnership as the key to delivery.
> (Tony Blair, Prime Minister, communicating with Sir Richard Wilson, Head of the Home Civil Service and Cabinet Secretary, October 1998)

To achieve these aims the Blair government welcomed, indeed encouraged, new forms of governance.

CHANGING GOVERNANCE STRUCTURES AND THE EFFECTS ON ACCOUNTABILITY

Although the use of the concept 'governance' has attained currency within the past decade, at the expense of the concept 'government' (Hirst, cited in Pierre 2000: 13), despite its widespread usage it remains a concept with different dimensions and applications (Guiliani, cited in Salet *et al.* 2003: 9). 'Governance' lacks precision and is used in a variety of disciplines and in different discourses (Southern 2002: 16). It is generally perceived as an alternative to government, and it is argued that the following reasons account for this:

- National governments all over Europe during the post Second World War period took a proactive role in expansion of the Welfare State.
- During the 1980s, and thereafter, dramatic shifts altered the balance between government and other agencies.
- Common features such as a reduction in the proactive role of government in the economy and society.
- Diversification of decision making throughout a wide range of organizations. Restructuring of inter-governmental relationships became evident.

(Salet *et al.* 2003: 6)

Hirst offers a definition of governance as 'a means by which an activity or ensemble of activities is controlled or directed, such that it delivers an acceptable range of outcomes according to some established social standard' (Hirst 1997: 3). Whereas government has traditionally been thought of as the formal institutional structures of decision making, new forms of 'governance' have blurred the boundaries between the state, the market and civil society (Geddes 1997). This new system of governance engages a plurality of institutions and organizations alongside state agencies to solve particular problems and multi-agency partnerships are regarded as the most effective means of achieving common goals (Taket and White 2000: 19–20).

There is no real agreement on why governmental institutions have been replaced by new forms of governance. The following have been offered as explanations:

- Rapid global and technological changes and the resultant international interdependence, coupled with declining growth rates and increasing competitive pressures within states.
- Shrinking budgets for social programmes.
- Blurring of boundaries between business and government.
- Dissatisfaction with legal processes for solving complex problems.

We have argued elsewhere that very little can be accomplished by a single organization acting alone, and in an era when organizational boundaries are loosening and becoming more complex and problematic, most organizational problems need partners, not only horizontally in alliances but also vertically around relationships with users and consumers (Attwood *et al.* 2003: 143). Increasingly, new standards

153

of delivery are now matched by exhortations to join up practice and involve service users (Hutton, cited in Attwood *et al.* 2003: x). Indeed the Labour government's aim for radical modernization of public services depends on its ability to make a reality of 'holistic' government, 'joined-up thinking', and achieve better outcomes across a wide range of policy areas, as successive governments have failed to tackle deep-seated problems (Wilkinson and Appelbee 1999: 1). In the drive to join up policy areas, however, ever increasing gaps in lines of accountability are exposed, as we shall now discuss.

TRADITIONAL OR NEW FORMS OF ACCOUNTABILITY?

The origins of accountability may be political, constitutional, statutory, hierarchical or contractual and may consist of four components:

- Assignment of responsibilities.
- An obligation to answer for those responsibilities.
- Surveillance of performance to ensure compliance with direction.
- Possible sanctions and rewards.

(Norman 2003: 144)

and involve answering the following questions:

Outputs, what has been achieved with resources allocated?.
Ownership, is a department (or part of the government/organization) well placed to meet the demands placed on it now and in future?
Strategic alignment and collective interests, are the goals consistent with the government's strategic goals?
Contribution to outcomes, how well is the organization doing in contributing to better outcomes?

(Norman 2003: 144)

MULTIPLE ACCOUNTABILITIES

Accountability in the UK is managed at multiple levels, and traditionally those exercising power were held to account through a line of accountability to elected persons, who were in turn held to account by citizens in periodic elections, and based on a presumption of due processes and the observance of procedures to ensure responsible public action. Most public servants have multiple accountabilities, and their freedom to use discretion is governed by the rules, regulations and guidelines emanating from central government or a higher authority (Friend *et al.* 1974). Moreover, their understanding of the general rules, conditions and knowledge governing their own professional arena (such as land use, social services, education) leads to more complex and dynamic forms of scrutiny, accountability and legitimacy.

The Local Government Code of Conduct and, at central government level, the Civil Service Code of Conduct have both developed as a result of the Nolan principles on conduct in public life. Moreover, all appointments to public bodies follow Nolan guidelines, and are monitored very closely by the Office of Public Appointments, overseen by the Parliamentary Standards and Privileges Committee. Public servants are also accountable to their own ethical standards (because accountability is considered to be intuitive), but much of their work is now enshrined in the Nolan principles, of which accountability is but one of the key elements that should guide their activities (the other six are selflessness, integrity, objectivity, openness, honesty and leadership). Accountability may have little validity without some clear evidence about the other six principles, and as well as being accountable to their own professional training, public servants are accountable upwards to central government by regular inspection:

- Audit Commission or District Audit or the Standards Board of England (in the case of local government).
- The Commission for Health Audit and Inspection and Commission for Social Care Inspection (health and social care systems).
- HM Inspectorate of Constabulary (the police).

This huge regulatory system across all aspects of UK public service is designed to ensure no misappropriation of funds or untoward behaviours.

Professional accountability in which public officials drew their codes of conduct from a body of professional knowledge and expertise is being undermined, as individuals and groups are expected to put aside their professional training and experience in the interests of the common weal. By increasingly working across professional boundaries and in completely new jurisdictions it is clear that the professional perspective on standards and guidance that governs behaviour is in retreat, as professional bodies attempt to offer guidance to public servants working in completely new contexts and environments. Within these changing contexts and environments there is an ever growing burden of scrutiny and inspection.

SCRUTINY AND INSPECTION

Scrutiny through inspection and audit has become more prominent in the UK system and Moran points to the rise of surveillance, audit and regulation (Moran 2000). Where once the audit function would have been seen as the prerogative of service professionals it is now in the hands of arm's-length (and supposedly independent) regulatory bodies. The command and control systems of accountability have been replaced by a regulatory mode. There are now public auditors, professional inspectorates and ombudsmen, and in theory they are independent, objective and assess measurable indicators of performance to nationally established standards (Rogers 1990: 129). The regulatory mode of accountability is based on managerialism and control and downplays democracy, pluralism and the conventional view that government ministers are at the apex of democratic accountability and control (McGarvey 2001: 24). Public service regulation is a control mechanism by which central government seeks to govern the activities of those agencies providing public services. Agencies such as the Audit Commission, the National Audit Office and central government inspectorates allow the centre to govern increasingly fragmented governance. They monitor, influence and control the performance of agencies delivering public services (Cope and Goodship 1999: 10). The Audit Commission has developed an array of performance indicators (and use the Best Value Regime or Comprehensive Performance Assessment to benchmark local authorities against each other), HMI Constabulary issues certificates of efficiency, OFSTED (standards in schools) constructs league tables of schools, and the District Audit, National Audit Office, Audit Commission and IDEA (Improvement and Development Agency) audit the spending and performance of local authorities and schools, as well as spreading best practice. There is a big question mark over where audit ends and inspection begins as regulatory agencies often have different remits, agendas and styles, and compete with each other, resulting in frequent turf wars. Cope and Goodship (2001: 14) see moves towards more joined-up government hindered by the way in which state agencies are still functionally and vertically organized, and the fact that there are still entrenched interests of politicians, bureaucrats and professionals (p. 14). Scrutiny processes are likely to stay fractious between central government with its desire for reform and service providers who are trying to lessen the burden that scrutiny brings, and concentrating their limited resources on service provision. The audit explosion has challenged delivery agencies, increased tensions and led to either increased use of management consultancy or prescriptive models of best practice. The future of regulation and audit depends very much on the potential for a lighter touch or the development of greater trust between the parties (Clarke, cited in Bovaird and Loffler 2003: 157).

Public servants expect to be vertically accountable by political, managerial and financial interests and other processes of inspection and regulation, but they are also internally accountable to their own organizational scrutiny and accountability mechanisms, as well as vertically and horizontally to a variety of stakeholders (of an increasingly multi-governance level and multi-professional, multi-constituent and multi-agency nature).

Until recently, for all day-to-day purposes civil servants had loyalty and duty to the Crown and Queen's Parliament, and if they were unhappy with this line of authority they could resign (Chapman 1993: 29). However, many high-profile cases such as the Ponting case in 1985 (a civil servant who leaked information to Parliament because he believed his minister was lying to Parliament) have increased the sensitivity for individual civil servants. Ministerial accountability to Parliament was of a higher order than nowadays and ministers rarely resign over issues. Such cases have led to:

- Reforms of Parliamentary Select Committees, where MPs can examine officials and ministers and probe minute details. Various documents of guidance were issued to civil servants (1977).
- The Croham directive on the Disclosure of Official Information, which was followed by the Osmotherly Rules.
- A 1985 statement by Sir Robert Armstrong (revized in 1987), Head of the Home Civil Service and Cabinet Office, on the duties and responsibilities of civil servants in relation to ministers.

There is a draft Civil Service Bill being considered currently by the Public Administration Select Committee of the House of Commons, and there are demands for a Civil Service Act (mainly to clarify the relationship and codes of conduct between civil servants and ministers and between civil servants and the many special advisers or external experts being used by ministers; House of Commons, Public Administration Select Committee, 2003–4).

Traditionally accountability has been, nationally, through cabinet ministers, civil servants, select committees, central departments, Members of Parliament, the National Audit Office, the Audit Commission or other regulatory agencies, HM Treasury, the Parliamentary Ombudsman, or locally through cabinet or committee systems in local government via local members. Direct accountability in local government was via officials to elected members, and nationally via civil servants to ministers, and indirectly appointed boards were accountable through ministers to Parliament and through council members to full council. However, traditional forms of public accountability no longer provide a sufficient basis for explanation, and the complexities of public life and the greater demands placed on officials and elected members raise further doubts (Stewart 1992: 4).

In the traditional perspective on national political accountability there is a coherent chain of accountability, from official to official in the Weberian bureaucracy, from official to minister, from minister to Parliament, and from Parliament to the people, but it is largely illusionary (McGarvey 2001: 18). Accountability is still at the heart of public policy and politics, but recent changes have created many tensions and difficulties as normal channels of accountability between the governors and the governed become strained, and difficult to disentangle. Nevertheless we should not entirely dismiss the traditional view of accountability, because civil servants still derive their own code of ethics from an understanding of their place

157

in the hierarchy and their relationship to ministers, other civil servants, Parliament, the Cabinet, and the general public interest (Chapman 1993). Since 1997 the Labour government has pushed the Modernising Government agenda of change affecting many constitutional structures, practices and procedures. Unlike other countries, the UK system of government lacks a written constitution, a Freedom of Information Act or a Bill of Rights and this has enabled the government of the day (Labour have remained in power since 1997 and now enjoy a 160-seat majority in Parliament) to instigate changes that have affected lines of accountability. Parliamentary accountability has been traditionally through the channel of representative MPs who question the action of the Executive through parliamentary questioning and scrutiny and select committee. The Prime Minister, as *primus inter pares* (first among equals), is responsible for choosing a Cabinet and the leading government ministerial teams. Under the current government the duration of both Cabinet meetings and Prime Minister's Question Time has been shortened, leaving many backbench MPs to use the select committee system as their only legitimate way of bringing the Executive to account, and leading many commentators to suggest a more presidential style of politics than has hitherto been experienced in a UK context.

Individual citizens still have the right to write to their MP on any issue of public concern, and verbal or written questions will be put to the PM and ministers, if parliamentary time allows, but the scale of new legislation leaves little time for individual concerns when manifesto promises or other issues of national importance take precedence. An MP still has the option of suggesting that an individual constituent writes to the Parliamentary Ombudsman to obtain redress of grievance, or failing all else the voter can show his (her) displeasure with the government of the day, or a constituency MP, by voting them out of office at the next general or by-election. A major problem in the UK system of government is the fact that MPs are elected and seek re-election after a four- to five-year period, meaning that their horizons are short term.

Decentralization of decision making and budgets has strengthened the need for central co-ordination and HM Treasury has become more powerful, but there has been a fine balancing act between exercising strong central leadership and fostering a model of decentralization On the one hand there is the rhetoric of decentralized decision making, but on the other hand little guidance on how to achieve outcomes. Accountability becomes blurred when the central agencies (in particular the ultimate funder, HM Treasury) fail to give clear instructions and delivery agencies are left to guess how to interpret the guidance. HM Treasury remains the most important line of accountability because of the requirement of the accounting officers of the spending departments to give regular updates on spending. It has the ability to influence spending priorities in departments. The key role as co-ordinator of overall government spending gives the Treasury and the Chancellor of the Exchequer a powerful role as the key agents of accountability. Many chief executives of Next Steps agencies have short-term contracts and have strictly limited room for manoeuvre. This means that they can be removed when necessary, and are continuously challenged to provide an account of their activities.

It has been argued that traditional notions of political accountability have changed for ever (McGarvey 2001: 25) but still inform political behaviour. The professional accountability of the post-war period, in which technical and apparently depoliticized solutions to public services were in fact an attempt to increase resources available to professionals, went into retreat. Managerialist accountability, based on the notions of New Public Management, replaced both political and professional notions of accountability, and had at core the belief that accountability required a clear statement of objectives and target setting, that a direct relationship between administrators and users of public services would improve management, and that choice and empowerment would deliver more responsive, effective and accountable services (McGarvey 2001: 20). However, the new governance framework involving non-state actors and agencies is threatening the managerial perspective, and requires reworking of our traditional ideas and views of the role of the state and the effectiveness of representative democracy (Hirst 1997: 33). There is a greater need for improved representativeness, but also service quality improvements.

QUALITY OF SERVICE IMPROVEMENT AND PERFORMANCE MANAGEMENT

Quality of service improvement is based on the idea that greater accountability and transparency for consumers will enable them to engage more effectively and demand higher standards. Since the 1980s countless quality initiatives have been introduced by central government, such as market testing; Citizen's Charter; Service First; Public Sector Excellence (based on the EFQM, the European Foundation for Quality Management model); CCT; Best Value; IDEA and Audit Commission Reviews; CPA (Comprehensive Performance Assessment); accreditation of local strategic partnerships (such as local strategic partnerships and New Deal for Communities); and the Partnership Diagnostic being developed by the Audit Commission.

The context within which these initiatives have taken place includes:

- Worldwide competition for shrinking markets.
- The domination of industrial, technological and managerial ideas by Far Eastern companies.
- Rising demands from a more highly skilled workforce.
- A shortage of the world's resources.

159

■ The need to eliminate waste.
■ A dominant political ideology in the UK focused on a wasteful bureaucratic state, inadequate public service delivery and cradle-to-grave state dependency.

The need to measure performance against central government targets, against performance in previous periods and against other departments or benchmark against other agencies is at the heart of the performance regime. The aim is to allow organizations to develop benchmarks, norms and targets of their own to improve policy, planning and budgeting, monitor and implement improved standards of service delivery, but at the same time review the distribution of resources and ensure access to all users. Nevertheless it is clear that the performance management systems imposed on the public sector are also designed to increase central control and influence over how decisions are taken.

The new performance culture of NPM, in which (apparently) autonomous and accountable managers have challenged the traditional Westminster view of anonymous or neutral civil servants who offer objective advice to ministers, increasingly (and especially with the increasing use of special advisors, think tanks or external policy forums) has to act in contractual and competitive ways to deliver services. The traditional language of civil servants based on stability, rules and procedures has been replaced by a new vocabulary based on managerialism, change, decentralization, responsiveness, creativity, innovation, performance outputs and impacts.

Governments have adopted the model of NPM in attempts to shift from funding organizations and institutions to funding performance (Norman 2003: 27), and public services traditionally delivered through government-owned bureaucracies are now delivered through a 'mixed economy' (Gray 1998) of public and private organizations competing for available funds. Government bureaucracies have been 'reinvented' in attempts to reduce costs to taxpayers and increase responsiveness to clients and citizens (Osborne and Gaebler 1992), but amidst the controversy generated by NPM methods there has been surprisingly little in-depth information about how they work in practice (Norman 2003: 28).

Innovative service delivery involving partnerships has been a core theme of many of the 'joined-up and citizen-focused' legislative changes since 1997. Indeed the case of local economic development, social cohesion and regeneration of local communities has been an issue of public debate for many years. Partnership has been seen as a recognizable way to solve economic and social decline, given that no one agency, such as a local authority, can be expected to take sole responsibility for addressing these problems. The public policy system is replete with issues and problems that lie outside any one area of professional expertise or department, and the multi-organizational model of decision making recognized by Friend et al. (1974) offers useful guidance in a contemporary setting. In recognising that it is not always possible to plan strategies top down owing to turbulent environments, multi-accountabilities and technical aspects of implementation and execution, Friend *et al.*'s model moved beyond formal democratically elected agents and agencies and offers considerable appeal for establishing the subtle relationships between representatives in decision-making forums now prevalent across the whole UK public sector.

JOINED-UP POLICY MAKING AND ACCOUNTABILITY

Joining up policy and service provision made a reality of 'holistic' government, to achieve better outcomes (Wilkinson and Appelbee 1999: 1), whereas democratic renewal was the response to the perceived problems in existing local institutions and was integral to the modernising agenda. Pratchett (2000) argued that the entire role and purpose of local government and the nature of local democracy were under threat, so that local authorities were urged to pursue policies in collaboration and partnerships with other agencies as a way of extending local autonomy and local leadership, to reverse voter apathy, functional impotence and arcane decision-making structures. There was considerable experimentation with new modes of governance which combined components of traditional representative democracy with a more participatory, responsive and consultative polity. Questions have arisen on how well traditional forms of responsiveness and accountability are serving citizens, and recent writers are calling for more effective means of involving citizens

TRADITIONAL PUBLIC ADMINISTRATION, NEW PUBLIC MANAGEMENT OR NEW PUBLIC GOVERNANCE?

Denhardt and Denhardt (2000) present a new public service (NPS) approach as a viable alternative for the dichotomy between the 'old' public administration and the 'new' public management. It seeks to balance the advantages of NPM with the emerging requirement for greater public participation in public service improvement. NPS theorists emphasize democratic citizenship, models of community and civil society as viable alternatives to both the traditional and the now-dominant managerialist models (Denhardt and Denhardt 2000). According to this approach, public sector organizations should be organized in such a way that public servants are not responsive to 'constituents and clients' (traditional public administration), nor to 'customers' (NPM), but to 'citizens'.

With citizens at the forefront, the emphasis in NPS should not be placed on either steering (NPM) or rowing (public administration) the governmental boat (Osborne and Gaebler 1992), but rather on building public institutions marked by integrity and responsiveness. Denhardt and Denhardt (2000) suggest that NPS is built on six principles:

1   Serve rather than steer, because public policies are no longer simply the result of governmental decision-making processes.
2   The public interest is the aim, not the by-product. It is necessary to establish shared interests and shared responsibilities based around a vision for the community and a single set of goals.
3   Think strategically, act democratically. Collective effort and collaborative processes should exist within open and accessible government.
4   Serve citizens, not customers, and have a concern for the larger community. Accountability is not simple and involves complex constellations of institutions and standards.
5   Value people, not just productivity. Processes of collaboration and shared leadership should be based on respect for people.
6   Value citizenship and public service above entrepreneurship.

Schedler (2002) goes further in showing the loss of credibility in NPM due to market failure in delivering public services, and sees a future in which citizens, rather than customers, achieve prominence, but points out that greater clarification on the role of the state as guarantor and/or regulator will be vital. A new public governance, it is argued, would strengthen democratic control over decision making and citizen involvement, as well as improving public trust in government institutions and types of services provided. NPM, based on a managerial rationality, was perceived as lacking sensitivity to the misuse of power, and of ignoring the fact that political rationality has an inherent drive to increase, limit or control power.

CHANGING LOCAL GOVERNANCE

In terms of local accountability the notion that elected local governments have a legitimate and automatic role in making authoritative local decisions on behalf of their communities is challenged. In the UK, like most of its Western European counterparts, local governance evolved from earlier nineteenth- and twentieth-century institutionalized forms, in which public decisions were institutionalized in public bureaucracies and political parties largely created and legitimized by central states, to a 'more variegated, independent and more experimental form of local politics offering the potential for politicians, bureaucrats, interest groups and publics to express their local identities, different from, but complementary to higher tiers of governance' (John 2001: 2). As a consequence, political authority is now being devolved to groupings of wider agencies, which are exhorted to work in collaboration with formerly marginalized community groups.

Under the Local Government Act of 2000 local authorities with a population of more than 85,000 were asked to choose, after broad consultation, from four alternative internal decision-making mechanisms:

162

1   Streamlined Committee Structure.
2   Elected Mayor/Council Manager.
3   Cabinet and Scrutiny Committee/Panel.
4   City Manager and administration.

Prior to these changes all local authorities were organized around a committee structure with members acting as representatives of their voters, and officers recruited on the basis of technical expertise to advise the politicians.

To date 12 local authorities have opted for an elected mayor; 1 chose the Mayor/Council Manager option; approximately 70 chose a streamlined committee structure; but by far the majority of all local authorities opted for cabinet leadership with a series of scrutiny committees or panels (Leach and Norris 2003: 4). In the last option the Cabinet makes most of the decisions and has direct overall control of the work of the council. Membership is drawn from the majority or ruling party, and each cabinet member is designated a policy portfolio, and in a departure from traditional committee/departmental scrutiny, portfolio functions cut across council services to encourage joined-up thinking. Many councils have established area committees or panels to bring the council and communities closer together, for the purpose of making decisions on a range of different local issues, such as traffic schemes, parking or monitoring and evaluating the progress of local regeneration schemes. In some, but not all, instances area forums link town and parish forums into a plethora of partnerships, consortia or other joint working arrangements.

The ruling party holds cabinet positions with some local councils allowing a restricted number of opposition parties to have a seat in the Cabinet, and each member has a portfolio of service responsibility. Unlike the traditional committee structure where committees followed the council departmental structure with a view to ensuring direct accountability, many cabinet systems are organized along cross-cutting themes (such as Lifelong Learning, Regeneration or Sustainability) and cross-departmental boundaries. Under the traditional committee structure, all councillors would carry a caseload of ward business and be part of the overall council decision-making body, but under the cabinet system, most 'backbench' members have lost their intimate role in decision making. Instead, some have been drawn into scrutinising the role of the full Cabinet.

The change from having a committee structure directly aligned to service departments, and in which members could call officers to account, has altered the direct relationship between members and officers, and most officers are now deployed in servicing the work of the senior cabinet members of an authority, leaving few resources for the ordinary backbencher who wants to ask pertinent questions of the Executive of cabinet members. Most local authorities have established scrutiny panels but there is no real evidence to suggest that they are being run along the lines envisaged by central government; that is, similar to the

163

Parliamentary Select Committees with the capacity to call upon expert witnesses, external advice or commissioned research, to bring the Executive to account. Very few local authorities that have adopted the Cabinet and scrutiny system have the resources or staff to service the system. In theory this revolutionary new system was designed to allow the citizen to be brought closer to the governed, but in reality there is little evidence of lay people or community representation on any scrutiny panels as most are led by a backbench member who lacks the officer support or capacity to bring the cabinet members to account for their actions. Some local authorities have hired costly consultants, and attempt to have a scrutiny panel to oversee all scrutiny panels, but there is no evidence to show any real independent scrutiny. The main problems are insufficient training of members on what the scrutiny role is supposed to achieve, insufficient funds and poor officer support to challenge decisions. Moreover, although some scrutiny panels can instigate an investigation, in most cases the chief officer and cabinet members will determine the scope of business to be scrutinized, which rather defeats the object of the exercise. All local authorities also now have a standards panel to monitor the behaviour of members, and are being asked to carry out audits of governance and develop procurement strategies to ensure fair distribution of contracts for work.

Internally, in addition to scrutiny committees/panels, local authorities have also established the following:

- Standards committees.
- Regulatory and other committees.
- Area committees/panels.
- Joint arrangements.

Scrutiny committees review all council policies, proposals and performance, but they can suggest their own proposals and consider the outcomes of commissioned research. Under call-in procedures, the Scrutiny Committee can investigate any cabinet decision. Six ward councillors, the Shadow Cabinet and other opposition groups are able to scrutinize any area of local government business providing the Scrutiny Committee agrees to the investigation.

Each local authority has different types of scrutiny committees, and they all differ in size, scope of activities and resources devoted to them. For example, Ealing Borough has a borough scrutiny committee to investigate physical or infrastructure policies; an area committee scrutiny panel to respond to local needs (normally it is chaired by councillors and can involve community representatives); a regulatory committee to make decisions on planning, trading standards, consumer protection or environmental health (this body oversees the work of all regulatory bodies and acts as a link between the bodies and the council); and a planning committee that scrutinizes all planning applications.

Joint arrangements committees allow the Cabinet to enter into arrangements or collaborate with any person or body to promote the economic, social or environmental well-being of the area.

Rules governing the conduct of local government council members are enshrined in the Standards Board for England's guidelines, and every local authority must adopt specific codes of conduct to guide behaviour. Many have also established standards committees for promoting and maintaining high ethical standards and investigating allegations that members' behaviour may have fallen short of required standards. Every local authority was required by May 2002 to develop a code of conduct setting out the expected behaviour of members. This code covers all elected, co-opted and independent members of local authorities, including parish councils, police, fire and joint authorities and national park authorities. The code requires individual members to have rules and procedures on how not to abuse their position or authority resources. Additionally there are rules governing disclosure of interests and withdrawal from meetings due to vested interests or poor behaviour. A record must also be kept of all financial and other interests. The Standards Board for England oversees the process and deals with any disputes or specific transgressions, by instigating procedures, nationally or at the local level. Local lay people and external experts are appointed nationally to serve locally, and they act as a mediator in any disputes in a quasi-legal role.

Turnout in local elections is low (generally below 30 per cent) but central government is experimenting with new electronic forms of voting (and recent evidence has shown that this can improve voter turnout). Local governments have few powers to raise taxes, other than council tax and business rates, so still rely on a block grant from central government for 50 per cent of their spending, though beacon councils and others that receive high ratings on Best Value and Comprehensive Performance Assessment have been given greater financial freedoms since April 2004. The low turnout at elections, coupled with the overarching financial dependency, leaves local government still highly accountable to its central government 'master'.

There is also a panoply of regulatory and inspection mechanisms to maintain standards, transparency and good governance. These are all aimed at improved service, customer orientation and value for money, and include Best Value and Comprehensive Assessment; Area Panels and Area Committees; LSPs, New Deal for Communities or other partnerships; and Primary Care Trusts (to identify local health care needs). Democratic accountability is also facing huge challenges, in particular as local members and officials are expected to work in collaboration with a variety of stakeholders to achieve commonly agreed objectives. This is true in the case of LSPs where all main agencies in a particular locale are brought together for the purpose of mainstreaming funding to satisfy local needs within nationally determined floor targets. Traditionally, local members would act as the funnel of representative views to the council, but as many decisions are taken outwith the council chamber it has become increasingly difficult to determine who is responsible and accountable for actions.

One of the major problems facing anyone attempting to oversee and scrutinize the work of local authorities or health bodies is the fact that much of their business is conducted in partnership, collaboration, consortia or joint working arrangements that cross traditional boundaries. Most local authorities took an early lead in bringing together partnership agencies to work in completely new ways to achieve the central tenets of the Modernising Government agenda, but the partners are also required to work within a Best Value regime and develop suitable PSAs (Public Service Agreements) and measurable targets based on UK Treasury floor targets. Furthermore, during the summer of 2002, 150 upper tier local authorities were subjected to a 'Comprehensive Performance Assessment'. This public scrutiny may have profound implications for elected local governments, as their legitimate and automatic role in making authoritative local decisions on behalf of their communities becomes threatened. A central question is 'if local authorities lack the corporate capacity to drive the new agenda, how can communities make up that shortfall?'

ENGAGING COMMUNITIES IN PARTNERSHIP

Government has urged community engagement and empowerment, but the extent to which community participants are allowed into mainstream policy-making structures is still rather limited. Representatives of the community may be self-selecting, and not always connected to, or representative of, the wider community. Some breakthroughs have been made, within some LSPs, but as far as the citizen moving centre stage, generally local authorities are still the dominant force, so one needs to ask whether they still represent their communities, given the low turnout at elections. The Improvement and Development Agency (2001) showed that nationally elected members are predominantly male (71 per cent) and aged over 45 (86 per cent), and it is debatable whether the voluntary and community sectors are more representative of the community than elected members. There are enormous problems in switching from a local-authority-led approach to one controlled by communities, not least because communities currently lack the capacities to take on these new challenges (Hutton 1997; Miliband 1999). Indeed local politicians are sceptical, because community representatives are seen as self-interested individuals seeking resources, mainly monetary, for the furtherance of their own goals (Colenutt and Cutten 1994). Community partnerships are diverse but still have only a small number of people assuming leading roles, and they are held in overall low regard by officers in public sector agencies (Balloch and Taylor 2001; North 2001).

There are practical difficulties of community involvement and some way to go before citizen-based advocacy becomes the norm. To involve people is extraordinarily difficult, in part because there is no agreed methodology on how to achieve this. Many local authorities have made efforts to increase community capacities; however, local politicians are very realistic in managing aspirations in communities for fear of not being able to deliver against new, higher expectations. Some politicians have seen the new structures of local governance as a slow erosion of local democracy and concern is already being expressed that care needs to be taken not to create an alternative democratic system. Many politicians see themselves as community activists responding to views and issues within their communities, and this has changed the role of elected members who now spend less time in committee meetings. The shift from representative to participative democracy is not entirely proven, as some members believe that their legitimacy comes from working on behalf of communities. The ballot box is still seen as a useful mechanism of accountability, but the growth in community partnerships and networks calls for other forms of accountability.

On the positive side of partnership working, there are various attempts to unite around a shared agenda, and delegate responsibility for delivery nearer to communities. Less positively, some public servants are only just starting to cross their own organizational boundaries, despite the fact that future judgements about local government's success will be based on its ability to work in partnership (Improvement and Development Agency, 2001). Partnerships can be very effective in communities as a way of harnessing energy; they also allow agencies and communities to share agendas and constraints, or to receive feedback on plans. Joint working is essential if issues are to be addressed holistically, but undeniably there will be conflicts between partners.

There are local politicians who welcome the opportunity to provide 'grassroots' views and enlighten communities. Conversely partnerships can detract from strong leadership and increase demands. Furthermore, unwilling partners adopting a passive stance can sabotage progress. There is a real concern that local authorities continue to dominate and a desire to see more active involvement from the voluntary and business sectors, and LSPs, is being encouraged to involve broader representation. They were created to agree a common set of priorities based on an understanding of an area's specific difficulties; as a springboard for creative ideas; and as a way of joining up services at a local level while acknowledging the difficulties this presents. Moreover, some local authorities think that the partnerships exist to validate their hastily made decisions, or to access new funds.

Government policy is directed towards increasing levels of community participation in policy making, but a proven methodology is lacking and existing approaches conspire to limit aspiration and nurture dependency. Community leaders are increasingly being given opportunities to voice opinions, but there is a tendency towards community 'consultation' and limited signs of 'involvement'. 'Delegation' of responsibility is rare and occurs at the margins of policy making, or in discrete and relatively small-scale community regeneration initiatives. The number of active community leaders varies and may be defined by existing initiatives, and they need mechanisms for validating their personal leadership role and the mandate they represent. There are considerable barriers that continue to exclude them from active participation.

Local authorities remain the dominant organizations, but legitimacy is challenged owing to low voter turnout and the demographic profile of councillors. Elected members have emerged as community representatives, but they do accept that benefits can accrue from community involvement. There are links between participative and representative forms of governance. Regeneration has resulted in more partnership working spanning different sectors, but most are concerned with the sharing of information and plans, or consultation with other partners or communities. Actual decisions about activities tend to be made intra-organizationally rather than inter-organizationally. Little progress has been made on joint planning, commissioning or procedures; there is no discernible shifting resources or responsibilities.

The slow pace of progress, coupled with the concerns on measuring performance of partnership working, is a real concern with a distinct need for rationalization and clearer objectives. Some partnerships provide the opportunity for financial gain, while others provide opportunities for under-represented groups, but good leadership is essential to manage inclusiveness. In future, how well individual local authorities work in partnership will be a key criterion of their overall performance.

LSPs are a main plank of UK government policy and through active community involvement they are designed to overcome a perceived culture of dependency. They are acknowledged forums to agree shared priorities relating to an area's specific problems, and provide a mechanism for joining up public services at a local level, but they will take some time to mature, though the requirement for a positive impact is immediate.

ARE TRADITIONAL LINES OF ACCOUNTABILITY APPROPRIATE?

It is self-evident that the traditional lines of accountability are no longer appropriate for modern-day governance, and in the case of regeneration the complexities and blurred organizational boundaries lead to issues of who has responsibility or who is accountable for what. As has already been explored in Chapter 1, very little is now accomplished by a single organization acting alone. This has the consequence of creating complex and problematic 'action spaces', and the need to make a reality of holistic and joined-up thinking has created a position in which multiple agencies and professionals are seeking consensus through multiple agendas to achieve commonly agreed goals. As partnership has become recognized as the most effective means of bringing together state, market and civil society, regeneration managers have difficulties in deciding who to account to, and which level of authority they must respond to. Are they responsible to:

- customers;
- consumers;
- citizens;
- their own organizations;
- multi-organizational forums/partnerships;
- their professional code of conduct or rules and guidance;
- local or national bodies;
- quangos;
- some other body?

When asked to describe his own accountabilities, a regeneration manager suggested the following:

- All stakeholders, but most importantly my staff to whom I owe a duty of care.
- External agencies I collaborate with, in particular other local authorities.
- My own local authority, for quality of service and appropriate use of resources.
- My professional body.
- Commercial accountability (if we are working with private companies we must act according to commercial propriety).
- In the case of using private contractors we must be accountable to their rules and regulations.
- Office of Deputy Prime Minster and other government departments.
- Sub-regional and regional governance agencies.

In this chapter we suggest that it is no longer certain where accountability and responsibility lie. The traditional lines of accountability are more strained than in the past, not least because of the scale of partnership activities, and the possible duplication of effort and need to mainstream budgets.

Given this new context of governance and accountability it seems to us that regeneration managers have a more difficult role in 'sense making', managing within new lines of accountability, as they adjust the move from a hierarchical, top-down command system of control and accountability (based on a unitary state, where it was expected that an account would be made upwards) to a more fluid system where accountability is varied and multifarious. Accountability can be horizontally from below or above, vertically across organizational boundaries as well as to citizens, consumers or customers of service, but also increasingly managers are required to provide other types of accountability.

New forms of service delivery, especially those carried out in collaboration and partnership, have increased the scope for things going wrong, or for mistakes being made. This adds to an already confused picture for regeneration managers, whose professional training will include some aspect of ethics, namely:

- personal codes of conduct;
- professional rules and regulations;
- organizational requirements;
- multi-organizational needs;
- other elements of accountability.

Hierarchical and organizational forms of accountability are embedded in a traditional governmental system that we argue is no longer appropriate to the experimental world of regeneration. Indeed we suggest that as regeneration is now centred on experimental forms of governance, the risks involved offer greater potential for mistakes to be made or misappropriation. While we do not argue that the new system of governance necessarily leads to more corrupt or underhand activities, it is our contention that gaps in coverage do create the potential for mistakes and errors, and, therefore, there is an increased need for managers to present an account of the resources used to achieve commonly agreed objectives.

In pursuit of achieving central government's many initiatives to regenerate impoverished locales, local authorities have been urged to restructure their internal mechanisms of decision making and forms of scrutiny and accountability, as has already been explained.

At the same time the Local Government Act of 2000 gave local authorities the opportunity to work in partnership with external agencies to comply with a duty of care for the overall economic, social and environmental well-being of local communities. However, despite urging local authorities to create new 'action spaces' managers were given no guidance or regulations on types of governance arrangements beyond the local authority boundaries. Moreover, the lines of accountability when working in collaboration with other partners are very unclear. We suggest that as managers from different levels of hierarchy (and members too) begin working outside of the normal channels of scrutiny and lines of accountability, they become immersed in a new, experimental world where few rules and regulation apply, where guidance is limited, and in which they have to work horizontally and vertically with other agencies to bring about changes. This means that as they pool resources and expertise, there is a greater need to explain their activities to more stakeholders, but the traditional mechanisms they would normally use are becoming obsolete and inadequate forms of scrutiny and accountability. On the one hand internal mechanisms on scrutiny and accountability have been enhanced, but the fact that regeneration managers work mainly beyond their organizational boundaries leads, on the other hand, to 'virtual action spaces' where few controls exists. We argue that this increases the need for personal and professional accountability, and a code of ethics governing actions.

There are obvious dangers in requiring regeneration managers to take more risks and be more innovative, creative and entrepreneurial, without providing the vital guidance, new rules and regulations to shape behaviour. We argue that in working within experimental ways, beyond organizational boundaries, there is a greater need for professionalism and self-regulation. In this way new training and education in codes of ethics, ways of conducting business and how to manage within new forms of governance are essential.

It is our view that the blurring of boundaries at the following levels of governance

- area based;
- local;
- sub-regional;
- regional;
- national;
- European.

leaves regeneration managers with choices, challenges and dilemmas in choosing which level to respond to and how to provide an account.

Accountability may be

- financial;
- political;
- regulatory by scrutiny or audit;
- managerial;
- administrative;
- professional;
- personal.

and the requirement to present an account to various stakeholders (to which we might add other agencies, such as private and civic agencies, quangos, citizens) clearly creates uncertainty. We would argue that transformative governance creates problems and tensions, not only between regeneration managers and other partners, but also between those managers working on competing or other initiatives, within or beyond the partnership, or organizational boundaries, but (what were traditionally considered to be) higher levels of governance, such as regional, national or European levels of governance. Regeneration managers continually have to make choices on whom they need to inform and communicate their decisions to, and what the mechanism, level and frequency of engagement should be. There are, we argue, statutory requirements to give an account and be responsible for actions, but regeneration managers are now expected to broaden their reporting or communication of what they do to a varied group of stakeholders. As the requirement to consult with stakeholders is enshrined in

171

guidance notes or new legislation, regeneration managers are placed in a position of developing mechanisms for doing so, but many may have little experience of the types of engagement, or have an understanding of the purposes or frequency of interaction.

In a very real sense managers are attempting to address the democratic deficit while at the same time gather evidence that they are providing good-quality service provision. However, many are experiencing difficulties in achieving true stakeholder participation or involvement in decision-making structures, due to the cost, officer time and other resources needed to do so.

As we discuss, the emerging forms of governance are not yet fixed and this fluidity adds to the gaps in accountability, as regeneration initiatives become the site of struggle for power and resources. Regeneration managers are continually navigating their way through the maze of existing accountability mechanisms, without a clear understanding (for few are forthcoming) of the new forms of accountability or reporting mechanism. Because new 'action spaces' exist at the area-based level, as well as at local, sub-regional and national levels, the potential for duplication has escalated. Moreover, as professionals, politicians and practitioners move between networks and partnerships, and promote or articulate the interests of their own agencies and the community, civic and voluntary sectors, the lines of responsibility and accountability become more complex. LSPs, CENs and NDCs have to be set beside other cross-agency partnerships and networks, all with their own forms of accountability.

As decisions are made inter- and intra-organizationally, with no real discernible shift in resources (despite the exhortations to mainstream), and as agencies share information and plans, and involve stakeholders, we can observe the tensions and challenges to traditional forms of accountability. For those managers at the heart of such initiatives we can see how they need to make sense of and align their understandings of existing forms of accountability with the uncertainty of, as yet ill-developed, new forms. As new 'action spaces' begin to develop and evolve new forms of accountability, practitioners need to seek clarity, and distinguish between those areas of activity where they are statutorily obliged to present a report and those where there is a level of discretion. They also need to understand how to present an account, and to which body, agency or individual. We argue that currently there is a lack of clarity on what must be communicated upon and reported to a variety of stakeholders, and until a clearer picture emerges, regeneration managers will perhaps continue to expend energy and resources on accounting for all activities to as many stakeholders as they can, when, in fact, if new clearer lines of accountability were developed the level of reporting might be significantly reduced.

The complexity of regeneration activities means that each professional regeneration manager will seek to limit the damage to their own organization, as initiatives intervene across known and defined boundaries. We argue that as each manager makes sense of what is needed and how an initiative will be delivered, they also have a sense of how and to whom they will be accountable. They will have an understanding of their own external reference points of accountable bodies. As they seek to achieve consensus on strategies, they must also come to an agreement on what the partnership (or their own sponsoring agency) is accountable for, and to whom. We want to argue that the complexity of accountability leaves scope for tensions, and that most regeneration managers will have an understanding (probably now out of date, or obsolete) based on their previous work experience of how they should account for their actions. As a consequence, they may resort to the more convenient and traditional mechanisms (based on reporting back to their agencies, or through hierarchical mechanisms to sub-regional, regional or national demands) but the demands placed upon them have changed. The goal posts on accountability are continually shifting.

Arguably, some of these mechanisms may have been superseded by, or augmented by, newer forms of accountability. If we are right in this assumption, then this enhances the case for training and staff development on new forms of accountability, and raises issues about who should be trained, and by what means. Should training be given just to professionals or practitioners, or broadened out to other participants? Should this be the responsibility of the sponsoring agency or the partnership? More significantly, do governance bodies at higher levels of authority have any responsibility to provide some new rules and regulations, or offer some guidance in these ambiguous areas?

As has been shown in Chapter 1, the NRS has recruited a significant number of 'advisers' to liaise with local initiatives, but we would suggest that little evidence exists to show that any training or expertise has been forthcoming on showing partners how to understand new systems of accountability. We argue that managers need more clarity on whom they are accountable to, for what, as well as the types of mechanisms and forms of reporting and communication beyond existing audit/reporting and regulatory systems.

The particular set of skills we suggest these managers need are as follows:

- Sharing best practice of their own internal systems of accountability with partners.
- Understanding new forms of scrutiny and accountability.
- Clarifying statutory and mandatory obligations.
- Identifying where there is scope for discretion.
- Varieties of stakeholder and the types of reporting mechanisms.
- New forms of communication and participation.

We are not suggesting that in some cases this sharing of best practice is not already happening, but we identify a clear need for embedding the transfer of such implicit knowledge more widely, in order to make it more explicit and understandable across agencies. There would be positive benefits associated with making explicit the implicit codes of behaviour, rules of engagement and types of scrutiny and accountability that participants must adhere to in their organizational settings, and if these became shared knowledge, this, we argue, would enhance the overall effectiveness of partnership working.

In a real sense then, in this chapter we seek to raise the issue of the dilemmas, challenges and choices regeneration managers are continually dealing with as they cope with the transformation from more traditional forms of accountability towards as yet not fully fledged new systems. Managers are being asked to make sense of new forms of scrutiny and accountability within new governance spaces of decision making, and as each of them comes to a partnership with their own preconceived ideas of who and what they are accountable for. We are demonstrating that existing knowledge is now threatened, as managers face more fluid and complex arrangements. We started from the assumption that existing knowledge may be insufficient to cope with the changing agenda, and that those who have worked in certain agencies with prescribed forms of accountability may be ill-prepared for the new challenges, as they are scrutinized and accountable to more stakeholders vertically and horizontally across sectors and boundaries. We suggest that many of the implicit types of accountability should be made more explicit, and there is a real need for training and expertise between agencies, and a responsibility on both sponsoring agencies and higher levels of governance to recognize the importance of this to improve the overall effectiveness of partnership working. The demands placed on regeneration managers are greater and the expectations to be accountable to a wider group of stakeholders make it imperative for training to be undertaken. Systems of accountability within organizations are changing, the need for personal and professional codes of conduct and appropriate behaviours are vital, but significantly, as we have argued, managers now operate in new 'action spaces' with limited guidance and fewer rules and regulations. It is therefore essential to provide adequate support and training.

We agree with Eden and Ackerman (1998: 7) that in the public sector issues of accountability need to be placed alongside the need for blueprints driven by

- Central government's determination to centralize control.
- The need to achieve efficiency savings and cut costs within a market economy.

To these we would add:

- The need to drive to increase customer satisfaction and stakeholder involvement in shaping service delivery.

And as Watson (2000: 5) suggests:

- Each public sector entity has special circumstances, rules, regulations and mandates governing activities.
- Some actors become powerless to act.
- Other actors need to motivate fellow participants and maintain morale in the face of cuts to budgets, dramatic changes to the external environment and increased scrutiny and accountability.

SUMMARY

This chapter has located the complexities of accountability, scrutiny and legitimacy within the new governance arrangements in the UK. Like many nation states, the UK has undergone massive transformation with the drive towards modernising its public services, and the traditional lines of accountability are ever more complicated, and are now as blurred as the boundaries within which state actors are exhorted to work alongside non-state actors.

The managerialist state based largely on neoliberal assumptions and business-like policies, both innovative and experimental, and reconfigured and re-engineered forms of governance fostered by the Blair administration and given expression through New Public Management, has replaced the traditional top-down, command hierarchies, but increased the ambiguities about which agencies or individuals should provide an account of activities, and to whom they must be accountable.

New arrangements in which state and non-state actors work together across organizational boundaries to achieve commonly agreed objectives have exposed gaps in institutional coverage and challenged the democratic legitimacy of both state and non-state actors, as scrutiny and accountability remain key unresolved issues at the heart of modernization of the UK state. As state officials now draw in personnel, resources and information from non-state actors and share 'democratic action spaces', the new relationships and responsibilities have altered democratic engagement and patterns of legitimacy.

Many of the problems facing the UK state cannot be solved solely by state agencies, and the multi-faceted social, economic and environmental nature of intractable problems, the rapidity of global changes, the escalation in citizen and consumer demands, and broader variety of partnerships have apparently become the new drivers of effective and efficient resource distribution. However, the need to encourage more creative and innovative ways of working and new approaches to problem solving have challenged how we view democratic legitimacy, scrutiny and accountability, by bringing them into sharper focus.

The chapter has argued that despite the ongoing conceptual debates surrounding democratic legitimacy, scrutiny and accountability, there is evidence to suggest that as the context of governance continues to change, and more and more state functions are contracted out, privatized or delivered by combinations of state and non-state actors or agencies, we need to rethink our views on legitimacy, scrutiny and accountability. While states continue to divest financial and managerial responsibilities and measure performance on market-driven criteria such as consumerism, competition, efficiency and value for money, questions remain on issues of equity and public interest.

It has been suggested that New Public Service or New Public Governance offer viable alternatives to counteract the dichotomous relationship between the traditional public administration and New Public Management. They would also provide a way of developing new forms of legitimacy, scrutiny and accountability. The emerging requirement for greater public participation in public service improvement enhances democratic citizenship, and models of community and civil society, and provides a model quite different to those traditional bureaucracies controlled top down

Both New Public Service and New Public Governance are viable alternatives to both the traditional and the dominant New Public Management, because both state and public sector organizations should be organized in such a way that public servants are not responsive to 'constituents and clients', nor to 'customers', but to 'citizens'. With citizens at the forefront, the emphasis in New Public Service should not be placed on either steering (New Public Management) or rowing (public administration) the governmental boat (Osborne and Gaebler 1992), but rather on building public institutions marked by integrity and responsiveness. Because accountability involves complex constellations of institutions and standards, there is a need to collaborate on shared decision making, but this must be based on a notion of strengthening democratic control and increased citizen involvement, as well as improving public trust in government institutions and types of services provided

DISCUSSION POINTS

By the end of this chapter we hope that you will be able to:

■ Determine what are the structures and systems present in your initiative to ensure accountability.
■ Map these structures and try to identify how governance is exercised.
■ Select one project and trace its progress (from development to implementation) and review how the systems and structures of accountability and scrutiny were played out. How effective were they?

CASE STUDY

An Environmental Services Partnership Concordat and accountability

A cross-boundary concordat partnership was established between three district authorities with the key objective of developing a joint approach to delivering high-quality, but cost-effective environmental services. Initially a core team, all senior environmental services officers, met to determine roles, responsibilities and future activities, while the political leaders made public statements in support of the venture. The local authority responsible for developing the idea of a concordat took the lead and provided the secretariat in the early stages. Over a period of 18 months the same core team of officers met regularly in each authority on a rotating basis, to share best practice and ensure consistency.

A firm of consultants was appointed to take an independent and objective assessment of the various procurement options available to the three collaborating authorities with regard to managing their waste management operations. This initiative was considered to be such an innovative and creative approach to service delivery across traditional organizational boundaries that the ODPM (Office of the Deputy Prime Minister) was keen to offer support, both financially and in other ways. There were a number of important barriers to overcome throughout the whole development process, including:

- Cultural and political issues.
- Financial aspects.
- Existing operating styles.
- Managing conflict.
- Risk assessment.
- Controlling and managing the project.
- The Boundary Commission (an impending report on local government reorganization).
- The suitability of existing accountability mechanisms.

This final barrier on whether or not existing mechanisms of accountability were appropriate for this type of cross-boundary working proved to be the greatest impediment as the project moved into its final stage, and led to its eventual collapse. After working together successfully for almost two years in a concordat relationship, with very harmonious relationships and most conflicts smoothed over, a decision had to be made on the setting up an arm's-length limited company to take the project ahead. This required substantial financial outlay and other resources from each authority as well as a commitment to second staff on a full-time basis for the first year of operation. The officers who had met together regularly in concordat meetings then began to make decisions on how the company should be constituted, organized and operated. Each had to take legal and financial advice from their

177

treasurer's and legal departments, and highlight any potential problems of operating in an arm's-length relationship to the sponsoring authorities. The issues of accountability then came to the fore, and when officers involved (from all three collaborating local authorities) were asked to say who they were accountable to, they chose the following (in no particular order of importance):

- General public, as the Council Tax payers and recipient of services.
- Own council members through the Cabinet.
- Own staff, because of a duty of care.
- Other collaborating local authorities.
- ODPM and other government funding agencies.
- District Audit and Audit Commission.
- Broader stakeholders such as businesses.
- Commercially, the companies from which services would be procured.

CHALLENGES, CHOICES AND DILEMMAS

All three collaborating authorities had recently instigated risk assessment strategies, and though the Local Government Act of 2000 encouraged partnership working across traditional boundaries, it became evident that this innovative project was doomed to failure owing to the lack of agreement on exactly what form, and to which body, the arm's-length company would be accountable. Council members from the lead local authority, although very supportive in the initial stages, began to get nervous when it came to spending large sums of Council Tax finance on this untested and experimental project. The idea of bringing together three small waste management and environmental services departments into a more strategic operation had the potential for greater efficiency and cost-effectiveness, but demonstrated that existing accountability mechanisms located within organizational boundaries were not sufficiently robust to deal with cross-boundary operations. The stakes were simply too high for the competing authorities and sharing good practice and collaboration were fine, but once there was a need to devote finance and other resources to such schemes, the importance of accounting for the use of these resources became paramount.

Chapter 8

An international dimension

KEY THEMES

- Impact of globalization.
- Learning from outside the UK.
- Restructuring of the public realm: lessons from other places.
- Reflecting on international experiences.

LEARNING POINTS

By the end of this chapter we hope that you will be able to:

- Identify the ways in which globalisation has shaped the regeneration of urban areas.
- Begin to identify whether the needs and practice of rural regeneration can 'learn' from the urban model.
- Reflect upon the ways in which UK policy and practice has been influenced by practice elsewhere.
- Begin to evaluate whether models of regeneration can be 'transplanted' from one locality to another.
- Think about how and in what ways your own experience and thinking has been influenced by practice outside the UK.

INTRODUCTION

Throughout this book we have focused on the practice and experience of those involved in regeneration management in the UK. This has been a deliberate choice on our part. While there are important lessons to be learnt (as we try to show below) from the choices made by others in Europe and North America the sheer scale and scope of these developments could be a book in itself! In this chapter we want to identify what seem to us to be the important points of difference and similarity. We have selected a number of specific examples for you to reflect upon and you will find these at the end of the chapter.

In this section of the book we want to introduce you to the ways in which the models of regeneration management adopted in the UK have been shaped by experience elsewhere and have over time contributed to a wider debate across Europe and between practitioners and policy makers.

SETTING A CONTEXT

While this chapter is intended to provide a context or a 'taster' of the debates and practice present within regeneration management outside the UK context, we can start by drawing very deliberate parallels between the UK and the USA.

In Chapter 1 we discussed the development of UK regeneration practice and we identified the introduction of the Urban Programme in the late 1960s as a key starting point. As Higgins *et al.* (1983) point out, the Urban Programme drew very significantly on the US War on Poverty initiative. Policy makers and civil servants went from the UK to visit their counterparts in Washington to 'learn' about the War on Poverty. There are a number of features of the Urban Programme which can be seen as a direct lift from the US experience.

The reasons for this policy transfer can be explained away by the following:

- The closeness of the UK and the USA after the Second World War.
- The assumption that both countries shared the same problems.
- The equal assumption that Europe had nothing to teach the UK.
- The belief that policy and practice transfer were easy to achieve.

In some ways we could argue that nothing has changed since the late 1960s except that the European Union is now seen as representing an opportunity to share learning and practice and does itself promote regeneration as a tool to address industrial and economic decline and social exclusion. Indeed we can include a number of key international agencies and organizations which now promote partnership and collaboration as a necessary feature of their practice. These agencies include the World Bank, IMF and OECD (2001).

To a large extent we want to suggest that the significance of the EU as a promoter of a particular model of urban regeneration has been underestimated over the past decade, and this applies, in the main, to those living in the UK. In the case of the UK, in particular this is in part because of:

- The ambivalent attitude of UK national governments to the 'value' of EU membership.
- The extent to which the work of the EU is understood within the UK.
- The capacity of practitioners and policy makers to 'learn' from the EU experience.

On the other hand, you may be aware of the ways in which (especially after 1997) key regional and city leaderships have actively sought to promote their relationship with the EU. This has become particularly evident in the ways English Regional Development Agencies have established a presence in Brussels to lobby for support. Indeed, prior to the creation of RDAs, most regions, notably the north-east and north-west, set up a Brussels office through consortia of local authorities, and welcomed the creation of the Committee of Regions to disseminate and share good practice on regeneration and other activities. It is, also, evident in the way the key cities across the UK have actively participated in EU initiatives which brought together urban and city regions.

GLOBALIZATION AND REGENERATION

There are a number of levels in which we can think about the relationship between 'globalization' and local regeneration initiatives. We have identified the following and you may wish to add others to our list. We think it is important to reflect upon the following (as a start):

- Globalization as a negative force which directly impacts upon local economic factors.
- Globalization as an agent of change in local, regional and national methods of governance, administration and management.
- Globalization as a catalyst for breaking national boundaries and the concept of the nation state.

The Westminster model no longer provides a comprehensive account of how the UK is governed and with a maxim 'what matters is what works' New Labour have created administrative arrangements at local, sub-regional and regional levels. John (2001) explains current governance as variegated, independent and experimental forms in which politicians, bureaucrats, interest groups and the public operate within an emerged internationalized economy and Europeanized polity. This form of governance is far removed from legitimately accepted economic compacts, bureaucratic routines, party hierarchies and political traditions of the period following the Second World War because flexible patterns of decision making and diverse, loose networks based on longevity have developed. He identified four key factors to explain the changes: (i) institutional reform created multiple levels of governance; (ii) a multiplicity of agencies and networks were necessary to carry out privatization and contracting out, whereas micro delivery required partnership; (iii) the requirement of long-term coalitions or regimes; and (iv) the capacity to transfer ideas between European states and the retreat of the state.

We discuss (briefly) each of these below.

Globalization as a negative force which directly impacts upon local economic forces

The experience of the UK over the past 30 years would suggest that the impact of globalization has been a negative experience. Arguably the 1970s/1980s provide real evidence of the ways in which processes of economic and industrial restructuring experienced in the UK were entirely negative.

Millions of jobs were lost in traditional industries and the rise in levels of unemployment, poverty and the decline in urban centres across the UK conceal individual and family stories of family breakdown, rises in drug and alcohol abuse, crime and social dislocation.

The very focus and purpose of this book is a reminder that the growth in UK urban regeneration is one consequence of these processes. Across the UK we can identify particular sub-regions and cities which have the direct impact of labour market restructuring and de-industrialization.

As such the impact of such changes can be looked at right across the population as a whole. No section of the population escaped the impact of these changes. They were either directly affected or bore indirect consequences of change. The legacy of these changes has informed current UK policies on education, training, policing, health and regeneration practice.

Globalization as an agent of change in local, regional and national methods of governance, administration and management

We have already discussed the ways in which regeneration management needs to be contextualized in a much broader and international debate (see Chapter 1). Here we want to make a slightly different point for you to consider. As Batley and Stoker (1991) have argued, we can make the link between economic and industrial global restructuring by thinking about local and national structures of governance as 'post-

Fordist'. At its most basic this suggests that in the UK the organizational form of governance and administration remained relatively stable over a long period. This is to say that as the role and responsibilities grew they were accommodated into a particular organizational form: the department. Services were developed, added to and absorbed into this model. They remained relatively immune from change. To some extent they reflected the model developed in traditional industries with:

■ relatively high levels of unionization;
■ clear levels of accountability and management;
■ known bureaucratic structures;
■ weak systems and processes to take account of users' needs;
■ cautious and risk-averse decision making.

Despite these negative features by the late 1970s and early 1980s a number of practitioners, policy makers and academics had identified ways in which change was not only necessary but could be introduced (Hambleton and Hoggett 1984). The introduction of decentralization or 'going local' initiatives within a significant number of UK local authorities illustrated this attempt to reform. They were influenced by changes in the private sector (Hoggett 1991).

The changes which were being promoted included:

■ challenges to unionization;
■ flatter hierarchies;
■ attempts to break down 'departmentalization';
■ greater user and community participation;
■ flexible forms of management.

We can see how, over the past 20 years, reforms of decision-making systems and bureaucratic forms of management have been replaced by more flexible forms of governance (Jackson and Stainsby 2000).

But we can, also, view the impact of globalization in a much more direct way on systems/structures of governance. As UK cities and regions experienced the negative impact of de-industrialization local government (in the period from 1979 to 1987) looked to respond to their local and particular experiences. While they were also adjusting to the ways in which the UK central government adjusted to these changes, at a local level strategies were being developed which explicitly promoted local solutions or placed a particular place and locality in direct competition with another locality (John 2001). Globalization in this sense accentuated differences and encouraged local/regional/national competition for investment and restructuring. As Le Gales and Harding (1998) argue, globalization creates opportunities and constraints for local political leaders and their coalitions as they choose appropriate policies for regeneration.

183

Globalization: as a catalyst for breaking down national boundaries and the nation state

If we have been through a process of change as defined and explained by Batley and Stoker (1991) then we are also in a period of transition from the nation state to the transnational. What do we mean by this? At its simplest we can see evidence of it in the way the EU has sought to create spaces and structures to direct funds to specific regions or in the way it facilitates greater city co-operation and urban collaboration.

We can see how the processes and practice of globalization move across and within national state boundaries with increasing flexibility. If regions seek to increase inward investment from large multinational corporations then they do so with the risk that such investment is for a relatively short time frame. There is also greater demand for the private sector to be involved in public decisions, and these new directions can circumvent the traditional mechanisms of representative democracy. In the era of greater competitiveness, policy makers and business representatives have to operate in more cut-throat and changeable national and international markets (John 2001: 11). The degree of changes to governmental forms across Europe varied between countries, but in the post-1980 period common features such as a reduction in the proactive role of government in the economy and society, diversification of decision making throughout a wide range of organizations and a restructuring of inter-governmental relationships became evident (Salet *et al.* 2003).

Regional agencies and urban centres need to be much 'freer' to enter into conversations with multinational organizations as well as having the capacity to learn from elsewhere.

It is this latter point that we now want to discuss.

LEARNING FROM OUTSIDE THE UK

We started this chapter by going back to the 1960s and the introduction of the Urban Programme by the then Labour government of Harold Wilson. We made the point that the Urban Programme had been significantly influenced by the War on Poverty initiative in the USA.

It is debatable whether the USA or the EU remains the more significant in terms of its influence on contemporary regeneration practice in the UK. We would suggest that it is now the case that:

- Regeneration practice has become 'normalized' and that it is possible to point to growing evidence of policy/practice transfer between the UK/EU, UK/USA and USA/UK.
- Policy transfer evidence is likely to relate to specific initiatives.
- Regeneration practice has become more 'uniform'.
- Regeneration practice has been influenced by transnational organizations.

Before we explore ways in which we think the above is the case it may be useful to identify ways in which the 'globalization' of the regeneration experience is evident in the UK.

While it is necessary to point to the ways in which the forces of globalization have shaped the UK experience, it is equally important to reflect upon how these forces are present elsewhere. To a large extent we can identify certain key features which are common in certain parts of the USA and Europe. In particular, we can say that regeneration initiatives are present when:

- Addressing levels of unemployment.
- Developing strategies to improve educational attainment levels in poor neighbourhoods.
- Making urban areas safe and environmentally friendly, by investment and through policing strategies.
- Reducing levels of crime and anti-social behaviour.
- Drawing in local community and voluntary sector agencies.

At the same time these strategies are, often, underpinned by seeking to reform the practice and 'culture' of public welfare agencies by:

- Developing area-based strategies.
- Designing 'targets' which these agencies/initiatives have to meet.
- Imposing reforms in the organization and structure of public agencies at the local level.
- Enhancing the status and decision-making process of area-based/neighbourhood teams.
- Breaking down inter-agency rivalries through establishing project teams to lead on initiatives.
- Securing private sector involvement through partnerships.
- Dedicating resources to improve the physical infrastructure.
- Anchoring such initiatives in the shadow of a major public/private investment.

While the experience may differ across the UK, USA and Europe over time we can see some or all of the above present in most urban regeneration initiatives. Whether we are looking at Barcelona (post the Olympics), Pittsburgh (in the USA) or Manchester, these processes are in place. They have been informed by a local urban 'crisis', which has brought local and regional agencies together with the private sector and, in the UK, the national government to address the particular problems which are presented.

In the UK throughout the 1980s (and beyond) these initiatives have often centred on the redevelopment of the urban/industrial core of the city as a prerequisite for the revival of the city. In the UK (in London and Liverpool specifically) these initiatives were based upon redeveloping the former waterfront/docklands areas of the cities. The 'waterfront' model is an example of 'borrowing' from the USA and Holland (Jacobs 2000). Such 'flagship' projects are seen as sending important messages to outside investors. They signal a commitment to redevelopment on a large scale but they are also about demonstrating the intent of those proposing the initiative that cities are 'safe' for inward investment and professional middle-class interests. We can see how the process of gentrification gets played out (and is encouraged) in regeneration initiatives. Alongside such projects investment usually follows in housing, schools, leisure and retail development. And in part this often leads to a uniformity of design, appearance and experience. On the back of such developments, whether on the site of such change or in the revival of the urban business and retail centres, comes the uniformity and predictability of specific global brands in retailing and the 'coffee bar' culture.

The key missing element in this process of change still remains the capacity to sustain such change and the extent to which those who were economically disposed through globalization are able to secure their presence in the regeneration experience.

RESTRUCTURING THE PUBLIC REALM

As we have already suggested, these changes are accompanied by changes in the way policies are decided, managed and monitored. We have outlined the ways in which partnership working and the involvement of third-sector agencies are central to the UK experience.

The experience outside the UK cannot be directly compared in the same way. There is a really important reason for this which we feel is critical in appreciating the extent to which policy/practice transfers can be 'read off' easily. There is a real danger that we miss the essential 'local' features which are present in each initiative. While it is the case that we can discern patterns of commonality in the forms of regeneration which are introduced and in the models of governance which are emerging, how they are experienced and understood by all participants will reflect *real* differences in culture, history, politics and the social and economic features of each locality.

It is the dynamics present in the complex inter-relationships between these factors which will shape the particular experience, and this will differ within nations as well as between cities/regions on a transnational basis. In a sense, when different actors/practitioners come together they need to be aware of the differences between them as well as potential similarities. These differences will be evident in some important respects:

■ Systems for governance.
■ Political/administrative systems.

- Scale and capacity of third-sector agencies.
- Rationale/catalyst for change.

These differences should not be underestimated. Our own view is that if they are put to one side and the focus for discussion is left to a specific policy initiative then only a small part of the potential benefit of such exchanges will be achieved.

The particular historical, political, cultural and economic features of each place need to be shared, discussed and understood if policy transfer lessons are to be of benefit.

We have identified below a number of lessons which have informed practice in the UK. You may wish to reflect upon these in the light of your own experience:

- The concept of the UK Sure Start programme was developed from the Head Start initiative in the USA which was created in 1965, and now has 19,000 centres across all states, with 900,000 children and at a cost of $7 billion per annum. The US programme is financed by direct federal funding (thus bypassing state legislatures), and despite some success, recent scrutiny has suggested some Head Start Programmes may not be adequately preparing children for school. Nevertheless, the UK government's approach to the introduction of the Sure Start initiative emulated the US funding model by bypassing local authorities as traditional service providers, preferring to fund programmes direct. It provided a real opportunity for partnership with local communities to meet need more effectively. The management function for the Sure Start initiative was through a central Sure Start Unit (SSU) which was established in London with the task of co-ordinating the service delivery plans and performance management of the trailblazers and the subsequent waves of Sure Start Programmes. The SSU was established under the auspices of the Department for Education and Skills (DfES) with a remit to draft aims, objectives and clear measurable outcome targets for each Sure Start Programme. Guidance notes set parameters around the aims and objectives for programmes, but partnerships were given freedom to design their own customized community service frameworks to meet central government targets. It was acknowledged in government circles that there was no quick solution to achieving the ambitious target to eradicate child poverty by 2020; consequently the Sure Start initiative was seen as long term with the lifespan of individual programmes expected to be 7 to 10 years.
- The UK Core Cities Programme is an ongoing attempt to study cities in a wider context, and drive urban renaissance and competitiveness at national and regional levels by drawing on European comparisons. It was a recognition by the UK government that social exclusion and environmental decline were hampering economic competitiveness, so a partnership of representatives from all nine RDAs, departments of central government (ODPM, Treasury,

187

DTI, Transport, Culture, Media and Sport) and eight UK core cities (Birmingham, Bristol, Leeds, Liverpool, Manchester, Newcastle, Nottingham and Sheffield) was established. The main aims were to determine:

- The characteristics and criteria of urban economic competitiveness
- Why some cities perform better than others
- What the policy implications are for partners at national, regional and local levels.

What we can see as a dominant mode of governance is the emergence of the partnership model accompanied by tangible reforms in the systems to support public welfare bureaucracies and the role of welfare/social professionals. It does seem to be the case that some of the features we identified above are embedding themselves at a local level:

- A decline in the significance of political institutions as the key site of decision making.
- An enhanced role for strategic and managerial decision making through local boards.
- An increase in stand-alone agencies to deliver services.
- A rise in the significance of local champions of cities – through the role of mayors (already a factor in the EU and USA).
- A much more decentralized and flexible system of decision making at the local level.
- The co-option of key public agencies into strategic decision making.

The longer-term impact of these changes is hard to evaluate. But we can speculate that it might include the following:

- Potential conflict between different agencies over strategic decision making.
- A political vacuum at the local level.
- Lack of accountability over stand-alone agencies.
- A democratic deficit at the local level.

You may want to think about your own knowledge and experience and reflect upon whether these changes/challenges are present in your area/neighbourhood.

SUMMARY

This chapter has tried to point to the ways in which regeneration initiatives and experience have been informed by practice outside the UK.

188

We have suggested that:

- Policy transfer is not straightforward.
- Models of regeneration do share similar features.
- The EU does occupy a significant role in facilitating regeneration initiatives in the UK.
- The impact of globalization has had a real effect on the economic and material experiences of regions and localities.
- Globalization has also affected the institutions of governance established to manage regeneration projects.

DISCUSSION POINTS

- Is globalization a myth or reality? What are the major consequences for urban and rural areas?
- What impact are global changes having on local, regional and national governance?
- Globalization has both positive and negative impacts upon localities. Assess some of the main ones, by drawing on your own experience of regeneration.
- Privatization of formerly publicly owned goods and services has had tremendous consequences for regeneration practices. Consider your own experiences of privatization within regeneration and examine some of the pluses and minuses.

SUGGESTED READING

Jackson, P. M. and Staisnby, L. (2000) 'The public manager in 2000: Managing public sector networked organisations', *Public Money and Management* 20 (January–March): 11–22

Jacobs, B. (2000) *Strategy and Partnership in Cities and Regions: Economic Development and Urban Regeneration in Pittsburgh, Birmingham and Rotterdam,* Basingstoke: Macmillan

Katz, B. (2004) *Neighbourhoods of choice and connection,* York: Joseph Rowntree Foundation (www.jrf.org.uk)

Le Gales, P. and Harding, A. (1998) 'Cities and States in Europe', *Western European Politics* 21(3): 120–145

OECD (2001) *Local partnerships for better governance,* Paris: OECD Publications

Salet, W., Thornley, A. and Kreukels, A. (2003) (eds) *Metropolitan Governance and Spatial Planning. Comparative Case Studies of European City-Regions,* London: Spon Press

Conclusion

Throughout this book we have attempted to argue that the present (and future) cohort of regeneration managers needs to draw upon a range of skills which are informed by more nuanced understanding of the local context to regeneration initiatives. In particular, we have tried to show that local initiatives which are shaped by an explicit relationship between local agencies and community-based groups are more likely to develop a more informed and subtle understanding of how there can be a negotiated match between what is available and what is expected, and in particular how the tensions between what local communities may want and what may be available (including statutory obligations) can be reconciled.

These processes are not easy or straightforward. In part they are dependent upon enhancing the 'capacity' of regeneration managers to cope successfully with the multiplicity of demands placed upon them. As we have shown, this can be addressed by the provision of appropriate training, staff development and a progression through a variety of courses (at differing levels) to better equip managers for their role.

But this approach only addresses one aspect of the complexities and challenges we have discussed. While we cannot assume that there will be significant changes in policy objectives, we have tried to illustrate the dilemmas and choices faced by regeneration professionals in terms of the way centrally determined initiatives are framed, understood, introduced and promoted.

There are still real and fundamental gaps in the way experience from one initiative is shared, reflected upon and used to inform practice. Much regeneration practice is shaped, in our view, by ambiguity and contradiction in terms of its expectations, the relationship initiatives have with practitioners, and the way regeneration professionals are expected to shift their priorities in response to the next initiative and target group.

It is not that evidence and/or experience does not exist but rather that the expectation that a 'holistic approach' is much easier to state than to achieve. There remain real absences in our collective understanding which make the type of collaborative work envisioned in the NRS still problematic. A number of factors militate against this. These include the quality of leadership at a local and regional level, the 'turf wars' between different agencies at all levels, the number of initiatives which create tensions, policy and practice uncertainty, and the shift in levels of understanding required by a new generation of managers.

It seems to us that there are some key features which can be summarized thus:

- Area-based initiatives restrict inclusiveness and impose spatial definitions of community or neighbourhood.
- Guidance and understanding of 'mainstreaming' remain problematic.
- 'Capacity building' derives from a deficit model of understanding and defining community needs.
- Equalities: an absence of consistent good practice.
- Sustainability and succession strategies.
- Multi-agency work and tackling the 'wicked issues'.
- Local partnerships.
- Negotiating models of governance and accountability.
- Emerging forms of leadership.

As we discuss these we would like you to match your experience against each area, and to allocate a weighting to each. Finally, we would like you to reflect upon what strategies you are going to adopt in order to address them.

Area-based initiatives restrict inclusiveness and impose spatial definitions of community or neighbourhood

As we have explored earlier, successive evaluations of UK regeneration policy have identified the 'area-based approach' as containing a number of weaknesses. For local regeneration managers the challenge is to look for ways of breaking out of the restrictions this places upon them. The spatial definition of a 'community' effectively defines which groups will be consulted and confers on these groups a legitimacy which may not be appropriate and/or agreeable to all partners.

While the Home Office (2003) has recommended alternative approaches in framing regeneration initiatives, the assumption appears to be that they are just one element of a process. The guidance they are considering includes:

- Enabling those communities living outside of a regeneration project to see themselves as beneficiaries of improvements.
- 'Twinning' projects in a wider locality so that lessons are shared as well as seeking to avoid 'more confusion'.
- Controlled flexibility in devising projects so that streets or parts of a neighbourhood outside the regeneration boundary directly benefit.

191

Such 'guidelines' will only be of benefit if they are supported by flexibility in the defining and monitoring of targets and in the way resources are directed – and in acknowledging the need to embed the social networks of practitioners who can help shape the measurements by which they are judged. But much more significantly they need to develop a more supportive environment within which local managers find themselves. Local managers, also, will need advice, guidance and support in enhancing their skills to address these innovations in project design and delivery.

Guidance and understanding of mainstreaming remains problematic

As the Neighbourhood Renewal Unit (2003) evaluation indicates, there are competing and conflicting definitions of 'mainstreaming'. This remains a real difficulty for local managers. Even if it is resolved, in principle, there will be a transitional phase as each project makes a case for being transferred to the core budget of a particular service at the local level. Clarifying the definition does not of itself ensure that projects, staff and good practice will be absorbed by the local agency identified as representing the 'home base' of such projects. Indeed we can anticipate that at a local level this debate will be fiercely contested. It is in these situations that local managers may feel vulnerable and defensive. So, while guidance is necessary it is by no means sufficient to ensure a smooth transition. On the contrary, what we might expect is an expansion of not-for-profit organizations and local community trusts as both local managers and local-community-based organizations look for alternative ways of financing their work. We can also assume that such an approach will be welcomed at both the local and central levels of government.

Capacity building derives from a deficit model of understanding and defining community needs

The government has embarked on a process of consultation in terms of developing a longer-term approach to 'capacity building' (Home Office 2003). Whatever the outcome of that consultation the underlying approach still remains the same. While it does seek to enhance the skill and knowledge base of local communities by investing and financing directly staff, organization and their infrastructure, it is essentially about enabling local organizations to 'fit' into the world of local government and local partnerships. In a sense it is about facilitating their accommodation into a highly technical and professional world. This should be welcomed. But it does not go far enough. As we have tried to show, it does not engage local professionals with a need to reflect upon their practice and the assumptions they bring to the 'table'. A policy which stressed the need for both would be one which raised

192

an alternative set of questions from the ones reflected in the official literature. Local managers do, however, have an opportunity to link into well-established national organizations which promote these approaches. The choice they face is whether to make themselves take up these ideas and so begin the reform process at their level of organizational responsibility. As a consequence they will begin to shape and influence their organization and their partner agencies.

Equalities: an absence of consistent good practice

Again the Neighbourhood Renewal Unit (2003) evaluation noted the absence of good practice on equalities across a number of regeneration initiatives. There are a number of centrally directed approaches to encouraging agencies to reflect upon their practice. Our concern is that some local managers do not appear to be part of these networks or that their local partnership boards do not seem to be giving this work the priority it should have. One approach for local managers might be to investigate the networks available through the voluntary sector or their RDA. A really useful starting point would be to consult The Equality Standard for Local Government in England (Speeden and Clarke 2002). The advantage of this model is that it is not a straightforward 'tick box' which a number of checklists or guide-lines appear to favour. It is more dynamic than this and requires local managers to reflect upon their practice, priority setting and resource allocation processes in order to assess themselves where they are, and where they need to be. More signif-icantly, its absence reveals not only a failure to address the issue, but also that 'good practice' in some areas is not being translated across. Given that successive regen-eration evaluations have highlighted this, we want to express our real concern that *all* managers need to address this basic of issues.

Sustainability and succession strategies

We have already noted how the language of environmental sustainability is one which has been transferred to the regeneration experience and in so doing means something quite different. In the context of managing a regeneration initiative it is about what happens after the project comes to an end and the staff associated with it have moved on. We remain concerned that while some of these issues are directly linked to the mainstreaming and capacity building debates, there is still a policy and practice vacuum for local managers. It is uncertain how and in what ways local managers are supported in their development of a succession strategy. On one level it is evident that it needs to be part of the initial planning process and that it cannot 'appear' in the final phase of an initiative. This is one area where at a regional or sub-regional level local managers can benefit from being 'twinned' with other projects at a different stage in the cycle so that knowledge and skills can be shared/transferred in order to inform or shape local discussions and decisions. This is an area where direct investment in supporting local managers by both the GOR and the RDAs would be of benefit. An essential part of this could include 'scenario planning', 'where to now?' and 'what if?' approaches.

Multi-agency work and tackling the 'wicked issues'

We think that it is important to restate that the primary focus on multi-agency working has to address those issues which go beyond the scope of any one agency or department. These so-called 'wicked issues' encompass anti-social behaviour, drugs, child protection and social exclusion. Regeneration initiatives because of their location occupy a potentially significant role in addressing and supporting work in these areas. The challenge for local managers is not that they have to be 'expert' in any of these areas but that they seek to define the practice of their initiative within a context which supports locally based projects outside their line management responsibility. In other words, multi-agency working, while it will doubtless inform much of what happens within a neighbourhood regeneration initiative, must also be linked to practice outside the scope and remit of the initiative. Membership of local networks and task groups can consume the working life of most local managers. Setting priorities and clarifying their role is a central set of tasks for any local manager. But equally important is the need to 'keep up to speed' with local information and intelligence. Regeneration initiatives may therefore be ideally placed to host and to facilitate other agencies or groups of agencies in their work. It is here that we can see the relevance of local and political knowledge as a way of informing local managers on issues which are beyond the direct remit of their initiative but nonetheless shaping the lives and experiences of local communities. In addition, local managers (if supported) are well placed to develop local evaluation networks by drawing higher education, further education and the voluntary sector into collaborative activity. This would enhance the research capacity of local partnerships and strengthen their hand in regional forums.

Local partnerships

We have examined the real and potential significance of local partnerships for managers. These partnerships, whether confined to specific projects or the newly formed LSPs, occupy important points of contact, accountability and information for local managers. Local partnership boards have, as we have noted, an uneven history. Their experience will vary depending upon a range of variable factors. As a first task local managers will need to reflect upon the capacity and strength of their partnership as part of their initial assessment of their initiative. We know that some partnership boards will be 'weak' and dysfunctional. But local managers will have to invest their time in developing and building upon the capacity of their local board if their initiative is to have credibility within their local community. Equally

194

local managers will need to be able to develop a good working relationship with their board if they feel it is too assertive. Again we might look to GOR, the RDAs or other external agencies to provide support and advice. Local managers will also need to be aware of the political/professional dynamics contained with LSPs if they are able to negotiate a positive relationship with them. The knowledge base and skills set which local managers need to support them in this work will go beyond 'conventional' regeneration management skills. We have argued, in this book, that while practitioners acknowledge the importance of enhancing these technical skills, project management skills and strategic decision-making skills, it is these political/negotiating skills which need to be of equal status in the current environment. They also need to be actively reflecting upon the policy and practice relationship between local, regional, national and European initiatives.

Negotiating models of governance and accountability

We have already noted the complexities of decision making, accountability and governance which are inherent in regeneration management. In particular there is a real open debate on the role of locally elected councillors which either directly or indirectly will affect local regeneration initiatives. Even formal structures reveal these complexities and if we add additional layers or interested constituencies the complexity grows. We can identify LSPs, local community networks as well as neighbourhood-based voluntary organizations. Given the proliferation of networks and the ambiguities associated with them in terms of their status, ability to take decisions and shape policy, local managers need to be aware of not only the formal structures but also the informal ones too. It is this complexity and the ways in which experience is shared, understood and acted upon which accentuate the pressures felt by local managers. A key task for any local managers, we suggest, is to seek out the 'critical friend' to provide informed advice and to act as a sounding board as they seek to manage their initiative and try to make a difference.

Emerging forms of leadership

The complexities of governance are, also, reflected in the competing sites of leadership and decision making evident within regeneration initiatives. While issues of governance and accountability are inextricably linked to who exercises a 'leadership role', we can also observe new forms of leadership emerging. In the context of LSPs, for example, the role and capacity of local community networks to influence and to shape local decision making remains unclear. In those places with well-supported networks it is possible to anticipate that they will seek to exercise a greater influence over time. Additionally the diversity of local initiatives (some may say their complexity) may reveal new models of leadership as roles and responsibilities are shared and divided. The role and function of regeneration

195

managers within the process of multi-agency partnerships suggests that they will occupy a significant influence in the day-to-day delivery of specific programmes. But it is likely that they will find themselves acting as a local broker or facilitator bringing together different partners at different times. The need to be adaptable and flexible will increase and their importance as holders of local 'knowledge' will become ever more evident.

These challenges and choices do present real dilemmas for local managers. The potential to act as change agents within a highly contested environment is there. We feel passionately that local managers have an opportunity to make a significant difference at the local level. They occupy a key and strategic role. The challenge for future managers is to seek to work in ways which give personal and professional satisfaction but also to place some of these debates within a wider context which shifts the boundaries of decision making to a wider community of practitioners and residents.

Bibliography

Alford, J. (2001) 'The implications for "publicness" for strategic management theory', in Johnson, G. and Scholes, K., *Exploring Public Sector Strategy,* Harlow: Pearson Education, 3–9

Alkhafaji, A. F. (1989) 'A stakeholder approach to corporate governance. Managing in a dynamic environment and strategies for assessing and managing organisational stakeholders', *Academy of Management Executive* 5: 61–75

Aristotle (2000) *The Politics,* Book 4, Section 3 (Open University Strategy Guides)

Arnstein, S.R. (1969) 'A Ladder of Citizen Participation', *Journal of the American Institute of Planners* 35: 216–224

Atkinson, P. (1998) 'Countering Urban Social Exclusion: The Role of Community Participation and Partnership', in Griffiths, R. (ed.), *Social Exclusion in Cities: The Urban Policy Challenge,* Occasional Paper 3, University of the West of England

Attwood, M., Pedler, M., Pritchard, S. and Wilkinson, D. (2003) *Leading change: A guide to whole systems working,* Bristol: Policy Press

Audit Commission (1989) *A Fruitful Partnership: Effective Partnership Working,* London: Audit Commission

Bachrach, P. and Baratz, M. S. (1962) 'The two faces of power', *American Political Science Review* 56(3): 947–952

Bachrach, P. and Baratz, M. (1970) *Power and Poverty: Theory and Practice,* Oxford: Oxford University Press

Baddeley, S. and James, K. (1987) 'Owl, Fox, Donkey or Sheep? Political Skills for Managers', *Management Education Development* 18(1): 3–19

Balloch, S. and Taylor, M. (eds) (2001) *Partnership Working: Policy and Practice,* Bristol: Policy Press

Banks, S. and Shenton, F. (2001) 'Regenerating Neighbourhoods: A Critical Look at the Role of Community Capacity Building', *Local Economy* 16(4): 286–298

Banks, S., Butcher, H., Henderson, P. and Robertson, J. (eds) (2003) *Managing Community Practice*, Bristol: Policy Press

Barnett, R. (1998) ' "In" or "For" the Learning Society?', *Higher Education Quarterly* 52: 7–21

Batley, R. and Stoker, G. (eds) (1991) *Local Government in Europe*, London: Macmillan

Behn, R. D. (1988) 'Managing by Groping Along', *Journal of Policy Analysis and Review* 7(4): 643–663

Bennett, R. (1996) *Corporate strategy and business planning,* London: Pitman

Bockholt, P. (2002) Panel contribution to the European Trend Chart on Innovation, Trend Chart Policy Benchmarking Workshop, Improving Trans-National Policy Learning in Innovation, Luxembourg, 27–28 November. Available online: http://trendchart.cordis.lu/Benchmarking/index.cfm?

Boddy, M. and Fudge, C. (eds) (1984) *Local Socialism?,* London: Macmillan

Bogason, P. (2000) *Public policy and local government: institutions in post-modern society*, New Horizons in Public Policy Series, Cheltenham: Edward Elgar

Booth, M. (1997) 'Community Development: Oiling the Wheels of Participation', *Community Development Journal* 32(2)

Bovaird, T. and Loeffler, E. (eds) (2003) *Public Management and Governance*, London: Routledge

Brinkerhoff, D. W. (1999) 'Exploring State–Civil Society Collaboration: Policy Partnerships in Developing Countries', *Nonprofit and Voluntary Sector Quarterly* 28(Supplement 1): 59–86

Brownhill, S. and Darke, J. (1998) *Rich Mix: Inclusive Strategies for Urban Regeneration*, Bristol: Policy Press

Bryson, J. M. (1988) 'Strategic Management in Public and Voluntary Services: A Reader', *Best of Long Range Planning,* Second Series, Volume 4, Pergamon Press

Bryson, J. M. (1995) *Strategic Planning for Public and Non-Profit Organisations*, San Francisco: Jossey-Bass

Burgess, P., Hall, S., Mawson, J. and Pearce, G. (2001) *Devolved approaches to local governance*, York: Joseph Rowntree Foundation

Burns, D. (1991) 'Ladders of Participation', *Going Local* 18

Burns, D. and Taylor, M. (2000) *Auditing Community Participation*, Bristol: Policy Press

Burns, D., Hambleton, R. and Hoggett, P. (1994) *The Politics of Decentralisation: Revitalising Local Democracy*, London: Macmillan

Byrne, D. (2001) *Social Exclusion*, Buckingham: Open University Press

Cabinet Office (2003) *Innovation in the Public Sector,* Discussion Paper, October: 2–30

Cabinet Office and DLTR (2002) *Your Region: Your Choice*, Norwich: Stationery Office

Cantle, T. (2002) *The Report of the Community Cohesion Review Team*, London: Home Office

Carley, M. (2002) *Community Regeneration and Neighbourhood Renewal: A review of the evidence*, Edinburgh: Communities Scotland

Carroll, A. B. (1989) *Business and Society: Ethics and Stakeholder Management*, Cincinnati: South Western Press

Carter, A. (2000) 'Strategy and Partnership in Urban Regeneration', in Roberts, P. and Sykes, H., *Urban Regeneration: A Handbook*, London: Sage

Chanan, G. (1997) *Active Citizenship and Community Involvement* Luxembourg: Office for Official Publications of the European Communities

Channon, DF. (1973) *The strategy and structure of British Enterprise*, London: Macmillan

Chapman, R. A. (1993) 'Governance, Scrutiny and Accountability: Ethics in the public sector', *Politeia* 12(2): 28–42

Clarke, J. (2003) 'Scrutiny through inspection and audit', in Bovaird, T. and Loeffler, E. (eds), *Public Management and Governance*, London: Routledge

Clarke, J. (2004) 'Dissolving the Public Realm? The Logic and Limits of Neo-liberalism', *Journal of Social Policy* 33(1): 27–48

Clarkson, M. (1994) 'A risk based model of stakeholder theory', in *Proceedings of the Second Toronto Conference on Stakeholder Theory*, Centre for Corporate Social Performance & Ethics, Toronto: University of Toronto Press

Clarkson, M. B. E. (1995) 'A stakeholder framework for analysing and evaluating corporate social performance', *Academy of Management Review* 20: 92–117

Clegg, S. R. (1989) *Frameworks of Power*, London, Sage

Cmnd 5237 (2001) *Strong Local Leadership-Quality Public Services*, London: HMSO

Coaffee, J. and Healey, P. (2003) 'My Voice: My Place: Tracking Transformations in Urban Governance', *Urban Studies*, 40(10): 1979–1999

Cockburn, C. (1977) *The Local State: Management of Cities and People*, London: Pluto Press

Colenutt, B. and Cutten, A. (1994) 'Community empowerment in vogue or vain', *Local Economy* 9(3): 236–250

Coote, A. and Leneghan, J. (1997) *Citizens Juries: Theory into Practice*, London: IPPR

Cope, S. and Goodship, J. (1999) 'Regulating Collaborative Government: Towards Joined Up Government', *Public Policy and Administration* 14(2): 3–16

Cope, S. and Goodship, J. (2001) 'The Audit Commission and Public Services: Delivering for Whom?', *Public Money and Management* 22(4): 33–40

Cornell, B. and Shapiro, A. C. (1987) 'Corporate stakeholders and corporate finance', *Financial Management* 16: 5–14

Craig, G. and Taylor, M. (2002) 'Dangerous Liaisons: Local government and the voluntary and community sectors', in Glendinning, C., Powell, M. and Rummery, K. (eds), *Partnerships, New Labour and the Governance of Welfare*, Bristol: Policy Press

Crocker, S. (2001) *Competences for local and regional development*, High Wycombe: Institute of Economic Development

Dabinett, G., Lawless, P., Rhodes, J. and Tyler, P. (2001) *A Review of the Evidence Base for Regeneration Policy and Practice*, London: DETR

Dale, P. (2002) *At the Starting Blocks – Community Involvement in Local Strategic Partnerships*, London: CDF

Danson, M. W. and Lloyd, M. G. (1992) 'The erosion of a strategic approach to planning and economic regeneration in Scotland', *Local Government Policy Making* 19(1): 46–54

Denhardt, R. B. and Denhardt, J. V. (2000) 'The new public service: serving rather than steering', *Public Administration Review* 60(6): 549–559

DETR (1998) *Modernising Local Government*, London: HMSO

DETR (1999) *Local Leadership, Local Choice*, London: HMSO

DETR (2000) *Out towns and cities, the future*, CMN 4911, London: HMSO

De Wit, B. and Meyer, R. (1999) *Strategy Synthesis: Blending Conflicting Perspectives to Create Competitive Advantage*, London: Thomson Learning

De Wit, B. and Meyer, R. (2003) *Strategy: Process, content and context, an International Perspective*, 2nd edition, London: Thomson Business Press

Diamond, J. (1990) 'Local socialism as decentralisation: A study of the Neighbourhood Services Initiative in Manchester 1984–1988', PhD thesis, University of Salford

Diamond, J. (2001) 'Managing change or coping with conflict', *Local Economy* 16(3): 272–285

Diamond, J. (2002a) 'Decentralisation: New Forms of Public Participation or New Forms of Managerialism', in Mclaverty, P. (ed.), *Public Participation and Innovations in Community Governance*, Aldershot: Ashgate, 123–140

Diamond, J. (2002b) 'Strategies to resolve conflict in partnerships', *International Journal of Public Sector Management* 15(2): 296–306

Diamond, J. (2004) 'Capacity Building – for What?', *Community Development Journal* 39(2): 296–306

Diamond, J. and Liddle, J. (2003) 'Regional Governance: Some Unresolved Issues', *Public Policy and Administration* 18(2): 106–116

Diamond, J., Speeden, S., Cuff, M. and Loftus, C. (1997) 'Lessons from Performance Review', *Local Government Policy Making* 23(5): 27–30

Doherty, T. and Horne, T. (2002) *Managing Public Services*, London: Routledge

Donaldson, T. and Preston, L. (1995) 'The stakeholder theory of the corporation: concepts, evidence and implications', *Academy of Management Review* 20(1): 65–91

Duncan, P. and Thomas, S. (2000) *Neighbourhood Regeneration: Resourcing Community Involvement*, Bristol: Policy Press

Durham City Leisure Strategy (2003) Town Hall, Durham City

Eden, C. and Ackerman, F. (1998) 'Making strategy', in *Journey of Strategic Management,* London: Sage

Elcock, H. (2001) *Political Leadership*, Aldershot: Edward Elgar

European Trend Chart on Innovation, Trend Chart Policy Benchmarking Workshop, Improving Trans-National Policy Learning in Innovation, Luxembourg, 27–28 November 2002. Available online: http://trendchart.cordis.lu/Benchmarking/index.cfm?

Evan, W. M. and Freeman, R. E. (1988) 'Stakeholder theory of the modern corporation: Kantian capitalism', in Beauchamp, T. L. and Bowie, N. (eds), *Ethical Theory and Business*, Englewood Cliffs, NJ: Prentice Hall, 75–84

Fainstein, N. and Fainstein, S. (eds) (1982) *Urban Policy under Capitalism*, Beverly Hills, CA: Sage

Fainstein, S., Fainstein, N., Hill, R., Judd, D. and Smith, M. (1986) *Retrenching the American City*, New York: Longman

Filkin, G., Allen, E. and Williams, J. (2001) *Starting to Modernise: The change agenda for local government*, London: New Local Government Network

Freeman, R. E. (1984) *Strategic management: a stakeholder approach*, Boston: Pitman

Freeman, R. E. and Evan, W. M. (1990) 'Corporate governance: a stakeholder interpretation', *Journal of Behavioural Economics* 19: 337–359

Friend, J. K., Power, J. M. and Yewlett, C. J. L. (1974) *Public Planning: The Intercorporate Dimension*, London: Tavistock

Froud, J., Haslam, C., Suckdev, J., Shaoul, J. and Williams, K. (1996) 'Stakeholder Economy? From Utility Privatisation to New Labour', *Capital and Class* 60(Autumn): 119–134

Frost, R. (1995) 'The use of stakeholder analysis to understand ethical and moral issues in the Primary Resource Centre', *Journal of Business Ethics* 14(8): 653–661

Fulop, L. and Linstead, S. (1999) *Management – A Critical Text*, Basingstoke: Macmillan Business Press

Gaster, L. (1995) *Quality in Public Services*, Buckingham: Open University Press

Geddes, M. (1997) *Partnerships against poverty and exclusion*, Bristol: Policy Press

Glendinning, C., Powell, M. and Rummery, K. (eds) (2002) *Partnerships, New Labour and the Governance of Welfare*, Bristol: Policy Press

Goldsmith, A. A. (1997) 'Private sector experience with strategic management: cautionary tales for public administration', *International Review of Administrative Sciences* 63: 25–40

Gordon, R. D. (2002) 'Conceptualising leadership with respect to its historical-contextual antecedents to power', *Leadership Quarterly* 13: 151–167

Goss, S. (2001) *Making Local Governance Work*, Basingstoke: Palgrave

Government Office NE (2003) *A Skills and Knowledge Programme, 2002/3 by the NRU/SEU Source*

Grant, R. M. (1997) *Contemporary strategic analysis, concepts, techniques applications*, 2nd edition, Oxford: Blackwell

Gray, A. and Jenkins, W. (2001) 'Government and Administration: The Dilemmas of Delivery', *Parliamentary Affairs: A Journal of Comparative Politics* 54(2): 206–222

Gray, A. G. (1998) *Business-like but not like a business: The challenge for public management*, London: Public Finance Foundation/CIPFA

Greener, I. (2001) 'Social Learning and Macroeconomic policy in Britain', *Journal of Public Policy* 21(2): 133–152

Grint, K. (1997) *Fuzzy Management Contemporary Ideas and Practices at Work*, Oxford: Oxford University Press

Gyford, J. (1985) *The Politics of Local Socialism*, London: Allen and Unwin

Hall, P. (1993) 'Policy paradigms: Social learning and the State', *Comparative Politics* April: 275–296

Hambleton, R. and Hoggett, P. (eds) (1984) *The Politics of Decentralisation: Theory and Practice of a Radical Local Government*, Working Paper 46, School for Advanced Urban Studies, Bristol

Hartley, J. (1998) *Leading Communities*, London: Local Government Management Board

Hastings, A., McArthur, A. and McGregor, A. (1996) *Less than Equal: Community Organisations and Estate Regeneration Partnerships*, Bristol: Policy Press

Hax, A. (1990) 'Defining the concept of strategy and the strategy formation process', *Planning Review* May–June: 34–40

Hax, A. C. and Majluf, N. S. (1994) *Strategic Management: An integrative perspective*, Harlow: Prentice Hall

Hay, C. and Richards, D. (2000) 'The tangled webs of Westminster and Whitehall: The discourse, strategy and practice of networking within the British Core Executive', *Public Administration* 78(1): 1–28

Henderson, P. and Mayo, M (1998) *Training and Education in Urban Regeneration*, Bristol: Policy Press

Higgins, J., Deakin, N., Edwards, J. and Wicks, M. (1983) *Government and Urban Poverty*, London: Blackwell

Hill, C. W. L. and Jones, T. M. (1992) 'Stakeholder–Agency Theory', *Journal of Management Studies* 29(2): 131–154

Hirst, P. (1997) *From statism to pluralism*, London: UCL Press

Hoggett, P. (1991) 'A New Management in the Public Sector', *Policy and Politics* 19(4): 143–156

Hoggett, P. (ed.) (1997) *Contested Communities*, Bristol: Policy Press

Holden, A. (2002) 'Bomb Sites: The politics of opportunity', in Peck, J. and Ward, K. (eds), *City of Revolution*, Manchester: Manchester University Press

Home Office (2003) *Policing: Building Safer Communities Together*, London: Stationery Office

Home Office Active Community Unit (2001) *Learning from Action, Learning for Change*, May

House of Commons, Public Administration Select Committee (2003–4) *A Draft Civil Service Bill: Completing the Reform. First Report of Session 2003–4*, Volume One, London: Stationery Office

Hughes, O. (2003) *Public management and administration: An introduction*, Basingstoke: Palgrave

Hutchinson, J. (2001) 'The Meaning of Strategy for Area Regeneration', *International Journal of Public Sector Management* 14(3): 265–274

Hutton, W. (1997) *The state to come*, Chatham: Vintage

Huxham, C. and Vangen, S. (2000) 'What makes partnerships work?', in Osbourne, S. (ed.), *Public–Private Partnerships*, London: Routledge

Improvement and Development Agency (2001) *Benchmark of the 'ideal' local authority*, 3rd edition, August. Available online: www.idea.gov.uk

Imrie, R. and Raco, M. (eds) (2003) *Urban Renaissance? New Labour, community and urban policy*, Bristol: Policy Press

Jackson, M. (2001) 'Public Sector Added Value: Can bureaucracy deliver?', *Public Administration* 79(1): 5–28

Jackson, P. M. and Stainsby, I. (2000) 'The public manager in 2000: Managing public sector networked organisations', *Public Money and Management* 20: January

Jacobs, B. (2000) *Strategy and Partnership in Cities and Regions: Economic Development and Urban Regeneration in Pittsburgh, Birmingham and Rotterdam*, Basingstoke: Macmillan

Jacobs, B. and Dutton, C. (2000) 'Social and Community Issues', in Roberts, P. and Sykes, M. (eds), *Urban Regeneration: A Handbook*, London: Sage

John, P. (2001) *Local governance in Western Europe*, London: Sage

Johnson, C. and Osborne, S. P. (2003) 'Local Strategic Partnerships, Neighbourhood Renewal and the Limits of Co-Governance', *Public Money and Management*, July: 147–154

Johnson, G. and Scholes, K. (1993) *Exploring corporate strategy: Text and cases*, Harlow: Prentice Hall

Johnson, G. and Scholes, K. (2003) *Exploring corporate strategy: Text and cases*, 4th edition, Harlow: Prentice Hall

Johnston, G. and Percy-Smith, J. (2003) 'In search of social capital', *Policy and Politics* 31(3): 321–334

Jones, G. W. (1992) 'The search for accountability', in Leach, S. (ed.), *Strengthening local government in the 1990s*, London: Longman, 73

Joseph Rowntree Foundation (2002) *Networking Across Regeneration Partnerships*, York

Jowitt, A. and Chapman, J. (2001) 'Community Leaders and Community Regeneration:

A pilot project for neighbourhood renewal', Paper presented to the 5th Learning and Skills Research Conference, University of Cambridge, 6–7 December

Joyce, P. (1999) *Strategic management for the public services*, Buckingham: Open University Press

Joyce, P. (2000) *Strategy in the public sector*, Chichester: John Wiley & Sons

Kanter, R. M. (1994) 'Collaborative advantage: The art of alliances', *Harvard Business Review* July/August: 96–112

Kanter, R. M. (1995) *World class: Thriving in a global economy*, New York: Simon and Schuster, 151–160

Katz, B. (2004) *Neighbourhoods of choice and connection*, York: Joseph Rowntree Foundation

Kellerman, B. and Webster, S.W. (2001) 'The recent literature on public leadership reviewed and considered', *Leadership Quarterly* 12: 485–514

Langtry, B. (1994) 'Stakeholders and the moral responsibilities of business', *Business Ethics Quarterly* 4: 431–443

Lawless, P. (1996) *Urban Partnership in the Mid 1990s: The Evolving Nature of Urban Governance in Sheffield*, Sheffield: CRESR

Leach, R. and Percy-Smith, J. (2001) *Local Governance in Britain*, Basingstoke: Palgrave

Leach, S. and Norris, D. F. (2003) 'Elected mayors of England: A contribution to the debate', *Public Policy and Administration*, 17(1): 21–39

Leach, S. and Wilson, D. (1998) 'Voluntary Groups and Local Authorities: Rethinking the Relationship', *Local Government Studies* 24(2)

Leach, S. and Wilson, D. (2000) *Local Political Leadership*, Bristol: Policy Press

Leach, S., Davis, H. *et al.* (1996) *Enabling or Disabling Local Government*, Buckingham: Open University Press

Leadbeater, C. (2003) *The man in the caravan and other stories*, London: Improvement and Development Agency, 135–177

Leavy, B. and Wilson, D. (1994) *Strategy and Leadership*, London: Routledge

Le Gales, P. and Harding, A. (1998) 'Cities and States in Europe', *Western European Politics* 21(3): 120–145

Liddle, J. (2001) 'RDAs, Sub-Regional Partnerships and Local Regeneration', *Local Economy* 16(4): 312–323

Liddle, J. and Townsend, A. T. (2003) 'Reflections on the development of Local Strategic Partnerships: Key emerging issues', *Local Governance* 29(1): 37–54

Lindblom, C. (1959) 'The science of muddling through', *Public Administration Review* 2: 79–89

Local Government Information Unit (LGIU) (2003) *Advice on Community Cohesion and Area Based Initiatives*, Steer Policy Briefing

Lowndes, V., Nanton, P., McCabe, A. and Skelcher, C. (1997) 'Networks, partnerships and urban regeneration', *Local Economy* 11(4): 333–343

Lukes, S. (1974) *Power: A Radical View*, London: British Sociological Society (Macmillan reprint)

Luxembourg Conference (2002) The European Trend Chart on Innovation, Trend Chart Policy Benchmarking Workshop, Improving Trans-National Policy Learning in Innovation, Luxembourg, 27–28 November. Available online: http://trendchart.cordis.lu/Benchmarking/index.cfm?

Maddock, S. (2002) 'Making modernisation work: new narratives, change strategies and people management in the public sector', *International Journal of Public Sector Management* 15(1): 13–44

Mayo, M. (1997) 'Partnerships for Regeneration and Community Development', *Critical Social Policy* 52: 3–26

Mayo, M. and Taylor, M. (2001) 'Partnerships and Power in Community Regeneration', in Balloch, S. and Taylor, M. (eds), *Partnership Working*, Bristol: Policy Press

McGarvey, N. (2001) 'Accountability in Public Administration: A Multi-Perspective Framework for Analysis', *Public Policy and Administration* 16(2): 17–28

McInroy, N. (2001) 'A New Regeneration Agenda', *Local Work* 30

Miliband, D. (1999) 'This is a modern world', *Fabian Review* 111(4): 11–13

Mintzberg, H. (1987) 'Crafting strategy', *Harvard Business Review* July–August: 66–75

Mintzberg, H. (1990) 'The Design School: Reconsidering the Basic Premise of Strategic Management', *Strategic Management Journal* 11

Mintzberg, H (1997) 'Patterns of Strategy Formation', *Management Science* May: 34

Mintzberg, H., Ahlstrand, B. and Lampel, J. (1998) *Strategy Safari*, Harlow: Prentice Hall Europe

Mitchell, R., Agle, B. and Wood, D. (1997) 'Toward a Theory of Stakeholder Identification and Salience: Defining the Principle of Who and What Really Counts', *Academy of Management Review* 22(4): 853–884

Moran, M. (2000) 'The Frank Stacey Memorial Lecture: From Command State to Regulatory State', *Public Policy and Administration* 15(4): 1–14

Morgan, G. (1998) *Images of Organisations*, London: Sage

Mudd, J. (1984) *Neighbourhood Services: Big Cities Work*, Chicago: Chicago University Press

Mulgan, R. (2000) 'Accountability: An ever expanding concept', *Public Administration* 78(3): 555–573

Mumford, M. D., Connelly, S. and Blaine, G. (2003) 'How creative leaders think: Experimental findings and cases', *Leadership Quarterly* 14: 411–432

Neighbourhood Renewal Unit (2003) *New Deal for Communities – The National Evaluation Annual Report*, Research Report 7

205

Neighbourhood Renewal Unit (2004) 'Neighbourhood Renewal Delivery Skills', ODPM, April

Neighbourhood Renewal Unit, Skills and Knowledge. Available online: http://www.neighbourhood.gov.uk/sandk.asp?pageid=36

Nevin, B., Loftman, P. and Beazley, M. (1997) 'Cities in Crisis – Is Growth the Answer? An analysis of the outcome of the first and second round of the SRB Challenge Fund', *Town Planning Review* 68(2)

Newman, J. (2001) *Modernising Governance: New Labour, Policy and Society*, London: Sage

Noordegraf, M. (2000) 'Professional sense makers: managerial competencies amidst ambiguities', *International Journal of Public Sector Management* 13(4): 319–332

Norman, R. (2003) *Obedient servants? Management freedoms and accountabilities in the New Zealand Public Sector*, Victoria: University Press

North, P. (2001) 'Conflict within regeneration partnerships: a help or hindrance?', Paper delivered at the Second Regeneration Management Research Workshop, University of Durham Business School, 7 November

North, P. (2003) 'Communities at the heart? Community action and urban policy in the UK', in Imrie, R. and Raco, M. (eds), *Urban Renaissance? New Labour, community and urban policy*, Bristol: Policy Press

NRU (2002) *The Learning Curve*. Available online: www.nru.gov.uk

Nutt, P. C. and Backoff, R. W. (1992) *Strategic Management of Public and Third Sector Organisations*, San Francisco: Jossey-Bass

Nutt, P. C. and Backoff, R. W. (1993) 'Transforming public organisations with strategic management and strategic leadership', *Journal of Management* 19(2): 201

OECD (2001) *Local partnerships for better governance*, Paris: OECD Publications

Osborne, D. and Gaebler, T. (1992) *Re-inventing Government: How the Entrepreneurial Spirit is transforming the Public Sector*, Reading, MA: Addison-Wesley

Parna, O. (2002) Panel contribution to the European Trend Chart on Innovation, Trend Chart Policy Benchmarking Workshop, Improving Trans-National Policy Learning in Innovation, Luxembourg, 27–28 November. Available online: http://trendchart.cordis.lu/Benchmarking/index.cfm?

Partnership 10 Initiative in Teesside, unpublished programme

Pearce, G. and Mawson, J. (2003) 'Delivering devolved approaches to local governance', *Policy and Politics* 31(1): 51–67

Peck, J. and Tickell, A. (1995) 'Business goes local: dissecting the business agenda in Manchester', *International Journal of Urban and Regional Research* 19(1): 55–78

Peck, J. and Ward, K. (2002) *City of Revolution: Restructuring Manchester*, Manchester: Manchester University Press

Peters, G. B. (1988) *Comparing public bureaucracies: Problems of theory and method,*

Tuscaloosa: University of Alabama Press

Pfeffer, J. (1981) *Power in organisations*, London: Pitman, Harper Business

Pierre, J. (ed.) (2000) *Debating Governance: Authority, Steering and Democracy*, Oxford: Oxford University Press, 33

Porter, M. E. (1985) *Competitive Advantage: Creating and Sustaining Superior Performance*, New York: Free Press

Porter, M. E. (1990) *The Competitive Advantage of Nations*, New York: Free Press

Powell, M. (ed.) (1999) *New Labour, New Welfare*, Bristol: Policy Press

Pratchett, L. (ed.) (2000) *Renewing local democracy: The modernising agenda in British local government*, London: Frank Cass

Purdue, D., Razzaque, K., Hambleton, R. and Stewart, M. with Huxham, C. and Vargen, S. (2000) *Community Leadership in Area Regeneration*, Bristol: Policy Press

Quinn, J. B. (1980) *Strategies for change: Logical incrementalism*, Homewood, IL: Richard D Irwin

Regional Studies (2003) 'Debates on Conceptualising Regional Studies', *Regional Studies* 37(6/7): 699–751

Reich, R. B. (1991) *The Work of Nations: Preparing Ourselves for 21st Century Capitalism*, New York: Random House

Rhodes, J., Tyler, P., Brennan, A., Stevens, S., Warnock, C. and Otero-Garcia, M. (2002) *Lessons and evaluation evidence from 10 Single Regeneration Budget case studies*, London: DTLR

Rhodes, R. A. W. (1998) *Beyond Westminster and Whitehall: The sub-central governments of Britain*, London: Unwin Hyman

Ring, P. S. and Perry, J. L. (1985) 'Strategic management in public and private organisations: Implications of distinctive contexts and constraints', *Academy of Management Review* 10(2): 276–286

Roberts, P. (2003) 'BURA Skills for Regeneration Management', Internal Document, British Urban Regeneration Association, Liverpool

Roberts, P. and Benneworth, P. (2001) 'Pathways to the future? An Initial Assessment of RDA Strategies and their Contribution to Integrated Regional Development', *Local Economy* 16(2): 142–159

Roberts, P. and Sykes, M. (eds) (2000) *Urban Regeneration: A Handbook*, London: Sage

Robinson, F., Shaw, K. and Snaith, S. (2000) 'Who runs the NE Now?', Department of Sociology and Social Policy, University of Durham

Robson, B., Parkinson, M., Boddy, M. and MacLennan, D. (2000) *The State of English Cities*, London: DETR

Robson, B., Peck, J. and Holden, A. (2000) *Regional Agencies and area based regeneration*, Bristol: Policy Press

Rogers, R. (1999) *Towards An Urban Renaissance: Report of the Urban Task Force*, London: E & FN Spon

Rogers, S. (1990) *Performance Management in Local Government*, London: Longman, 129

ROOM (2001) *Improving Networks: Mapping networks used by regeneration partnerships*, London: Community Press

Rose, R. (1993) *Lesson drawing in public policy: A guide to learning across time and space*, Chatham, NJ: Chatham House

Russell, H. (2001) *Local Strategic Partnerships*, Bristol: Policy Press

Salet, W., Thornley, A. and Kreukels, A. (eds) (2003) *Metropolitan Governance and Spatial Planning. Comparative Case Studies of European City-Regions*, London: Spon Press

Schaecter, J. and Loftman, P. (1997) 'Unequal Partners', *City* 8: 104–116

Schedler, K. (2002) Keynote Speech, International Symposium of Public Sector Research, University of Edinburgh, April

Schneider, M., Teste, P. E. and Mintrom, M. (1995) *Public Entrepreneurs*. Princeton, NJ: Princeton University Press

Schuftan, C. (1996) 'The Community Development Dilemma: What is really empowering?', *Community Development Journal* 31(3): 260–264

Simon, H. A., Smithburg, D. W. and Thompson, V. A. (1950) *Public Administration*, New York: Knopf

Skelcher, C., McCabe, A., Lowndes, V. and Nanton, P. (1996) *Community Networks in Urban Regeneration*, Bristol: Policy Press

Skinner, S. and Wilson, M. (2002) *Assessing Community Strengths*, London: CDF

Smith, P. (1995) 'Performance indicators and outcomes in the public sector', *Public Money and Management* 15: 13–16

Smith, R. J. (1994) *Strategic Management and Planning in the Public Sector*, London: Longman/Sunningdale: Civil Service College

Social Exclusion Unit (1998) *Bringing Britain Together: A National Strategy for Neighbourhood Renewal*, Cm 4045, London: HMSO

Social Exclusion Unit (2000a) *National Strategy for Neighbourhood Renewal: Report of Policy Action Team 16: Learning Lessons*, London: HMSO

Social Exclusion Unit (2000b) *National Strategy for Neighbourhood Renewal: A Framework for Consultation*, London: The Cabinet Office

Social Exclusion Unit (2001a) *National Strategy for Neighbourhood Renewal*, London: HMSO

Social Exclusion Unit (2001b) *A New Commitment to Neighbourhood Renewal: A National Strategy Action Plan*, London: The Cabinet Office

Social Exclusion Policy Action Team (PAT 2) (2000) *Skills for Neighbourhood*

Renewal: Local Solutions SEU

Sosik, J., Kahai, S. and Avolio, B. J. (1999) 'Leadership Style, Anonymity and Creativity in Group Decision Support Systems: The Mediating Role of Optimal Flow', *Journal of Creative Behaviour* 33(1): 1–30

Southern, A. (2003) 'The management of regeneration: processes and routes to effective delivery', *Local Work* 50

Southern, R. (2002) 'Understanding multi-sector regeneration partnerships as a form of local governance', *Local Government Studies* 28(2)

Speeden, S. and Clarke, J. (2002) *The Equality Standard for Local Government in England and Wales: Guidance, Self Assessment and Audit*, London: Dialog

Speeden, S. and Diamond, J. (1993) 'Look Who is wearing the Emperor's Clothes', Paper delivered to the Urban Change and Conflict Conference, Sheffield University, September

Stacey, R. (1993) *Strategic Management and Organisational Dynamics*, London: Pitman

Stampfer, M. (2002) Panel contribution to the European Trend Chart on Innovation, Trend Chart Policy Benchmarking Workshop, Improving Trans-National Policy Learning in Innovation, Luxembourg, 27–28 November. Available online: http://trendchart.cordis.lu/Benchmarking/index.cfm?

Stewart, J. (1992) Speech to the Accountability to the Public Conference, Queen Elizabeth 2 Conference Centre, London

Stewart, M. and Taylor, M. (1995) *Empowerment and Estate Regeneration*, Bristol: Policy Press

Stoker, G. (1996) 'Theory and Urban Politics', Politics Studies Association Annual Conference, University of Glasgow, 11 April

Stoker, G. (1998) 'Governance As Theory: five propositions', *International Social Science Journal* 50: 17

Stoker, G. (ed.) (2000) *The New Politics of British Local Governance*, Basingstoke: Macmillan, 11–32

Stoney, C. (2001) 'Strategic Management or Strategic Taylorism? A case study into change within a UK local authority', *International Journal of Public Sector Management* 14(1): 27–42

Taket, A. and White, L. (2000) *Partnership and participation: decision-making in the multi-agency setting*, Chichester: John Wiley & Sons

Taylor, M. (1995) *Unleashing the Potential*, Bristol: Policy Press

Taylor, M. (2003) 'Another new dawn? Voluntary and community organisations and service delivery', Paper presented to the ESRC and Local Governance, University of Birmingham, 17 March, 1–29

The Smarter Partnership Toolkit. Available online:

http://www.lgpartnerships.com/howhealthy.asp?

Thompson, J. (2002a) *Community Education and Neighbourhood Renewal*, Leicester:

NIACE

Thompson, J. (2002b) *Re-rooting Lifelong Learning – resourcing neighbourhood renewal*, Leicester: NIACE

Tomlinson, M. (2002) Panel contribution to the European Trend Chart on Innovation, Trend Chart Policy Benchmarking Workshop, Improving Trans-National Policy Learning in Innovation, Luxembourg, 27–28 November. Available online: http://trendchart.cordis.lu/Benchmarking/index.cfm?

Vangen, S. and Huxham, C. (2002) 'Tensions and Dilemmas: How Partnership Managers Lend Collaboration', in Purdue, D. and Stewart, M. (eds), *Understanding Collaboration, Proceedings of the 8th International Conference on Multi-Organisational Partnerships and Co-operative Strategy*, Bristol: Policy Press

Van Heijden, K. (1999) *Scenarios. The Art of Strategic Conversation*, Chichester: John Wiley & Sons

Watson, D. (2000) *Managing Strategy*, Buckingham: Open University Press

Whittington, R. (2001) *What is strategy and does it matter?*, London: Routledge

Wilkinson, D. and Appelbee, E. (1999) *Implementing holistic government: joined-up action on the ground,* Bristol: Policy Press

Wolman, J. and Page, E. C. (2000) *Learning from the Experience of Others: Policy transfer among local regeneration partnerships,* York: Joseph Rowntree Foundation

Yin, R. and Yates, D. (1975) *Street Level Governments*, Boston: Lexington Books

Younge, G. (2002) 'Brickbats and Mortar', *Guardian* 10 June

Index